T0320334

Investigative Interviewing in the Workplace

Based on extensive interdisciplinary research and the author's over 30 years of experience in the field, this book provides best practice skills for auditors and investigators in any type of investigation and adapts them to ensure they are relevant to a corporate environment where the powers available to police are absent.

In addition to providing technical skills and practical advice on investigative interviewing, former police investigator Kevin Sweeney explains how to analyze information to assist in the investigation and to identify emerging trends to provide opportunities to prevent problems before they occur. Readers will come to understand legal concepts such as the chain of evidence, the psychological factors involved in questioning, and the sociological factors that can help to build a macro understanding of the organization and the event in question.

This book will become an essential resource for professionals involved in auditing or investigation work of any type in the corporate or public sectors, in contexts including human resources, employee relation investigations, auditing, or where criminal activity is suspected.

Kevin Sweeney is a former police investigator, with over 28 years of experience preventing and solving crimes, including terrorist offences, sexual assaults, fraud, intellectual property, organized crime, and cybercrime. Over the course of his police career, he received specialist training from agencies such as the Central Intelligence Agency, Interpol, and the Criminal Assets Bureau. Kevin also worked as a consultant assisting international pharmaceutical organizations with meeting regulatory compliance requirements as well as conducting investigations, building awareness and policies, and providing training before joining University College Cork as a lecturer in criminology. He holds a PhD from the Law Department of the University of Limerick.

Investigative Interviewing in the Workplace

Culture, Deviance, and Investigations

Kevin Sweeney

Routledge
Taylor & Francis Group

LONDON AND NEW YORK

Cover image: Ratchapon Supprasert

First published 2023
by Routledge
4 Park Square, Milton Park, Abingdon, Oxon OX14 4RN

and by Routledge
605 Third Avenue, New York, NY 10158

Routledge is an imprint of the Taylor & Francis Group, an informa business

British Library Cataloguing-in-Publication Data
A catalogue record for this book is available from the British Library

Library of Congress Cataloging-in-Publication Data
A catalog record has been requested for this book

ISBN: 978-1-032-21673-7 (hbk)
ISBN: 978-1-032-21671-3 (pbk)
ISBN: 978-1-003-26948-9 (ebk)

DOI: 10.4324/9781003269489

Typeset in Bembo
by Newgen Publishing UK

For Sinead, David, Sean, Rachel and Josh

Contents

Acknowledgments

As with every book, there is a back story about how the project developed. I am fortunate in having encountered generous people on my own journey who gave of their time and other resources to assist me on my way. My thanks in particular to Stan O'Neill and Mark McComish of The Compliance Group who convinced me that there was a broader interest out in the world about interviewing techniques and helped me make this book possible.

My thanks and appreciation also to Tom O'Connor, formerly detective in the Criminal Assets Bureau, who took the time to comment on the chapters and provided valuable insight. Finally, my thanks to Siobhan O'Leary who assisted me with her invaluable knowledge and patient editing suggestions. Any subsequent errors are mine entirely.

My thanks to you all for making this book possible.

Chapter 1

Introduction

What does a corporate investigation entail? Organizational investigations often have a financial component such as theft or embezzlement, but investigations will cover a broad array of different behaviors, ranging from occasional inaccuracies in day-to-day operations, bullying behavior, industrial espionage, safety violations, systematic sabotage, and sexually inappropriate comments or suggestions to outright violence.[1] Many investigations are initiated by complaints by whistleblowers and need to be comprehensively investigated to ensure that they are genuine. Alternatively, an investigator may be asked to evaluate a potential business partner through due diligence investigations or an investigator may be a court appointed liquidator, administrator, or auditor. Ensuring adherence to compliance regulations is another common task. In some industries, the very survival of the organization is dependent on their adherence to regulations, and therefore, they need to be especially cognizant of compliance obligations. Legislation, for instance, the Sarbanes-Oxley Act, places responsibility at the board level to ensure compliance, while regulators may give credit to companies who take voluntary steps to investigate, disclose, and halt any illegal or improper conduct.[2] Potential regulatory impact thus increases the need for competent investigations to forestall regulatory involvement. It is noteworthy that regulators have significant power to prevent a regulated business from trading, often with companies being required to prove compliance rather regulators having to discover problems.

Although an investigator may be external to the organization or part of its corporate internal structure, one thing many investigators have in common is that they receive little training in the investigation aspect of their work and, in particular, interviewing skills. Most investigators acknowledge gathering information from other people is the critical investigative skill as most investigations begin with talking to individuals to build knowledge and understanding of the issues.[3] Consequently, there may be certain situations where it may make strategic sense to use dedicated interviewers in combination with esoteric specialists, rather than trying to train experts in another field in interviewing. In such scenarios, it is possible to have the interviewers obtaining the information

DOI: 10.4324/9781003269489-1

from people while being guided by the technical expertise of the specialists. Whichever way it is done, investigators need to talk to people. This book focuses on that one skill set of obtaining information from people. This skill set is composed of a number of elements. As well as interviewing skills, it comprises the ability to gather information from other sources, and it includes evaluation of the information obtained. The gathering and evaluation of information feeds back into the interviews, and ultimately, it determines the outcome of the investigation, which in turn ultimately informs the decisions made by the commissioning client.

This book uses the term the forensic investigative interview technique (FIIT) to describe the combined skill set. The specific purpose of this book is to outline an effective investigation tool: first by presenting an ethical and efficient interviewing technique that can be used for any type of interviewing; second, presenting legal principles that should guide an investigator as there is nearly always the potential for some judicial involvement into an investigation; third, outline the importance of critical thinking tools to evaluate information to avoid many of the biases that too often have led investigators to come to erroneous conclusions with negative consequences for innocent people; and finally, an understanding of social dynamics will provide investigators with an insight that many problems in organizations result from the need of individuals to fulfill deep psychological needs including being part of a group and sometimes people will do anything to conform to the group values. With this knowledge, investigators may then be in a position to identify red flags or potential high-risk situations in organizations or deviant groups and thereby have the foresight to intervene before an adverse event occurs. This obviously goes beyond the usual job description of an investigator. Investigators usually arrive after the fact and assign blame. Nevertheless, investigation skills can also be used proactively to prevent negative outcomes. Naturally, both aspects may be combined in an investigation as an investigator may be called in to investigate but may subsequently be able to also offer solutions to both the specific problems as well as other potential problems identified. Thus, the comments made by investigators often form the basis of subsequent company remedial action plans. This problem-solving use of investigation tools is quite unlike public policing that is usually post-event only.[4] Therefore, although this book is focused primarily on the investigative process, this book will examine some aspects of organizational culture. This is to identify what safety experts refer to as the *signatures* or the common trajectories of deviance that have subtle and predictable patterns in many organizations.[5] Identifying trends and understanding the common trajectories of deviant behavior is a critical skill in preventing deviance early, minimizing losses, and ultimately protecting clients long term. This proactive use of investigations dovetails with the increasing concern in corporate security about the protection of financial, intellectual, and informational assets as well as the buffering of the organization from various forms of legal, regulatory, and prudential liability and risk.[6]

Many investigations will deal with premediated bad behavior but not every bad outcome is a consequence of malicious behavior, and many problems result from accident or unintentional behavior. However, once prepared for the worst-case scenario, an investigator should be able to tackle any assignment and scale up as appropriate and necessary. Rather than focus solely on criminal behavior, *deviance* is the term that will be used throughout to describe the matters under investigation and which can cover the range of interpersonal conflict and organizational issues. The FIIT interview tool itself is an investigative interviewing method which is focused on information gathering rather than accusation, which is more associated with interrogation. Interrogation usually begins with the assumption that the suspect is guilty but that suspects will rationalize, deny any involvement, seek to minimize their involvement or project blame on to somebody else to avoid accepting responsibility. Interrogation methods are heavily biased toward manipulating subjects to believe that there is nothing to be gained by refusing to confess.[7] Heavy-handed interrogations are still used worldwide, even in private investigations. For instance, in Australia, interrogation-style interviewing by private investigators involved in processing insurance claims have been criticized as unfair.[8]

The change to less confrontational interview techniques is a development that has been occurring throughout law enforcement in Europe over the last 25 years based on psychological principles to obtain information.[9] Investigative interviewing focuses on using social intelligence to build a connection with the interviewee, achieved through a focus on building rapport. The questioning method uses open questions to allow the interviewee to provide the narrative of the event as they perceived it. That is, the interviewee provides the information in their possession rather than only confirming the investigators prior beliefs. Once an account has been given, the method involves probing those narratives and, if necessary, challenging the account. The FIIT incorporates the use of evidence as a major component of the interview, to corroborate or to challenge the account, when needed. An organization must continue to function after an investigation. Lessons may need to be learned and applied. If the investigation process was unnecessarily harsh and dogmatic, it may have done more long-term harm than good, no matter the outcome, as people are very much driven by the concept of fairness. The concept of *procedural justice* suggests people are willing to accept a decision, even one that goes against them, if the process that led to the decision was fair.[10] This means that the process is seen as impartial and objective, while the person is treated with respect and given a genuine opportunity to give a response. Furthermore, creating harsh blame cultures with a zero tolerance for mistakes ultimately is counterproductive, as it simply encourages deception.

Behaving fairly and treating people with respect pays another important dividend. People will talk to you. This is not just during an interview; people will seek you out to impart information. This does not happen all the time, but it occurs frequently enough to be worth noting. Especially if the investigation extends over a few days, it appears that some employees who have concerns and information will come forward if they can trust the investigator to treat them fairly. Employees talk, and generally, an investigation is worth talking about. It provides an opportunity for some employees to come forward if they feel safe to do so. While there is always a potential risk that such information may be given malevolently, it can mean getting an insider's perspective and knowledge, built over years. It also provides useful avenues of enquiries and may lead to the discovery of important evidence.

The central premise of this book and the FIIT is that an investigator's job is to try to get to the truth in an investigation, and there are certain skills that will assist with this. However, an investigator must always operate within certain ethical and legal constraints. This book does not use or suggest any unethical or underhand tactics; all interviewing techniques are intended to be ethical, legal, and effective. The ends do not justify the means and every interviewee should be treated with respect. It is important to be able to stand over the investigation and interviewing methods used in any subsequent forum. Talent and ability are important, but so is character and integrity, perhaps even more necessary for an investigator than for most other professions.

This book does not offer any guarantees of foolproof methods to obtain information at an interview because investigations are complex, people are complex, and there can never be a guarantee that any single technique will succeed in getting everybody to talk. Reflection on using the techniques and feedback processes is essential to effective learning and, more importantly, what integrates new knowledge into new skills.[11] Reflective practice through linking theory and practice is an important tool in many practice-based professional learning settings where individuals learn from their own professional experiences.[12] Practicing in a deliberate way develops not only new neural pathways that become good habits but also develops a deep understanding of the process itself.[13] The willingness to learn and build from experience while remaining humble easily supplants any technical ability and together with integrity is fundamental to good investigative professionalism. Experience helps the new knowledge become embedded and while mastering the new skills is important, it is timing, the knowing when to do something that is critical. That is the hard part, and no one can teach you that, it comes from experience, which usually means learning from mistakes, to paraphrase Mark Twain.

Private Investigations

There are major differences between public and private investigations. Public investigation agencies such as law enforcement tend to focus on bringing persons who break laws before a court for adjudication and punishment. There are strict rules and protocols governing the process. Courts rarely tolerate police misbehavior in the gathering of evidence, although the many instances of wrongful convictions show this may be more aspirational than reality. Justice is administered in public, and the goal is usually punishment rather than restitution for damage suffered. Public justice thus often means informational access to internal organizational affairs including business practices and proprietary information, which cannot be prevented. Furthermore, the criminal justice process can move slowly, and it is not uncommon for years to pass before the conclusion of an investigation and judgment. Businesses are focused on doing whatever it is they do, but investigations can bring unwanted interruptions to workflow and may potentially bring challenging publicity, undermining profits. As a result, organizations can be reluctant to involve law enforcement. Other considerations such as the perceived lack of specific expertise among police investigators all influence the decision to opt for a private investigation.

Private investigations, on the other hand, can move speedily and can pursue varied solutions to issues that are more optimal and reputation saving.[14] Information can be kept confidential, with nondisclosure agreements routine, and there is more likelihood of recovering lost assets as well as rapidly stemming the losses. A speedy investigation may prevent the dispersal of illegally obtained funds.[15] While private investigators lack many of the formal powers of police, they are also less restricted by the formal rules of the criminal justice system. Because of the need for rapid efficient solutions, many organizational issues are approached as labor disputes to be resolved as effectively as possible and thus rarely enter the criminal justice system.[16] There remains the potential, nonetheless, for any private investigation to become the subject of judicial examination. Even where the matter is resolved informally and speedily, the subject of the investigation may feel aggrieved and unfairly treated. In which case, a person is entitled to take a legal case to seek compensation. In such an event, how the investigation was conducted, and the behavior of the investigator may be central to the case. Another possibility is that after commencing a private investigation, it uncovers criminal misconduct of such seriousness, that bringing in law enforcement is necessary or, in the case of a regulated industry, obligatory. In such instances, evidence that was gathered may become vital to the prosecution case; therefore, it needs to be done correctly.

Another major difference exists between private and public investigations; in private investigations, the commissioning client determines the scope of the investigation, which means they define the boundaries beyond which you are not allowed to go. A company may bring in outside investigators to simply determine who is responsible, and the investigator may be under considerable pressure to quickly assign attribution to some cause or individual. There is often a social and cultural need to blame specific, localized forces or events for outcomes that is part of the common assumptions around responsibility and failure.[17] This means in practice that someone closest to the issue at the time is blamed while systemic causes are ignored. Cultural expectations around failure also means there are sometimes strong forces preferring to keep the full truth hidden. An illustrative example is provided by the prosecution and conviction of 736 postmasters in the United Kingdom for fraud and theft offenses between 2000 and 2014.[18] Many received prison terms, and all lost their jobs and livelihoods. It later transpired that the internal computer system used by the post office was faulty, a failing that was known from the beginning but apparently concealed by senior management. The only evidence against the postmasters were data from the information technology (IT) system, and no other evidence of any financial shortfall was presented, although many accused pled guilty. It is unclear if investigative failings were responsible for not discovering this fact or if vital information was withheld from investigators.

The reality is that even where the investigators have a broad scope, the findings may not necessarily be welcomed, and an investigator needs to be prepared to encounter resistance. This may come from those responsible for the deviance, but unfortunately, it may also come in an institutionalized form. Businesses may vary in how they approach an investigation, and there may be major differences in the approach of an owner-operated business compared to a business with a large bureaucratic hierarchy, for example. A business owner may value a deep holistic approach, whereas managers may not. Managers have multiple responsibilities, some of which may conflict with the resolution of an investigation, and it may mean managers have divided loyalties. An investigator may thus meet considerable opposition in trying to identify the full causal chain leading to the event in question. While it may make long-term sense to understand this causal process to prevent reoccurrence and develop better processes, senior management may simply not wish to know. Many reasons may account for this. Sometimes, there is involvement in the deviance but not necessarily. In my experience, it is not unusual for senior management to pull the plug on an investigation rather than have it proceed beyond that immediately necessary. There may be no culpability of those managers for the deviance; nevertheless, there was a failure, perhaps ongoing over a considerable time, to recognize or intervene to solve the underlying problem. Stopping an investigation short may be done to protect those who should have been aware of the ongoing activity but for one reason or another were not. That is, until it became unavoidable to notice. Consequentially, often one of the most important interviews is the initial briefing that is received from a client, scoping the expectations of the investigation. It is not uncommon to be given only partial information, enough to do the job required. This is a choice the investigator makes if he or she is aware of the deficit, one that is perfectly within the remit of any investigator to make. It is not a reasonable choice to make if one is deliberately deceived, however.

Individuals, Organizations, and Systems

In my experience, the FIIT is both a suitable tool to respond to incidents retrospectively, as in a traditional law enforcement response, but it can also be used to prevent adverse outcomes by gathering information and identifying trends. This is achieved by understanding that while obtaining information is important, it is also important to understand the information received in the overall context of the organization under investigation. Sometimes, issues begin and end with one or a few individuals, but it is not unusual that that is only the tip of the iceberg, and an organization has deep systemic issues. By systemic causes, I primarily mean the culture of the organization, which are the norms, values, and beliefs that bind a group together. While people want to have autonomy, to act independently, to feel as if they have control over their lives—even if often illusionary—they also have a need to belong to a group, a need that can provide meaning in their lives.[19] For many, our occupational life is a critical part of our personality. Organizational culture is thus layered onto our own deep beliefs and cultural values created through religion, education, and nationality. People use these to negotiate their way through life, and these values may determine if a person is actively engaged in work or whether a person engages in some form of only ritual compliance.

Individual differences are important in any organization and different personality types behave differently in similar situations. Influencers are particularly important in any organization. Personality differences may have relevance for obtaining information at an interview, but FIIT is sufficiently adaptable that such differences can be accounted for. In terms of responsibility for deviance, the negative personality traits known as the *Dark Triad* of traits can be important. These include Machiavellism, psychopathy, and narcissism, and all share some behavior tendencies toward self-promotion, emotional numbness, duplicity, and aggressiveness.[20] It has even been suggested that the business world has more psychopaths than the normal distribution in the population; apparently, the cutthroat nature of business is attractive to them.[21] Machiavellians are more likely to lie to friends and to take revenge against others, while narcissists can be hostile and aggressive, especially when their egos are threatened.[22] Individually or collectively, these personalities may, in turn, have an outsize impact on organizational outcomes as well as other people's behaviors, more so when the individual concerned has a leadership role. Unfortunately, outside of generalizations, such information is of little practical use, as the indicators of personality disorders are not precise; for example, a lot of people exhibit selfish behaviors in certain situations and not in others. Moreover, only psychological testing can establish such traits for certain. Of much greater relevance for investigators is the phenomenon of motivated reasoning that applies to everyone and will be examined in more detail in this book. People will basically behave in certain ways because they have emotional reasons for believing that this behavior serves a purpose. Through the phenomenon of holding objectively false beliefs, people can maintain self-esteem and rationalize their behavior as acceptable, justified, or warranted. The power of people to rationalize behavior is incredible, as is the power of emotions to drive behavior. Therefore, an investigator should recognize that everyone has the potential to be involved in deviance, as Aleksandr Solzhenitsyn warns, the dividing line between good and evil cuts through the heart of every single person, and it is often fate that determines which side comes out.[23]

Consequently, while individual behavior is important, the primary determinant of behavior is usually the context it occurs in. This suggests that an investigator must take multiple perspectives. Edgar Schein, one of the leading authorities on systemic problems in organizations, suggests that to understand organizational problems, three different perspectives, in particular, are necessary: an *individual perspective* based on psychology; a *systemic perspective* based on anthropology, sociology, political science, and systems theory; and an *interactive process perspective* based on social psychology, sociology, and other theories of dynamic processes.[24] Although this book will be mainly on the practical level and not delve deeply into theoretical constructs, it is important to appreciate that organizations are dynamic entities in themselves or continuous adaptive systems.[25] Like all complex adaptive systems, an organization has many interacting factors that contribute to eventual behavior. Organizations, like any complex system, does not stand still, and is capable of constant adaptation. These changes can occur gradually and incrementally, so time is an important factor in understanding deviance. This concept of small incremental steps accumulating into major changes is fundamental to biological evolution, as well as systems thinking, and developmental psychology.[26] Different layers of influence therefore act on individuals, often subconsciously. Cultural beliefs and expectations, together with individual experiences, cognitive style, personality traits, and epistemic and existential needs, combine to generate mental models of how the world works. These mental models generate a personal worldview that are the lens through which people perceive and view the world, interpret behavior, and justify their actions. Some beliefs are fully conscious such as 'I dislike fish' but older and deeper beliefs are subconscious and become a part of one's personality but remain buried under layers and layers of later experiences. These older beliefs may nevertheless continue to influence contemporary behavior.[27]

Every organization has a culture. Every culture enculturates new arrivals, and over time, individuals in an organization must come to share at least some mental models and come to internalize the common norms, values, and ways of seeing the world, or else leave.[28] Culture can represent a positive force where learning, respect, efficiency, and a positive work environment are the values highly regarded. On the other hand, many companies embody the exact opposite values. Additionally, as culture is dynamic, even initially strong organizations may deteriorate over time. Schein developed an iceberg concept to identify the important cultural factors in an organization and their observability.[29] At the top, Schein describes how some aspects of culture such as the artifacts—the obvious and tangible manifestations—are readily visible, while others such as the espoused values among employees are deeper and more difficult to discover, but possible if effortful enquiry is made. At the lowest level, the deepest aspects, the hidden beliefs and the underlying assumptions, are often hidden from the organization and individuals themselves, making it difficult to identify them. These hidden values contribute nonetheless to an organization's worldview. This worldview is how the organization sees the world and interprets all information. Once an organization has developed a cultural acceptance of shortcuts, systems rarely evolve toward good processes. Diane Vaughan called this process the *normalization of deviance* whereby small decisions lead to small deviances being accepted as standard practice that over time lead to greater deviations because small errors compound, often dramatically.[30] Organizations operate on all levels simultaneously and understanding the relationships between different levels such as structural institutions and personal agency can be used to enhance our understanding of situated action; that is, behavior that takes place in socially organized settings. Culture, therefore, mediates between institutional forces, organizational goals and processes, and individual illegality, so that deviance can become normalized in organizational settings.[31] The financial industry is slowly recognizing the importance of culture in implementing regulatory supervision. The Dutch Central Bank (DNB), for instance, believes social dynamics is the nexus of the interaction between behavior and culture, with a recognition that public trust is difficult to achieve and slow to build, while being easy to destroy.[32] DNB acknowledges that poor culture and bad business practices erodes good governance and are a major source of mistrust by the public in the financial system.

Consequently, for an investigator to move deeper than blaming an individual and to truly understand issues in an organization, there is a need to understand the system that the organization is. A culture of deviance creates a systemic problem in the organization, known as a *criminogenic environment*, so it hardly matters who the individual was or what happened to him or her, because there is an inevitability that some other individual will produce a similar outcome through that same deviant criminogenic culture.[33] Fortunately, the deviation process is usually a gradual one, and this suggests that if early warning signs are caught, intervention is possible. Post-event analysis often reveals early warning signs, but opportunities to intervene were neglected because such early signs were either ignored, misinterpreted, or missed completely. Few organizations adopt the 'no blame culture' of the airline industry, so in most organizations, individuals who make mistakes, even inadvertently, move to protect themselves. It may be as simple as protecting self-esteem by refusing to acknowledge responsibility or protecting one's job by disguising the fault.[34] On some occasions, this cover-up may then have to evolve to become deliberate deception. The interaction between individuals and the culture of the organization is therefore important to understand. Matthew Syed argues that the high quality of air-crash investigators has been fundamental to improved airline safety.[35] Such investigations are comprehensive encompassing contributing human factors as well as technical causes. This combined with the willingness to report mistakes and learn lessons makes the airline industry an exemplar of safety. On the other hand, the failure to recognize red flags that are available means problems often have to be highly visible before they become apparent, and investigators, auditors, or regulators all have had the ignominy of missed opportunities to identify deviance in progress. Syed references the medical and healthcare profession as being very culturally resistant to full investigations, sometimes driven by the perceived infallibility of medics but often being fearful of litigation as reasons why many investigations either never happen or are conducted to protect individuals rather than uncover the truth.[36]

Theranos and Enron are two examples of organizations where failures by investigators resulted in major losses. It is perhaps unfair, therefore, to criticize any investigator for failing to recognize deviance; after all, this is not the natural sciences, and those involved in fraud or other deviance are what Malcolm Sparrow refers to as *conscious opponents*, people who disguise their activities and who react and adapt to any efforts to uncover their activities.[37] Nevertheless, some failures are sufficiently egregious that they are difficult to defend or explain within any reasonable framework. In early 2022, Elizabeth Holmes was convicted of fraud because while CEO of Theranos she promised a radical new blood test capable of testing for hundreds of different diseases concurrently. The technology did not actually exist, and it appears it was never close to reality. Instead, an elaborate deception utilizing commercially available blood testing technology gave the Theranos company market capitalization of around $9 billion at one point, with Holmes herself listed as a billionaire. Some investors employed due diligence investigators, and while at least one raised some concerns, it did not prevent the investments being made, and ultimately lost, or identify the ongoing fraud itself.[38] The bigger the scale of fraud, the easier it is to continue the deception, it appears. Investigators, both private and state, failed to perceive that such a widespread fraud was possible and failed to investigate the company fully.

Another example even more pernicious is Enron, originally an energy company and once the seventh-largest Fortune 500 company in the United States, whose collapse and bankruptcy wiped $70 billion off shareholder value and led to defaults on tens of billions of dollars.[39] Despite espoused values including respect, integrity, communication, and excellence, Enron is a case study in criminogenic environments in corporate crime, particularly how deviant culture permeates an organization, and perverse incentives serve to corrupt it further. Enron encouraged performance aggression and a survival of the fittest mentality among employees with yearly reviews where the lowest performers were automatically fired.[40] Even though this Performance Review Committee known as 'rank and yank' created some paranoia as peers reviewed peers, there was nevertheless a strong loyalty toward company leadership.[41] Share price was a prime motivator for management, and risk-taking employees were praised. Enron used ambiguous regulations, dubious accountancy practices, and special purposes entities (SPEs) to disguise its large debt that it had acquired and its toxic assets. Misuse of mark to market accountancy practices allowed potential profits to be claimed as real earnings in order to deceive the regulator and the public. Any realized losses went unreported. Aggression and greed became core values. Identification with and loyalty to the company meant many individuals even put company welfare ahead of their own personal well-being.[42] The eventual collapse of Enron also brought down its auditor, the large accountancy firm Arthur Anderson. Despite a long involvement, Arthur Anderson had failed to ever uncover the ongoing fraud or identify the risks inherent in Enron's business model, although in this instance, it appears Arthur Anderson was complicit. It is irrelevant whether the failings of Arthur Anderson resulted from the cleverness of Enron in hiding the deceit and fraud, if Arthur Anderson were careless or negligent in failing to find the problems, or the worst-case scenario, where the situation was one of 'regulatory capture' where those responsible for oversight had themselves become corrupted, as seemingly was the case here. The consequence was the same, a failure to uncover seemingly obvious truths about deception before it becomes too late.

Using This Book

This book is intended for anyone who wants to achieve the best possible results in getting information from people. Each chapter follows logically in a progressive manner from simple to more complex interviews and then examines other aspects of the FIIT. Chapter 2 examines some basic principles of the common law such as what do we mean by evidence, what we need to prove, what is hearsay, and voluntariness. The purpose of this chapter is to set the FIIT in the context of the criminal justice system. Again, it is acknowledged that many private investigators are not setting out on criminal justice investigations. There are good reasons to investigate to this standard, nonetheless. It avoids basic and simple errors that can contaminate evidence or even an entire investigation. It also provides a comprehensive framework within which to operate that can become habitual. It is easier to develop good habits at the beginning than trying to unlearn bad behaviors.

Chapter 3 looks at the basic interviewing concept. This book seeks to enhance communication skills, particularly listening skills. Asking the right questions and knowing what type of questions to ask are important, but good listening is one of the key skills in any type of interviewing. The building of rapport is another key skill, where the ability to introduce an atmosphere where communication can take place together with a willingness to listen to somebody is incredibly effective in investigative interviewing. This applies in any type of interview situation but even more so in investigations in the corporate environment. The emphasis will be on respecting the interviewee, establishing good communication, behaving ethically, but while maintaining a skeptical cognitive attitude that pays attention to the details and keeps curious until all relevant lines of enquiry have been exhausted.

Chapter 4 discusses forensic interviewing where an investigator has to ask questions of important persons from an investigative standpoint. The investigative interviewing model is not about getting confessions, it is a fact-finding model. In essence, the interview strategy suggested is based on developing a deep knowledge of the issue and asking questions to uncover the truth. The questions generally begin broad and are open questions, and the interviewee provides a narrative or account. Once an account has been obtained, then it is probed by asking more focused questions until any ambiguity is resolved. It requires patience, determination, and skill to cover all matters and to over-come any resistance. The foundational structure for the interviewing aspect of FIIT is an interviewing model that is a non-accusatory suspect and witness interview model initially designed for police forces in the United Kingdom (PEACE). The approach taken throughout the entire process is the assumption that the person may be innocent, and interviewing is a fact-gathering exercise, not an accusatory process. It is an important element of natural justice that a person suspected of deviance be allowed an opportunity to respond, and even in circumstances where there is a preponderance of evidence, the interviewer should approach any interview with an open mind.

Chapter 5 takes a deeper look at obtaining an account from an interviewee in a forensic interview. The theoretical foundations of PEACE itself are the cognitive interview (CI) and the conversation management (CM) concepts. I have also included an additional model, motivational interviewing (MI) in this chapter. Combined, they provide an escalation technique to respond to any type of interviewee. The CI technique is about building social connection and using that to help access memory to improve recall. MI is built around using active listening skills to overcome reluctance and avoiding confrontation. CM, on the other hand, can also be used with a resistant interviewee, although it is also applicable to cooperative interviewees.

Chapter 6 then moves to obtaining evidence. It discusses the importance of the chain of evidence and why care must be taken in recovering evidence. Evidence must be kept securely, and any interference must be accounted for. In principle, any court should be satisfied that the evidence is in the exact same state as when it was seized. This chapter explores some tools for maintaining records to manage evidence. The ultimate record is the investigation report which is the outcome of the investigation and the reason the client hired the investi-gator. Impartiality, objectivity, and professionalism are important components, but ultimately, the report must answer the questions asked by the client.

Chapter 7 explores the importance of analysis of the evidence. Evaluation and analysis are critical components of FIIT. Evidence is important as it can be used to corroborate or challenge an interviewee's account as well as tending to prove, or disprove, some aspect of the investigation independently. It is vital that all information or evidence encountered be examined through a critical and objective lens. This chapter looks at why biases can arise before introducing some tools to use to help alleviate the effects of biases. This includes the ana-lytical tool of analysis of competing hypotheses, whereby evidence is examined from different perspectives. The goal is to make explicit any biases rather than try to eliminate them, as that is virtually impossible.

Chapter 8 follows on from the analysis of evidence to using evidence in the interview as well as detecting deceit. This chapter explores methods to present evidence in a tactical way. This is particularly important in uncovering efforts to deceive the interviewer. Some methods of detecting deceit are discussed, including changes in verbal and nonverbal behavior. Although it is acknowledged that despite many claims to the contrary, there really is no magic bullet to detecting deceit. Furthermore, getting to the truth is about more than knowing the person is lying. It is necessary to get that person to move to giving a truthful account. The tactical use of evidence alters the perception of the interviewee that deception is no longer a valid strategy, and the truth may become the best option.

Chapter 9 takes altering the perceptions of the interviewee a stage further. In certain situations, it may be necessary to use persuasion to alter the interviewee's perceptions. It is important to emphasize that this is about framing the available evidence to be as salient and relevant as possible in the interview situation. It is not about manipulation, which is either presenting false information, alluding to fictitious evidence, or otherwise lying to the interviewee. This chapter does not alter the ethical imperative that the interviewer has to treat interviewees with respect. Nonetheless, motivated reasoning on the part of the interviewee can be difficult to dislodge, and when it is based on a false perception of reality, it may be necessary on some occasions to shift perceptions by using the tools of persuasion. This approach tends to bypass the use of logical argument, which can not only be ineffective but even counterproductive, and utilizes instead the emotional brain's decision-making. This chapter looks deeper at the emotional brain and how it is shaped by a fundamental human need to belong to a group. This has a profound effect on behavior, but because much happens beneath conscious awareness, we may be unaware both of its power and the beliefs we must hold to conform to the values of the group. The need to maintain self-esteem and belong to a group can result in people getting involved in deviant behavior. Leveraging the exact same phenomena permits the interviewer to apply subtle influencing tools in trying to get the truth.

The penultimate chapter is an overview of the court videotape evidence in a multiple murder investigation in Canada. It is difficult to adequately describe an interview technique by only writing about it. I would strongly recommend watching a similar technique in actual use. I suggest watching the Canadian police interview of air force Colonel Russell Williams. Detective sergeant Smyth utilizes a similar PEACE-type interviewing method to get admissions to murder from this Colonel during a voluntary interview.[43] This video is available widely online, and the review of it is offered as an example of the interview style and tone that is the fact-finding interview. The non–accusatory nature of it may make it seem underwhelming, but the technique is very effective, while remaining ethical throughout. The fact that it is a real-life case, involving very high stakes, makes it invaluable as a learning opportunity on the use of fact-finding interviewing in the hands of a skilled investigator. This chapter is followed by some final concluding remarks.

Notes

1 Meerts, C., "Corporate Investigations: Beyond Notions of Public–Private Relations", *Journal of Contemporary Criminal Justice*, (2020), 36(1), pp 86–100: 87.

2 Missal, M., Fishman, E., Ochs, B. and Kline Dubill, R., "Conducting Corporate Internal Investigations", *International Journal of Disclosure and Governance*, (2007), 4(4), pp 297–308.

3 King, M., "Financial Fraud Investigative Interviewing—Corporate Investigators' Beliefs and Practices: A Qualitative Inquiry", *Journal of Financial Crime*, (2021), 28(2), pp 345–358.

4 I am referring here to the traditional criminal justice police role of police to investigate and prosecute crime. Investigation skills are used to prevent and predict problems in intelligence-gathering organizations and are becoming more prevalent in police forces. In police forces, it is normally known as a strategy of intelligence-led policing, where serious criminals are monitored with active intervention into their criminal plans before completion.

5 Syed, M., *Black Box Thinking: Marginal Gains and the Secrets of High Performance*, (John Murray, London, 2015) p 12.

6 Williams, J. W., 'The Private Eyes of Corporate Culture: The Forensic Accounting and Corporate Investigation Industry and the Production of Corporate Financial Security', (eds) Walby and Lippert, in *Corporate Security in the 21st Century: Theory and Practice in International Perspective*, (Palgrave Macmillan UK, London, 2014) pp 56–77.

7 Leo, R., *Police Interrogation and American Justice*, (Harvard University Press, Harvard, 2008): 319, Leo, R., "From Coercion to Deception: The Changing Nature of Police Interrogation in America", *Crime, Law & Social Change*, (1992), 18(1–2), pp 35–59.

8 King, M., "Financial Fraud Investigative Interviewing—Corporate Investigators' Beliefs and Practices: A Qualitative Inquiry", *Journal of Financial Crime*, (2021): 347.

9 Police interviewing developments in the United Kingdom have been fundamental in this shift. Although other European countries are developing similar models around the same time. See Clarke, C. and Milne, R., *The National Evaluation of the PEACE Investigative Interviewing Course*, (Institute of Criminal Justice Studies. Report No. PRAS/149, Portsmouth University, 2001); Kohnken, G., Milne, R., Memon, A. and Bull, R., "The Cognitive Interview: A Meta-Analysis", *Psychology, Crime & Law*, (1999), 5, pp 3–27; Milne, R. and Bull, R., *Investigative Interviewing: Psychology and Practice*, (Wiley, Chichester, 1999). North America has also seen developments particularly in Canada, see St. Yves, M. and Deslauriers-Varin, N., 'The Psychology of Suspects Decision-Making during Interrogation', (eds) Bull, Valentine and Williamson, in *Handbook of Psychology of Investigative Interviewing*, (Wiley-Blackwell, Chichester, 2009), pp 1–16. However, even in the United States, there is a recognition of the advantages of the practices of investigative interviewing, e.g., see Borum, R., Gelles, M. G. and Kleinman, S. M., 'Interview and Interrogation: A Perspective and Update from the USA', (eds) Milne, Savage and Williamson, in *International Developments in Investigative Interviewing*, (Willan, Cullompton, 2009), pp 111–125.

10 Tyler, T. R., "Enhancing Police Legitimacy", *The Annals of the American Academy of Political and Social Science*, (2004), 593(1), pp 84–99.

11 Brown, P. C., Roediger III, H. L. and McDaniel, M. A., *Make It Stick: The Science of Successful Learning*, (Harvard University Press, Cambridge, MA, 2014).

12 Thompson, N. and Pascal, J., "Developing Critically Reflective Practice", *Reflective Practice*, (2012), 13(2), pp 311–325.

13 Cabrera, D. and Cabrera, L., *Systems Thinking Made Simple: New Hope for Solving Wicked Problems, 2nd ed.*, (Plectica Publishing, 2018) p 68.

14 Williams, J. W., "Governability Matters: The Private Policing of Economic Crime and the Challenge of Democratic Governance", *Policing and Society*, (2005), 15(2), pp 187–211.

15 A number of civil routes for the recovery, freezing of assets, or the prevention of destruction exist such as Anton Piller orders and Mareva injunctions in the United Kingdom. Such recourses require as much information as possible to be gathered to convince a court of the propriety of such actions.

16 Meerts, C., "Corporate Investigations: Beyond Notions of Public–Private Relations", *Journal of Contemporary Criminal Justice*, (2020).

17 Cook, R. I., "How Complex Systems Fail: (Being a Short Treatise on the Nature of Failure; How Failure Is Evaluated; How Failure Is Attributed to Proximate Cause; and the Resulting New Understanding of Patient Safety)", *Cognitive Technologies Laboratory, University of Chicago*, (2000), https://ckrybus.com/static/papers/how_complex_systems_fail_cook_2000.pdf

18 See "Post Office Scandal: What the Horizon Saga Is All About". Available at www.bbc.com/news/business-56718036. [Accessed February 15, 2020]. See also government inquiry into issue referred to as "England's Biggest Ever Miscarriage of Justice" at www.gov.uk/government/publications/post-office-horizon-it-inquiry-2020; Court of Appeal cases quashing convictions include Hamilton & Ors v Post Office Ltd [2021] EWCA Crim 577; and Ambrose & Ors v Post Office Ltd [2021] EWCA Crim 1443.

19 Langer, E., 'The Illusion of Control', (eds) Kahneman, Tversksy and Slovic, in *Judgement under Uncertainty: Heuristics and Biases*, (Cambridge University Press, Cambridge, 1982), pp 231–238. On the need to belong to group, see Tajfel, H., "Social Psychology of Intergroup Relations", *Annual Review of Psychology*, (1982), 33(1), p 1, Tajfel, H. and Turner, J. C., 'An Integrative Theoty of Intergroup Conflict', (eds) Austin and Worchel, in *The Social Psychology of Intergroup Relations*, (Brooks/Cole, Monterey, CA, 1979) pp 33–47. Also the need for meaning in belonging to group, see, for example, Sageman, M., *Misunderstanding Terrorism*, (Pennsylvania University Press, Philadelphia, PA, 2017).

20 See Paulhus, D. L. and Williams, K. M., "The Dark Triad of Personality: Narcissism, Machiavellianism, and Psychopathy", *Journal of Research in Personality*, (2002), 36(6), pp 556–563; O'Boyle, E. H., Forsyth, D. R., Banks, G. C. and McDaniel, M. A., "Meta-Analysis of the Dark Triad and Work Behavior: A Social Exchange Perspective", *Journal of Applied Psychology*, (2012), 97(3), pp 557–579.

21 Babiak, P. and Hare, R. D., *Snakes in Suits: Understanding and Surviving the Psychopaths in Your Office*, (Harper Collins, New York, NY, 2019).

22 O'Boyle, E. H., Forsyth, D. R., Banks, G. C. and McDaniel, M. A., "Meta-Analysis of the Dark Triad and Work Behavior: A Social Exchange Perspective", *Journal of Applied Psychology*, (2012).

23 Solzhenitsyn, A., *The Gulag Archipelago*, (The Harville Press, London, 1986).

24 Schein, E. H., "From Brainwashing to Organizational Therapy: A Conceptual and Empirical Journey in Search of 'Systemic' Health and a General Model of Change Dynamics. A Drama in Five Acts", *Organization Studies*, (2006), 27(2), pp 287–301: 287.

25 Cabrera, D. and Cabrera, L., *Systems Thinking Made Simple: New Hope for Solving Wicked Problems*, 2nd ed., (2018).

26 See, e.g., Cabrera, D. and Cabrera, L., *Systems Thinking Made Simple: New Hope for Solving Wicked Problems*, 2nd ed., (2018), Gleick, J., *Chaos: Making a New Science*, (Vintage, London, 1987). On developmental psychology, the reference is to the chronosystem elucidated by Bronfenbrenner, U., *The Ecology of Human Development: Experiments by Nature and Design*, (Harvard University Press, Cambridge, MA, 1979).

27 See, e.g., Greenman, P. S. and Johnson, S. M., "Process Research on Emotionally Focused Therapy (EFT) for Couples: Linking Theory to Practice", *Family Process*, (2013), 52, pp 46–61. This discusses therapy based on John Bowlby's Attachment Theory.

28 Schein, E. H., "Culture: The Missing Concept in Organization Studies", *Administrative Science Quarterly*, (1996), 41(2), p 229, Schein, E. H., "From Brainwashing to Organizational Therapy: A Conceptual and Empirical Journey in Search of 'Systemic' Health and a General Model of Change Dynamics. A Drama in Five Acts", *Organization Studies*, (2006); Schein, E. H., *Organisational Culture and Leadership, 5th ed.*, (Wiley, Hoboken, NJ, 2017).

29 Schein, E. H., *Organisational Culture and Leadership* 5th ed., (2017).

30 Vaughan, D., *The Challenger Launch Decision: Risky Technology, Culture, and Deviance at NASA* (Chicago University Press, Chicago, 2016).

31 Vaughan, D., 'Beyond Macro- and Micro-Levels of Analysis, Organizations, and the Cultural Fix', (eds) Pontell and Geis, in *International Handbook of White-Collar and Corporate Crime*, (Springer, New York, NY, 2007), pp 3–24: 4. Vaughan suggests levels include macro (large-scale social structures and institutions), meso (formal and complex organizations such as business corporations, industries, states, and government agencies), and micro (human agency in the form of face-to-face interaction as well as the process of acting toward things based on social meanings created as well as the interaction with macro processes) are all operating concurrently. See also Bronfenbrenner, U., *The Ecology of Human Development: Experiments by Nature and Design*, (1979) for a discussion of a similar distinction between different systems operating in a child's life and development.

32 DNB, *Supervision of Behaviour & Culture: Foundations, Practice, and Future Developments*, (DeNederlandscheBank, Amsterdam, 2015). The iceberg model of culture developed by Schein is a major part of DNB's approach, that by understanding the deep drivers of behavior, particularly those social norms that arise in relationships, risk managers can prevent problems arising by anticipating behavior in certain situations.

33 McBarnet, D., "After Enron will 'Whiter than White Collar Crime' Still Wash?", *British Journal of Criminology*, (2006), 46(6), pp 1091–1109.

34 It is important to note that there may be times that professionals accept responsibility and assume guilt simply because the incident happened on their watch. This may be unjustifiable on objective grounds as systemic causes may have contributed much more to the situation. This can lead to what Dekker describes as "secondary victimization" when while suffering from guilt and remorse, employees receive no emotional support from their organization. See Dekker, S., *Second Victim: Error, Guilt, Trauma, and Resilience*, (CRC Press, Boca Raton, FL, 2013): viii.

35 Syed, M., *Black Box Thinking: Marginal Gains and the Secrets of High Performance*, (2015).

36 Syed, M., *Black Box Thinking: Marginal Gains and the Secrets of High Performance*, (2015): 56. Syed highlights a number of NHS hospital deaths that were never investigated plus a general unwillingness to investigate throughout the system. Where investigations did happen, frequently cover-ups were involved. Finally, lessons learned, (in rare cases) are not adopted broadly throughout the sector because of both cultural issues and the deluge of information already in the system.

37 Sparrow, M. K., *The Character of Harms: Operational Challenges in Control*, (Cambridge University Press, Cambridge, 2008).

38 Steven Burd, CEO of Safeway, which planned to install the technology in 900 stores testified in October 2021 at the trial of Elizabeth Holmes that they had done a "thorough investigation" with over 100 hours of due diligence before signing their deal. Despite this, and the obvious failings of test trials, the deal was signed worth $400 million. See www.cnbc.com/2021/10/12/safeway-ex-ceo-we-did-at-least-100-hours-of-diligence-on-theranos.html. [Accessed October 13, 2021].

39 McBarnet, D., "After Enron Will 'Whiter than White Collar Crime' Still Wash?", *British Journal of Criminology*, (2006); McLean, B. and Elkind, P., *The Smartest Guys in the Room: The Amazing Rise and Scandaous Fall of Enron*, (Penguin, New York, NY, 2003).

40 Fusaro, P. C. and Miller, R. M., *What Went Wrong at Enron*, (John Wiley, Hoboken, NJ, 2002).

41 Turnage, A. and Keyton, J., 'Ethical Contradictions and E-mail Communication at Enron Corporation', (ed) May, in *Case Studies in Organizational Communication: Ethical Perspectives and Practices*, (Sage, Los Angeles, CA, 2013), pp 87–98: 90.

42 Turnage, A. and Keyton, J., 'Ethical Contradictions and E-mail Communication at Enron Corporation', (ed) May, in *Case Studies in Organizational Communication: Ethical Perspectives and Practices*, (2013): 93.

43 Available on YouTube at www.youtube.com/watch?v=bsLbDzkIy3A. [Accessed September 11, 2021].

Bibliography

Babiak, P. and Hare, R. D., *Snakes in Suits: Understanding and Surviving the Psychopaths in Your Office*, (Harper Collins, New York, 2019).

Borum, R., Gelles, M. G. and Kleinman, S. M., 'Interview and Interrogation: A perspective and update from the USA', (eds) Milne, Savage and Williamson, in *International Developments in Investigative Interviewing*, (Willan, Cullompton, 2009) pp 111–125.

Bronfenbrenner, U., *The Ecology of Human Development: Experiments by Nature and Design*, (Harvard University Press, Cambridge, MA, 1979).

Brown, P. C., Roediger III, H. L. and McDaniel, M. A., *Make It Stick: The Science of Successful Learning*, (Harvard University Press, Cambridge, MA, 2014).

Cabrera, D. and Cabrera, L., *Systems Thinking Made Simple: New Hope for Solving Wicked Problems*, 2nd ed., (Plectica Publishing, New York, 2018).

Clarke, C. and Milne, R., *The National Evaluation of the PEACE Investigative Interviewing Course*, (Institute of Criminal Justice Studies. Report No. PRAS/149, Portsmouth University, 2001).

Cook, R. I., "How Complex Systems Fail: (Being a Short Treatise on the Nature of Failure; How Failure is Evaluated; How Failure is Attributed to Proximate Cause;

and the Resulting New Understanding of Patient Safety)", *Cognitive Technologies Laboratory, University of Chicago*, (2000), https://ckrybus.com/static/papers/how_complex_systems_fail_cook_2000.pdf

Dekker, S., *Second Victim: Error, Guilt, Trauma, and Resilience*, (CRC Press, Boca Raton, FL, 2013).

DNB, *Supervision of Behaviour & Culture: Foundations, Practice, and Future Developments*, (DeNederlandscheBank, Amsterdam, 2015).

Fusaro, P. C. and Miller, R. M., *What Went Wrong at Enron*, (John Wiley, Hoboken, NJ, 2002).

Gleick, J., *Chaos: Making a New Science*, (Vintage, London, 1987).

Greenman, P. S. and Johnson, S. M., "Process Research on Emotionally Focused Therapy (EFT) for Couples: Linking Theory to Practice", *Family Process*, (2013), 52, pp 46–61.

King, M., "Financial Fraud Investigative Interviewing—Corporate Investigators' Beliefs and Practices: A Qualitative Inquiry", *Journal of Financial Crime*, (2021), 28(2), pp 345–358.

Kohnken, G., Milne, R., Memon, A. and Bull, R., "The Cognitive Interview: A Meta-Analysis", *Psychology, Crime & Law*, (1999), 5, pp 3–27.

Langer, E., 'The Illusion of Control', (eds) Kahneman, Tversksy and Slovic, in *Judgement under Uncertainty: Heuristics and Biases*, (Cambridge University Press, Cambridge, 1982) pp 231–238.

Leo, R., "From Coercion to Deception: The Changing Nature of Police Interrogation in America", *Crime, Law & Social Change*, (1992), 18(1–2), pp 35–59.

Leo, R., *Police Interrogation and American Justice*, (Harvard University Press, Harvard, 2008).

McBarnet, D., "After Enron Will 'Whiter Than White Collar Crime' Still Wash?", *British Journal of Criminology*, (2006), 46(6), pp 1091–1109.

McLean, B. and Elkind, P., *The Smartest Guys in the Room: The Amazing Rise and Scandaous Fall of Enron*, (Penguin, New York, NY, 2003).

Meerts, C., "Corporate Investigations: Beyond Notions of Public–Private Relations", *Journal of Contemporary Criminal Justice*, (2020), 36(1), pp 86–100.

Milne, R. and Bull, R., *Investigative Interviewing: Psychology and Practice*, (Wiley, Chichester, 1999).

Missal, M., Fishman, E., Ochs, B. and Kline Dubill, R., "Conducting Corporate Internal Investigations", *International Journal of Disclosure and Governance*, (2007), 4(4), pp 297–308.

O'Boyle, E. H., Forsyth, D. R., Banks, G. C. and McDaniel, M. A., "Meta-Analysis of the Dark Triad and Work Behavior: A Social Exchange Perspective", *Journal of Applied Psychology*, (2012), 97(3), pp 557–579.

Paulhus, D. L. and Williams, K. M., "The Dark Triad of Personality: Narcissism, Machiavellianism, and Psychopathy", *Journal of Research in Personality*, (2002), 36(6), pp 556–563.

Sageman, M., *Misunderstanding Terrorism*, (Pennsylvania University Press, Philadelphia, PA, 2017).

Schein, E. H., "Culture: The Missing Concept in Organization Studies", *Administrative Science Quarterly*, (1996), 41(2), p 229.

Schein, E. H., "From Brainwashing to Organizational Therapy: A Conceptual and Empirical Journey in Search of 'Systemic' Health and a General Model of Change Dynamics. A Drama in Five Acts", *Organization Studies*, (2006), 27(2), pp 287–301.

Schein, E. H., *Organisational Culture and Leadership*, 5th ed., (Wiley, Hoboken, NJ, 2017).

Solzhenitsyn, A., *The Gulag Archipelago*, (The Harville Press, London, 1986).

Sparrow, M. K., *The Character of Harms: Operational Challenges in Control*, (Cambridge University Press, Cambridge, 2008).

St. Yves, M. and Deslauriers-Varin, N., 'The Psychology of Suspects Decision-Making during Interrogation', (eds) Bull, Valentine and Williamson, in *Handbook of Psychology of Investigative Interviewing*, (Wiley-Blackwell, Chichester, 2009) pp 1–16.

Syed, M., *Black Box Thinking: Marginal Gains and the Secrets of High Performance*, (John Murray, London, 2015).

Tajfel, H., "Social Psychology of Intergroup Relations", *Annual Review of Psychology*, (1982), 33(1), p 1.

Tajfel, H. and Turner, J. C., 'An Integrative Theory of Intergroup Conflict', (eds) Austin and Worchel, in *The Social Psychology of Intergroup Relations*, (Brooks/Cole, Monterey, CA, 1979) pp 33–47.

Thompson, N. and Pascal, J., "Developing Critically Reflective Practice", *Reflective Practice*, (2012), 13(2), pp 311–325.

Turnage, A. and Keyton, J., 'Ethical Contradictions and E-mail Communication at Enron Corporation', (ed) May, in *Case Studies in Organizational Communication: Ethical Perspectives and Practices*, (Sage, Los Angeles, CA, 2013) pp 87–98.

Tyler, T. R., "Enhancing Police Legitimacy", *The Annals of the American Academy of Political and Social Science*, (2004), 593(1), pp 84–99.

Vaughan, D., 'Beyond Macro- and Micro-levels of Analysis, Organizations, and the Cultural Fix', (eds) Pontell and Geis, in *International Handbook of White-Collar and Corporate Crime*, (Springer, New York, NY, 2007) pp 3–24.

Vaughan, D., *The Challenger Launch Decision: Risky Technology, Culture, and Deviance at NASA*, (Chicago University Press, Chicago, 2016).

Williams, J. W., "Governability Matters: The Private Policing of Economic Crime and the Challenge of Democratic Governance", *Policing and Society*, (2005), 15(2), pp 187–211.

Williams, J. W., 'The Private Eyes of Corporate Culture: The Forensic Accounting and Corporate Investigation Industry and the Production of Corporate Financial Security', (eds) Walby and Lippert, in *Corporate Security in the 21st Century: Theory and Practice in International Perspective*, (Palgrave Macmillan UK, London, 2014) pp 56–77.

Chapter 2

Criminal Proofs and Concepts of the Common Law

Introduction

An interviewer is conducting an investigation for a specific purpose and whatever is being investigated is usually a breach of some written code, whether policy or law. A criminal offense means that a law has been broken. Likewise, a breach of company policy means that some deviation from a specified behavior has occurred. In such a case, the specificity of the policy or law is important. The criminal law is built on the concept of free will and that everyone is responsible for their actions, hence, culpability is examined around the intentions of the person doing the behavior. There is little or no examination of context or circumstances that created a potential criminogenic environment. Obviously, in some crimes, there are certain defenses dependent on context, but there is no focus on systemic contributors. In truth, this keeps the law sufficiently cogent and manageable as to do otherwise would create excessive obligations in terms of proofs.

In the case of a criminal offense, for instance, the law will clearly define the behavior that is illegal and the sanction it will attract. It is a foundational tenet of the common law that a person is considered innocent until proven guilty. In a criminal trial, it must be proved *beyond a reasonable doubt* that the person is guilty of that specified crime. In a civil case, the standard is somewhat lower, the requirement being the *balance of probabilities*. In either case, evidence that the person is responsible for some act or omission must be presented, and this must include evidence covering all the necessary elements to be proved. While the actual requirement to present before a court may never arise, it is important to understand some basic principles of the common law. This avoids simple mistakes that can have a major impact on the subsequent investigation, prosecution, or other sanction. This chapter covers some basic terms from the laws of evidence and is included to provide the context that an investigation is occurring in. The interview is not a conversation or counseling session, it is designed to discover the truth about some alleged deviation or breach. The interviewer, therefore, must be familiar with what he or she is trying to achieve in the context of their investigation. Understanding how they are constructed will assist in conducting any interview, not just investigating potential criminal offenses.

DOI: 10.4324/9781003269489-2

The common law applies to most English-speaking countries, although considerable differences have evolved. Consequently, this chapter is not meant to be legal advice, and an investigator must understand the pertinent laws covering their specific jurisdiction to ensure accuracy and relevance.

Proof

Proof is offered through the presentation of tangible material called 'exhibits' or through intangible information such as scientific data or testimony by witnesses. When proofs are accepted and allowed to be introduced into the trial, they are referred to as evidence.[1] Tangible evidence is often referred to as *real evidence*, while intangible evidence includes *oral testimony* as well as *representative evidence*. Representative evidence is evidence such as a diagram or photograph that represents something else.[2] From our perspective, evidence is therefore any information, data, or material that tends to prove the existence of a particular fact or the truth of an assertion. In criminal justice, the purpose of proving facts through the presentation of evidence is to convince a court or a similar tribunal to accept a particular version of events.[3] Generally, these require any evidence to be relevant to the issue at hand and be probative rather than unfairly prejudicial or confusing. In a trial, it is the function of the judge to decide the admissibility of evidence although rules of evidence can vary considerably, even in the same jurisdiction. The judge may comment on the credibility of the witness, so it is important that the witness has been questioned carefully.[4] It is usual that criminal courts have higher standards in allowing in evidence compared to civil lawsuits.

The evidence itself can either be direct or circumstantial. Direct evidence tends to prove something directly, as in a witness who testifies that he saw the mugger/accused hit the lady before grabbing her bag and running away. Circumstantial evidence is evidence that requires an inference to be made to link the evidence to the crime. An example could be a witness who testifies that he witnessed the accused throw away a lady's handbag into the thrash. In such a situation, the evidence does not link the person directly to the crime but the disposal of the bag by that person might allow the inference to be made that it was he who stole it (context dependent). Circumstantial evidence may go toward corroborating other evidence. Corroboration is evidence that tends to strengthen other evidence. Corroboration is important as individual strands of evidence, although individually weak, may be woven together to form a strong rope capable of supporting the burden of proof. For instance, lies told by a person may serve to corroborate the other evidence against him or her. In one English criminal case, the defendant lied about his whereabouts at the time of the crime, and this evidence corroborated identification evidence offered by a witness.[5] Evidence can be a critical factor in proving any allegations, particularly where no verbal admissions are made. Evidence may be also exculpatory, and evidence should never be concealed or disposed of, even if its relevance is not fully appreciated or understood at the time. As previously noted, most private investigators operate outside the criminal justice arena, and unless someone seeks redress through the civil courts, there may never be judicial oversight. Nevertheless, it is vital to understand that evidence is the bedrock of building a case, and the process that is used in the criminal prosecution of a case provides a recognized methodology that is beneficial to any type of investigation.

Chain of Custody

Evidence is therefore vital and how it is collected is extremely important. Exclusionary rules in court determine what evidence members of the jury will even hear about.[6] Evidence can be excluded for a number of reasons, and one of the most important is if there is a doubt about the provenance of the evidence, known as the chain of custody. The chain of custody ensures evidence is collected and controlled thereafter in such a way that there is no possibility of it changing in nature, so the process used must give assurance that the evidence cannot have been altered or changed in any way from when it first came into existence. Therefore, the capture of evidence is an essential element to any successful investigation, and using a camera, exhibit bags, and maintaining accurate written records are essential to gathering and preserving evidence. Any evidence that is forensically examined must be tracked through all of the different stages so that every action taken is accountable, and the reasons for it can be explained. The custody chain of evidence is to ensure that there has been no potential for anyone to interfere with the evidence, and its current state is the same as its original state, unless otherwise accounted for. This principle is known as the *doctrine of documentary evidence*, and its purpose is to show a court that the evidence produced is no more and no less now than when it was first taken into the possession of law enforcement. That is, the evidence has not been altered or interfered with in any way. It is insufficient to establish that there was no deliberate interference; it must be shown that no one, other than authorized persons who had reason to, had access to the evidence.

The *best evidence* rule arose for a similar purpose to protect the integrity of evidence and may require the production in court of an original document in court as opposed to a copy of it. The rule dates from a time when copies were handmade and inherently unreliable. Although the rule still exists, the advent of large computer data storage methods makes bringing original documents impractical. Therefore, downloads of data are generally acceptable as accurate copies of information held digitally. The custody chain remains important, and the person who downloaded the data, their level of expertise to do so, the integrity of the data, and when it was done are issues that must be proved.

Criminal Offenses

Many investigators may never investigate a criminal offense. Nonetheless, an understanding of how criminal liability is constructed focuses an interviewer on questions that need to be asked to establish culpability or responsibility. There are certain elements that must be covered in the interview or investigation more broadly to ensure that culpability is made explicit, and sufficient evidence is gathered to prove that culpability.

An offense is written into law in a specific way, containing certain elements that must all be present before the law is broken. For instance, in the United Kingdom, the offense of theft under the Theft Act 1968 is defined as:

> A person is guilty of theft if he dishonestly appropriates property belonging to another with the intention of permanently depriving the other of it.

This deceptively simple definition of an offense is nevertheless constituted by various elements that are themselves the culmination of long-standing legal precedent and meaning. For instance, appropriates is not the same as 'misappropriates', and so there is no need to show in the United Kingdom that the property was taken without the owner's consent.[7] Generally, a statement from the owner outlining that there was no consent is used to show that the person took the property. The *dishonestly* element of the offense means that there is no legal right to take the property, or there is no agreement from the owner to take it, or the person did not take reasonable steps to find the true owner. However, the last part does not apply to people who are entrusted with the property as trustees or personal representatives.[8] The legal right to take the property is important as even if the person was been mistaken that they had a right to the property but where that is a reasonable and genuinely held belief, then it is not considered theft as they did not intend to steal it.[9] The meaning of *permanently deprived* is generally considered to be where the person intends to treat that property as their own and disregard the owner's rights, usually by keeping it or selling it on.

In criminal legislation, fraud is a specific form of theft, so there is considerable overlap between the two. The offense of fraud may be simply defined as when 'a person is financially cheated by another person as when an individual deceives another by inducing them to do something or not do something that results in a financial loss'. This definition essentially captures the two key elements present in fraudulent activity: the deception of a person, whether natural or legal, with the purpose of making a financial gain at the expense of that person or of another person. US wire fraud makes it a criminal offense for a person devising any scheme to defraud, or for obtaining money or property, by means of false or fraudulent pretenses, representations, or promises, to then transmit any writing, signs, or signals, for the purpose of executing the scheme, that is punishable by up to 20 years.[10] In the United Kingdom, Fraud Act 2006, states:

A person is guilty of fraud if he is in breach of

a   section 2 (fraud by false representation),
b   section 3 (fraud by failing to disclose information), and
c   section 4 (fraud by abuse of position)

Section 4 of the Act, for instance, deals with an abuse of position by someone who commits an act or fails to do something and who dishonestly abused the position and intended by that abuse to make a gain/cause a loss. In such an investigation, the matters of importance include the nature of the relationship, the specific abuse alleged, and how that caused a loss to the victim or made a gain to the suspect. The investigation, and specifically the interviewer, needs to cover each element to ensure that all constituent parts are contained within each offense. Failing, for instance, to show that there was an acknowledged relationship between the victim and the person who is alleged to have abused their position will mean there is no prospect of a criminal case proceeding.

Culpability

Aside from the specifics of the offense, criminal law generally requires that a person deliberately or knowingly commits the offense. Not, it must be emphasized, knowingly commits a crime but knowingly does an act that is a crime. Ignorance of the law is no excuse but doing something accidentally is not a culpable act, usually. For instance, someone who accidentally bumps into someone while walking along the pavement is innocent of an assault claim. This is the mental element of the offense, known as the intention. In legal terms, the *mens rea* or *guilty mind* establishes the *culpability* of the accused. The prosecution must usually prove that the accused had *intent* when doing the act and therefore acted maliciously. Sometimes an offense is constructed differently, and intent is not necessary, rather it is simply necessary that a person acted recklessly. Recklessly is where someone recognized the risks but proceeded with the action regardless. Negligence, on the other hand, does not need any consideration of the consequences. But the action is one that an observer would regard as careless or below the expected standard of behavior. Under normal circumstances, a person is expected to anticipate the consequences of their actions. Therefore, in any interview, questions around the preoffense behavior are important to establish if the person understood the likely outcomes from their behavior. In the corporate sector, the planning of an offense or efforts to conceal the crime from others such as managers or coworkers prior to committing them are necessary to establish that guilty-knowing mind. Efforts to conceal after, on the other hand, may be important but could simply show a desire to cover up a mistake.

Sometimes an offense can be committed without any type of intention on the part of the actor. In such a case, it is termed a strict liability offense. The very doing of the act is sufficient; there is no mental element. For instance, many traffic offenses are strict liability offenses. If I am caught driving over the speed limit, there is no need to prove anything except that fact. In an organizational setting, an offense such as bullying is a similar offense. Bullying is defined as behavior from a person or group that's unwanted and makes you feel uncomfortable.[11] Harassment, however, is bullying that is directed at a protected characteristic such as age, gender, disability, religion, or sexual orientation.[12] As such, harassment is against the law if it violated the person's dignity, whether intended or not or created a hostile environment for the person, whether intended or not. In some cases, one single incident is sufficient, or a catalogue of ongoing behavior, even if minor in themselves, may suffice. What is of note in relation to the bullying is how the person felt, not the intention of the offender. Accordingly, a series of relatively minor incidents may combine to generate evidence of bullying behavior. Where bullying has occurred and the additional element of it being conducted in the context of a protected characteristic is included, it becomes harassment. As such, this information forms an important aspect of the interviewing process, and the properly constituted questions need to be asked depending on the matter being investigated.

Finally, some offenses are *omission* offenses, where someone is expected by law to perform some action such as in certain legislation to prevent money laundering by ensuring training of officials and fails to do so. These are rare but becoming more common as a criminal law deterrent in areas such as the financial sectors. Even where criminal offenses defined by crimes of omission contrary to crimes of commission remain rare, it remains an important concept from a moral and ethical perspective in an organization. Managers and those in a supervisory role should be expected to take an active interest in the practices of employees. The notion of turning a blind eye to unsavory practices should be seen as unacceptable behavior. This can be used to counter any claims of no culpability based on strict legal criteria because the fact that the person ignored a moral obligation can be seen as abdicating responsibilities, either expressed or implied by nature of their supervisory role. Interview questions should focus on company policies and training received. In other words, what behavior was expected in the organization versus what occurred.

In sum, even where it is not breaches of law that are being investigated but company policy, a similar approach to breaking down the specific allegation into its elements should be done. This ensures that the investigation covers all the necessary elements of the breach to ensure the proper evidence is gathered to prove the offense or deviance and a full understanding of the breach can be established.

Hearsay

Hearsay is a term to cover a written, verbal, or nonverbal statement (such as pointing) made outside of court and is made to offer the truth of the matter asserted.[13] Normally, it means that a person makes a statement that someone else said something to them. There are a number of exceptions where it is allowed to be given into evidence, but generally, unless a person is available to make the original statement in court, it is excluded. The reasons for this are the inherent unreliability of such secondhand statements based on faulty perception, memory, the telling of the account (narration), or the intention to deceive (sincerity).[14] Nevertheless, it is acceptable practice (within limits) to allow hearsay into statements witnesses make. This is because in certain situations hearsay provides context and unless irrelevant can be included. There may even be consideration given to include it when it is unreliable if other evidence can be gathered to shows its inaccuracies, as it may show an effort to deceive. Moreover, it allows follow-up interviews to be arranged with the relevant individuals if sufficiently important.

Voluntariness

The major important legal consideration in conducting an interview is its perceived fairness and the lack of oppression. In most Western countries, people possess rights that protect them from State interference. These range from protection against arbitrary arrest and detention to the right and expectation of privacy. These rights have evolved over many years and strive to maintain a balance between the power of the State to intervene in someone's life to protect others or investigate crime and a citizen's right to be left in peace free from interference by the State. The criminal law sphere is particularly governed by a combination of legal precedent and legislation enshrining these rights. Generally, these provisions protect an individual from the overreach of the State or its agents. Interactions between individuals or between private organizations and individuals are not subject to the same protections. Obviously, individuals can seek protection from the criminal law or make a complaint if a law is broken; likewise, the civil process whereby someone can seek damages through torts is available if someone feels wronged. But generally, the responsibilities placed on the State are not replicated in the interpersonal sphere, so a company can set its own rules and policies and expect employees to follow them. Once there is not discrimination against individuals based on characteristics such as race, gender, religion, or sexual orientation, the company can govern its own business as it sees fit. Employees may be expected to adhere to certain behaviors or be made redundant.

Therefore, most organizations can set rules requiring employees to fully cooperate with an investigation and impart all information in their possession. So, unlike the situation with the criminal law in many countries, the 'right of silence' has no place in private investigations. This means that an employee may be expected to cooperate fully with an investigation by answering questions. However, it does not mean that an individual can be forced to remain in the interview room against their will. It is assumed to be voluntary cooperation, but if an employee decides to withdraw their cooperation, they are free to leave. The consequences in terms of employment are a separate matter and should not be within the remit of the investigator to decide. Under no circumstances should an investigator force a person to remain in an interview room when they wish to leave. That is detaining a person and depriving them of their liberty which may be a criminal act in itself.

The right of silence itself is fundamental to the common law criminal process that has been pretty consistent in the common law system over hundreds of years. It remains one of the most important legal rights that a confession must be voluntary, and that no one should be forced to confess has been established. A confession that is forced from a person is inadmissible in a criminal court.[15] This established legal doctrine enshrined the common law's aversion to judicial torture that was a feature of the European continental justice system until late in the eighteenth century. The doctrine is also known as the *right against self-incrimination,* and it remains the subject of ongoing debate and jurisprudence. In the United States, it developed to a constitutional right of silence which police must respect and includes the reading of the Miranda rights to any person they arrest.[16] A suspect must sign a waiver to actually permit police questioning to commence, as well as excluding a lawyer. However, the situation before an arrest is made is somewhat more complex. Broadly speaking, there is no need to warn a person about their right to silence if he or she is not under arrest.[17]

In other common law countries, a person who is not warned about the implications of speaking to police, even if not under arrest, cannot have any admissions made by them admitted as evidence in a criminal court.[18] Generally, the right to silence is interpreted slightly differently as an arrested suspect must submit to police questioning (if properly detained), although before questioning begins, he or she must be informed that they are not obliged to answer questions.[19] In a criminal case, an admission made to a police investigator or such a *person in authority* is considered an exception to the hearsay rule—which prevents statements made outside the courthouse being given in evidence—because it is a statement against interest. In other words, it is not to the benefit of the person making it, rather it is averse to their interest. A warning must be given to the person before he or she is questioned known as 'the caution', for instance, in England, it is stated as:

> You are not obliged to say anything unless you wish to do so, but anything you do say will be taken down in writing and may be given in evidence.[20]

Police in democratic countries operate under strict regulations, guidelines, and oversight to prevent mistreatment of prisoners and the obtaining of involuntary or unfairly obtained confessions. The purpose of the caution is to ensure that the person understands that they do not have to speak and is aware of the potential use of any statement if they choose to speak. In many common law countries, the law around using the caution will apply equally to regulators also or indeed any state investigator where there is even a slight possibility of a criminal court outcome. Even private investigators need to be aware of the rules around using the caution. In general, any person who is the subject of an investigation that uncovers alleged criminal behavior that subsequently may result in sanction before a criminal court should be reminded of their right to remain silent. Therefore, the caution should be given before every formal interview of a person who *might* be a suspect or during any witness interview when it becomes apparent to the regulator that the person is now making admissions that could see them before a criminal court.

While the freedom to remain silent is an important right in criminal law, this does not mean that the State never compels a citizen. The awesome power of the State is most often evident when the State is deprived of income. In any country, a citizen is compelled to provide full and accurate tax returns. So, compulsion, *per se,* is not invalid, but it depends on the use that is then made of the answer. In areas of administrative law such as personal or corporate tax compliance, company law, or road traffic legislation, it is used routinely. The European Court of Human Rights accepts that compulsion has its place but any answers obtained in such a process will probably not be admitted to a criminal court as evidence.[21] Therefore, regulatory bodies may have powers such as compelling an individual to produce documents or answer questions that police do not have. Where regulators do use compulsion powers to obtain answers, these are usually not admissible before a criminal court. It would be necessary for a police officer to caution the suspect in the course of a new interview which is necessary to obtain the evidence in a manner permissible by the courts.

The issue with compelling someone to answer questions is that their answers are not voluntary. To have an adverse statement or admission admitted into evidence, police must prove the statement was given voluntarily, even if the caution was administered. Both the Miranda warning and the caution alert people to the possibility of having anything they chose to say used against them, but the most important facet of any admission is that the person made it freely, of their own will, as opposed to being forced to make it by any inducement. Inducement is an umbrella term applied to threats of force, use of oppressive tactics, or promises made for the sole purpose of compelling the person to make admissions. A confession should come from free will as opposed to a coerced mind, coerced through either hope or fear.

Accordingly, in an interview situation where an employee is under an obligation to assist the investigation and answer questions, it is unlikely criminal courts would regard the confession as voluntary. Most private investigations are not conducted as part of the criminal justice process so the fact that they would be inadmissible in a criminal court is of little relevance. Nonetheless, whether or not the interview is to be used in a criminal case, it should be transparently fair. In other words, an interviewer should set aside the compulsion made to attend the interview and answer questions and should try to conduct the interview as fairly as possible. Inducements such as promises—of leniency, for instance, in return for an admission—must not be made to the interviewee. Furthermore, there must be no element of underhanded trickery, for example, the person should understand the seriousness of the investigation and not be misled that it is a minor matter when it is not. That means that the interviewee should not be tricked into believing that the interview is something that it is not. If the matter is serious or has potential serious consequences for the interviewee, it would be unfair to claim that it was only a minor chat. An interviewee should be informed ahead of time of the interview and its purpose. But in the interview room, the interviewer should again explain the matter under investigation, without minimizing the seriousness of it. The interviewee should be informed if there is potential for information gathered to be supplied to external agencies, if applicable, such as regulators. The purpose of the interview and its potential implications should be clear, at least in the context of the known information. If an interviewee chooses to seek legal advice, this must then be facilitated. It would be patently unfair to inform an interviewee of potential serious consequences of an interview but deny them the ability to obtain independent legal advice. If one is a legal counsel doing interviews in the United States, it is necessary to warn the interviewee that while the information they provide is privileged, the decision whether to retain that privilege rests with the employer who has mandated the investigation. Therefore, the decision whether to share the information with entities such as regulators or other state agencies rests with the employer.[22]

In relation to incentives such as promises of leniency or any kind of deal to obtain an admission, they should not be offered *if the admission is to be later admitted in a court*. In many organizational investigations, that is not an objective and the result sought may be the return of stolen funds or the name of another person involved in the deviance. In such cases, utilizing an industrial relations strategy to offer a deal can be acceptable. For instance, where company property has been stolen, but there is a reasonable prospect of recovering same, then offering a deal in return for cooperation may be acceptable.[23] If the deal succeeds in its objective, it is acceptable. If it fails, any admissions made after the offer was made will be problematic. However, sometimes it is a call worth making, but the rationale to do so should be laid out clearly.

Under no circumstances should threats of physical violence be made, but even threats about further employment may be problematic. Generally, the investigator should avoid the discussion of the consequences of the interview. It is normally sufficient to simply state that once a report is furnished, any further actions are in the hands of the relevant employers. It is not usually a threat to answer questions from the interviewee with answers that are factually correct and within common knowledge. It is usual that people seek information when they are trying to understand their situation or their world and are trying to reduce uncertainty.[24] Supplying genuine and honest information within the experience of the interviewer is normally acceptable, although one should be careful not to extend into legal advice. The interviewer should be careful to ensure the interview does not mistake any such comments as legal advice and should be advised accordingly.

Once again, it is important to remember that any person who loses his or her job because of an investigation would be entitled to take a legal case arguing the dismissal was unfair or disproportionate and challenge the propriety of the investigation. Hence, the interview process may attract judicial scrutiny and criticism even if there is no criminal complaint. As a result of this potential, a professional approach should always be taken, all interviews should be conducted fairly and respectfully, with best practice always followed.

Electronic Recording

Deciding whether to electronically record the interview is another important consideration. Certainly, if only one interviewer is conducting the interview, especially a formal interview, then the option of electronically recording the interview is the most feasible option. Such a decision will be based on the seriousness of the matter under investigation and possible future sanctions involved. Some people may object to being recorded, and the interviewer may choose to call this lack of cooperation and not continue although many companies will give an option of a scribe to the interviewee. In which case, the interview may need to be rescheduled for a scribe to attend. It is possible for the interviewer to take the handwritten notes, but this slows the process down considerably. It is difficult to maintain the question flow, train of thought, or explore unexpected utterances when one has to keep detailed notes. If a second interviewer is present, then it is an option for one to act as a scribe. In some situations, interviewees may also be allowed to bring an independent witness or scribe along. Independent witnesses and scribes should have no input into the interview, their sole purpose being record keeping. This extends also to a legal advisor to the interviewee if provision is made to accommodate the same. A legal advisor is there to observe, not to answer questions on behalf of the interviewee, although a discussion may ensue at the end of the interview. If a company HR representative is involved, they will usually scribe as they want a full record of the conversation. Electronic recording still retains a significant advantage as the scribe inevitably will have difficulty in keeping up and miss some remarks entirely. It is difficult to both listen and write at the same time, especially in a fast-paced interview. In my experience, even a good scribe can miss entire sentences; moreover, the questions and answers are paraphrased, so important context may be omitted, as in the tone of the interview. The tone or attitude of the interviewee is an important element to portray in a private interview. If an interviewee is exceptionally defensive or aggressive, or very reluctant with answers, then that is important information to convey to your clients. Where handwritten HR notes are taken, then the usual practice with HR is that the notes are typed up and parties then sign these typed notes. In other cases, where the interviewer takes his or her own contemporaneous notes, it is usual to read these back at the end of the interview, the interviewee may be then asked to sign that the notes are an accurate record of the interview, although the interviewee is also offered an opportunity to make any corrections or clarifications that they wish to make.

While the major positive of electronic recording is that it is a complete and accurate record of the conversation, which modern software can easily transcribe, the disadvantage is that it can be off-putting for some interviewees. When someone admits wrongdoing, an audiotape becomes a solid piece of evidence, that the admission was made and how it was made. Ultimately, the reality is that where a sole interviewer obtains admissions that are not recorded either in writing and signed by the interviewee or on tape, it will amount to one person's word against another that such admissions were ever made. Consequently, should an interviewee later seek judicial intervention in a disputed dismissal case, for example, an electronic recording of the interview is powerful evidence. Indeed, the very existence of such evidence may discourage these types of civil actions from being contemplated. I recommend that any type of formal interview should be electronically recorded. However, the interviewee should always be informed of this and the purpose of it should be explained to them as necessary to provide an accurate record of what was said. Another advantage of a recording, particularly a video recording, is that it permits a detailed review of the interview. Careful listening and watching of nonverbal behavior are important but can be very difficult in the real-time environment of the interview with the interviewer having a lot of information to process. The ability to review the videotape later may provide some signs of deception that were originally missed.

It is important to understand that not everyone interviewed is suspected of deviant behavior, quite often interviewees are spoken to with a view to understanding processes or events or as witnesses. The level of cooperation may vary, and some may have useful information that they wish to impart. It is a choice for the interviewer to decide at some stage to switch off the recording and go 'off the record', thereby allowing the interviewee to talk freely. I am happy to facilitate this, other investigators are not. If you do make an agreement to receive confidential information, then it should be kept. I do not disclose the source of my information in such cases, and sometimes, the information has to be carefully managed to avoid inadvertently disclosing its source. The balance and flexibility of allowing off the record conversations has paid dividends for me, but it is a personal choice. In my experience, if the organization has not become corrupted entirely, there are still many people in the organization who are concerned about behaviors and are willing to reveal their in-depth knowledge. This is not always the situation; over time, such honest people either leave the organizations to go elsewhere or give up and join the darkside themselves, in which case cooperation is scant throughout the organization.

Conclusion

A person need not have known that he or she was committing a criminal offense as ignorance of the law is no excuse. However, fraud is a legal term to describe a criminal act. Criminal acts have two elements, the physical act and the mental or fault element. Apart from discovering the physical act, it is also important to ensure that the mental element or *mens rea* of the person suspected must be examined and proved. The mental element means that most criminal offenses, other than strict liability offenses, require that the perpetrator knowingly intended the consequences of his or her actions or was reckless about the consequences. This is more relevant to police and regulatory interviews where it is essential that the individual elements of the offense are considered and evidence gathered to support each element as one would if one was moving to successfully prosecute in court. In an interview with a person suspected of committing a crime, the purpose of the interview is to obtain an account of knowledge and not just put the allegations and evidence supporting those allegations to the person. His or her response may neutralize such evidence, tend to confirm the evidence, or have no effect. The interview is the opportunity to respond, nonetheless, although the investigator has no control over whether someone takes that opportunity. In a private investigation, most employees have no choice but to cooperate. In all circumstances, an interview should still be conducted fairly. Evidence must be carefully and correctly gathered. The principles of criminal law may never be obvious for a private investigator, but these principles are important to pay heed to.

Notes

1   Friedland, S. I., Bergman, P. and Taslitz, A. E., *Evidence Law and Practice*, (Lexis Publishing, New York, 2000): 3.
2   Friedland, S. I., Bergman, P. and Taslitz, A. E., *Evidence Law and Practice*, (2000): 5.
3   Hannibal, M. and Mountford, L., *The Law of Criminal and Civil Evidence: Principles and Practice*, (Longman, Harlow, England, 2002): 31.
4   Consequently, it is preferable that a witness is challenged on his or her account at the interview stage rather than at trial where a loss of credibility may have a detrimental effect on the whole trial or civil case. Many cases of wrongful convictions in the criminal justice system are based on erroneous eyewitness identification. Therefore, an eyewitness might be assessed through the mnemonic ADVOKATE:

A is for the amount of time the witness had the person under observation,
D is for distance away,
V and **O** represent visibility and any obstructions inhibiting it,
K stands for previously known or seen before,
The next **A** stands for any particular reason to remember,
T is for time elapsed,
and **E** is for errors or material discrepancies noted (by interviewer).

In cases of organizational investigations, wrongful identification may be less of a problem, although it should still be borne in mind. But it is important that any potential in the witness for bias or veracity be fully explored and any possible affecting disabilities of the witness be noted. It is important that time be spent at the initial interviews carefully corroborating each witness's account and challenging, if necessary, and that the witness is carefully assessed at the interview as to reliability and confidence.

5   R v Goodway [1993] 4 All ER 894. See also R v Lucas [1981] QB 720 for conditions to be met in such cases.

6 Kiely, T. F., *Forensic Evidence: Science and the Criminal Law*, (CRC, Boca Raton, 2001); Twomey, A., "Poisonous Fruit from a Poisonous Tree: Reforming the Exclusionary Rule for Ireland", *Irish Law Times*, (2012), 30(19), pp 288–292.

7 Lawrence v Metropolitan Police Commissioner (1971) Cr App R 471. However, getting the owner to state that he or she did not give permission to the person to take the property is still the simplest way to prove the situation.

8 United Kingdom Crown Prosecution Service advices on charging suspects. Available at www.cps.gov.uk/legal-guidance/theft-act-offences. [Accessed September 30, 2021].

9 Ivey v Genting Casinos [2018] AC 391.

10 18 USC § 1343.

11 As defined in the United Kingdom. See www.acas.org.uk/if-youre-treated-unfai rly-at-work/being-bullied

12 Equality Act 2010.

13 Friedland, S. I., Bergman, P. and Taslitz, A. E., *Evidence Law and Practice*, (2000): 310.

14 Fisher, G., *Evidence*, (Foundation Press, New York, 2002): 337.

15 Common law countries refer to countries that use the criminal law system of England. Usually, this is for historical reasons as these were colonies of England. Interestingly, Scotland retains its own unique legal system although all members of the European Union were subject to the jurisdiction of the European Court of Human Rights (ECtHR). The ECtHR judgments are gradually introducing harmonization into criminal procedures between the civil law continental systems and the common law jurisdictions. As precedent is an important component of the common law, it is not unusual that case law from one common law jurisdiction, such as the United States, is used to make a legal argument in another jurisdiction.

16 As a result of Miranda v Arizona 384 U.S. 436 [1966]. The right of silence is guaranteed under the Fifth Amendment of the American Constitution. The Miranda warning states: *You have the right to remain silent. Anything you say can and will be used against you in a court of law. You have the right to an attorney. If you cannot afford an attorney, one will be provided for you.* Significantly in 2011, the Supreme Court of Canada rejected the argument that *Miranda* should be "transplanted in Canadian soil": R v Sinclair [2011] 3 S.C.R. 3.

17 Ciarelli, S., "Pre-Arrest silence: Minding That Gap between Fourth Amendment Stops and Fifth Amendment Custody", *Journal of Criminal Law and Criminology*, (2003), 92(2), pp 651–682.

18 There are some exceptions to this situation. For a considerable time, the Judges Rules guided interrogation practice in the United Kingdom. These first appeared in R v Voisin [1918] 1 KB. 531 at 539–40 and remained in force until new regulations were introduced in PACE 1984 that provided statutory powers to police to arrest people for interview.

19 While a person does not have to answer questions, recent legal developments have taken a European provision of *presumptions* to make failing to answer a question an unwise choice in certain scenarios. These adverse inference provisions can be used in certain circumstances to draw inferences from a failure or refusal to answer questions when being questioned.

20 In England and Wales, this is known as the old caution as under the Police and Criminal Evidence (PACE) Act 1984, the new caution places a certain onus on the

suspect to mention anything he or she may rely on in their defense to the police or risk harming their defense.

21 See cases such as Ibrahim v UK (application nos 50541/08, 50571/08, 50573/08, and 40351/09) Sept 2016 at para. 269; also Saunders v UK (1997) 23 EHRR 313; and O'Halloran and Francis v UK (2008) 46 EHRR 21.

22 Known as an 'Upjohn warning' from Upjohn Co v United States 449 U.S. 383 (1981). Held that attorney–client privilege between a company and counsel extends to communications between an investigating counsel and the employees of the company.

23 The old common law offense of Misprision of a Felony involved failing to report serious crimes to the proper authorities. It has been abolished in some countries but remains in others. For instance, in the United States, it remains an offense under 18 USC s.4. Moreover, many jurisdictions require notification about allegations involving financial crimes. Many regulated industries also have similar requirements. Offering an agreement not to report an offense to authorities might itself be a crime.

24 Jowett, G. and O'Donnnell, V., *Propaganda and Persuasion*, (Sage, Thousand Oaks, CA, 2012).

Bibliography

Ciarelli, S., "Pre-Arrest Silence: Minding That Gap between Fourth Amendment Stops and Fifth Amendment Custody", *Journal of Criminal Law and Criminology* (2003), 92(2), pp 651–682.

Fisher, G., *Evidence*, (Foundation Press, New York, 2002).

Friedland, S. I., Bergman, P. and Taslitz, A. E., *Evidence Law and Practice*, (Lexis Publishing, New York, 2000).

Hannibal, M. and Mountford, L., *The Law of Criminal and Civil Evidence: Principles and Practice*, (Longman, Harlow, England, 2002).

Jowett, G. and O'Donnnell, V., *Propaganda and Persuasion*, (Sage, Thousand Oaks, CA, 2012).

Kiely, T. F., *Forensic Evidence: Science and the Criminal Law*, (CRC, Boca Raton, FL, 2001).

Twomey, A., "Poisonous Fruit from a Poisonous Tree: Reforming the Exclusionary Rule for Ireland", *Irish Law Times*, (2012), 30(19), pp 288–292.

Chapter 3

The Fundamentals of Asking Questions

Introduction

An investigator's job is to find answers to questions about the unknown, in many ways like a scientist. Unlike nature though, people are conscious opponents, and they try to disguise their activities, misdirect investigators to confuse or dilute the truth, confabulate, and present false alibis or fabricated material. Interviewing is not the only method to gather information, and the perusal of documents, electronic data, and other artifacts can provide a lot of information, but few investigations have zero human interaction. Questions have to be asked in nearly all, even if it's only from the person briefing the investigator on the specific investigation requirements. Dealing with people is a specific skill, even if often taken for granted, and brings its own unique challenge and is therefore an essential element in a competent investigation.

This chapter discusses the basic skills which orientate around reciprocity, respect, and fairness and utilizes rapport and listening skills to achieve these. It is important to use the right type of questions, and understanding nonverbal behavior is also important. The ideal interview strategy is based on developing a deep knowledge of the issue, careful listening, and asking open broad questions before narrowing down into specifics and using more probing questions to examine details to uncover the truth. These skills require patience and determination to implement, nevertheless they are the most effective as well as being ethical and lawful, and usable in any interview situation, or any other form of interpersonal communication.

The Fundamentals of Interviewing

Interviews vary in complexity and responsiveness. Some will be friendly affairs and informal, no more than social interactions, but that provide useful information. At the other end are tense forensic interviews where someone is suspected for deviant behavior, and they are reluctant to answer questions. These can require additional technical skills. However, police interrogation techniques or interview tactics involving deception, aggression, or a narrow focus on obtaining

DOI: 10.4324/9781003269489-3

admissions of guilt should be avoided under all circumstances in organizational investigations. In the movies, police-suspect interviewing is often confrontational, with the cop shouting accusations. Sometimes threats are made, before the suspect cracks and makes admissions. Indeed, it is a real-life criticism as too often police interviewing has only one purpose and that is to obtain a confession. Because of this blinkered obsession, many innocent people have been convicted on the basis of false confessions.[1] To counteract this phenomenon, police training in many countries is moving toward a non-accusatory interviewing model, where the distinction is between a cooperative or uncooperative interviewee rather than witness or suspect. This is an investigative interviewing model of which forensic investigative interview technique (FIIT) is one. This model can be used in any circumstance, with minor adaptations.

The principal objective is to create a relationship with the interviewee that allows the person to disclose information in his or her possession without feeling judged or criticized. Some interviewees respond better to a more formal and business-like approach from the interviewer, while others respond better to a more casual approach, or even a caring approach, which may change during an interview. It is therefore important that the interviewer have good people skills with an adaptability to respond to different personalities and situations, as some interviewees can move between cooperative and noncooperative behaviors. It is this social interaction between the interviewee and interviewer that is paramount and that leads to the disclosure of useful information. Therefore, an interviewer must adapt his or her own interviewing style and personality to suit the interviewee. A curious mind as well as this emotional intelligence are essential attributes for an interviewer, and indeed, their presence alone may make up for the lack of technical interviewing skills. Demonstrating respect, kindness, and empathy to interviewees is part of emotional intelligence that facilitates information gathering. This includes humility and acknowledges a willingness to learn and recognize others as experts in their fields. It is also an awareness that you cannot know anything for certain; that you are subject to biases, make mistakes, and will not see or know everything; your personality type may not always gel well with an interviewee, this is not necessarily the interviewee's fault, and you are the one responsible for resolving the issue to move the interview forward. A determination to get to the truth is also a necessary attribute as there will be challenges and obstacles to overcome in discovering the truth. Finally, a critical aspect is to avoid a rushed interview, as it is unlikely to be effective. Time should be taken to do it right, including preparation.

Rapport

As noted, building a relationship with the interviewee is very important. Rapport is the term to describe seeking to build a personal connection which is essential for communication. Humans are fundamentally motivated to create and maintain meaningful social relationships with other people.[2]

Communication is a cooperative endeavor where understanding requires some element of trust, and demonstrating warmth and friendliness allows a relationship to develop. Rapport is part of normal social interaction that includes empathy and reciprocity. Reciprocity is a fundamental hardwired human response; when someone gives us something, then we feel socially obligated to return the favor.[3] It is the basis of human cooperation. Empathy is the ability to view a situation from someone else's perspective including understanding their emotional response and is the basic building block of morality.[4]

In the interview room, rapport should establish a respectful, empathic, and nonjudgmental atmosphere in seeking the truth by creating an atmosphere of positive connection between individuals through trust and respect. It avoids judging a person for what they have done, what they believe, or how they see the world to develop trust. These person-centered skills help to obtain cooperation and are the essential elements to a good interview.[5] This interview relationship does not have to be very deep, simply sufficient so that the person is not defensive or closed off from talking. Therefore, rather than a set of guidelines, it is a spirit of respectful interviewing that avoids confrontation—as much as possible—and does not use coercion to force answers. Instead, focus is put on positive communication skills, open-mindedness, flexibility, and an open-questioning structure, with the interview being non-accusatory, the only psychological pressure being created through the highlighting of inconsistencies in responses.[6]

First impressions are therefore important, especially as even a 100-millisecond exposure to a face is sufficient to create a lasting impression.[7] Showing warmth and friendliness is more important than competence, so a smile can achieve a lot. From the outset of the interaction, it is possible to establish both rapport and credibility immediately by conveying a combination of expertise, knowledge, and goodwill,[8] by simply using a confident introduction outlining your role as an investigator and then inquiring after the welfare of the interviewee. A good handshake may also be appropriate. Once this question of how they are has been asked, then the simplest and most effective way of actually building rapport with someone is simply to show the willingness to listen to what they are saying and be willing to express empathy with what they then communicate. Smiling, being pleasant (even in the circumstances of a forensic interview), referring to the interviewee by their first name, and trying to discover what he or she is interested in are basic people skills, as is avoiding criticism and condemnation.[9] Such behavior is simply good social skills while avoiding any hint of authoritative power, which keeps the relationship on a mutually respectful level and avoids power dynamics. Combined, these elements begin to build trust between both parties.

Do not rush or exhibit an impatience to get to the 'important' matters. Demonstrating an empathy with the interviewee's circumstances by showing an awareness of any nervousness and making efforts to relax the interviewee through simple questioning first are important. Ideally, particularly for potential extended interviews, the interviewer should attempt to find some shared common interests or backgrounds. Asking about sports teams, family members such as kids, schooling, and hobbies are all 'small-talk' subjects that can assist in building rapport and relaxing the interviewee. However, asking about the interviewee's career progression is probably the simplest question as it is nonthreatening, as well as relevant, and some people may not want to discuss personal matters. It may also be useful to share some personal information about yourself. Finding shared activities and interests builds commonalities and rapport as it makes the interviewer a similar person with shared interests. The objective is to heighten these similarities between interviewer and interviewee as people bond easier with people just like them. Importantly, it is unnecessary to spend too much time on this aspect as it is a natural process once you are friendly and respectful. Usually, one or two rapport-building questions are therefore sufficient for the beginning of most interviewing situations but be cognizant that maintaining rapport throughout the interview should be a priority.

Once rapport has been established, the next step is to tell the person what the purpose of the interview is and explain that you need to ask some questions. By asking permission in this way, it actively engages cooperation from the interviewee. Explaining that you need to ask some questions because you are conducting an enquiry into an incident provides a reason that people are generally willing to cooperate with. In fact, using the word *because* followed even by a nonsensical explanation appears to automatically engage cooperative tendencies.[10] The time taken to provide a complete explanation of the purpose of the interview is time well spent. As well as assisting in building rapport through ensuring the interviewee understands why he or she is there, it also enhances your professional image. It may also forestall issues such as reluctance from witnesses who may not fully appreciate the severity of the issue under investigation.

Preparing the Space

The decision where to conduct an interview may have a significant impact on the outcome. Informal interviews might be conducted at a person's workstation, while a formal interview will occur in a private room to which the interviewee is usually called to. In the initial phase of many investigations, the informal questioning method is suitable. This preliminary work may filter who is then called to a formal interview. Some types of audits only require informal interviews, but even in informal interviews, it is important that the subject has some privacy. Asking questions within earshot of others may inhibit the person and risks distraction reducing the ability to properly listen.

Where fraud or other potentially serious issues are being investigated, then the formal interview should be considered as more appropriate from the outset, certainly for investigatively important interviewees. A formal interview setting should take place in a room where privacy can be maintained. It is not suitable if employees are milling around outside, such as near coffee machines, water fountains, etc. If there is a phone in the room, it should be disconnected. Items like drinking water and tissues should be readily available and at hand. Consideration should be given to seating arrangements; generally, it is preferable that there is no desk barrier between interviewee and interviewer. It is sometimes suggested that a desk may place a defensive barrier between the interviewer and interviewee, thereby protecting the interviewee to some extent. The main reason I prefer a 'no desk' approach is it is less formal; therefore, the tone can be more conversational. In addition, I can scan the full body for nonverbal behavior. Monitoring nonverbal behavior is essential, and while many people tend to freeze their upper body to maintain posture when under stress, the lower limbs can be neglected and thus are very important sources of information. This does not mean there should be no desk. The advantage of a desk is that it is easier to make and review notes. Where a desk is present, seating can be arranged to accommodate this scanning by sitting the interviewee at a corner while allowing physically moving in closer as necessary.

Question Types

Once rapport has been established through some preliminary conversation, the next step is to ask questions in relation to the matter at hand. In simple matters, it may suffice to come straight to the point. In most other circumstances, the format of questioning needs to be considered more carefully, and a funnel-type approach, starting broad before narrowing in on specifics, is the optimal method to use. Consequently, the first questions asked are usually open-ended questions. Open questions encourage a fuller response than other types such as closed or leading question types, which tend to discourage or even close down dialogue. Open questions require a person to provide information to answer it properly. Such questions begin with a request for information such as 'tell me', 'can you describe', 'would you explain', 'show me', or other forms. The acronym used is TEDS for 'tell, explain, describe, show', but an individualized style can make it even more effective, for example, 'it would help me if you could describe …' as people generally respond well to requests for assistance and it maintains rapport. Questions may be asked in a neutral voice and business-like manner, and this provides a baseline to spot deception. Using this method, the person is not reacting to the interviewer's personality, rather it is the content of the question that generates the verbal or nonverbal signs of deception. That said, I have no problem adapting my style and voice as necessary. Generally, the tone should be calm and professional, but I rarely worry too much about voice inflection or prosody. It is important to ensure that you use appropriate or witness compatible questions.[11] This means ensuring that your questions are easily understood by the interviewee, although in general, avoid displays of thesaurus proficiency. It is often not possible to avoid the specific industry's technical jargon but be careful that the meanings are shared concepts. It's not unusual for technical terms and acronyms to have multiple interpretations, even in the same industry.

Once an answer to the first question has provided some type of narrative, another open question may be suitable, or it may appropriate to narrow in on the account given in the answer. Probing questions are therefore used to probe deeper into a subject when an answer has been given. Probing questions usually start with why, who, what, where, when, or how. The technique is to use probing questions to focus on ever-narrowing specifics in the funnel-type approach. Listening intently to the answers given and continuing to probe will inevitably surface any inconsistencies in the accounts, and these can then be explored further. The tone of this type of questioning is important, as it should not come across as an interrogation. Therefore, express your own confusion as you begin to uncover inconsistencies: 'I'm sorry, I must have missed something in what you said earlier' or 'I'm confused now because I thought you said …' are questions that offer a simple misunderstanding to be cleared up rather an accusation of deception. It is important that such accusations are normally avoided.

Using plain language that is easily understood is particularly important when using translators. Keep questions short and try to avoid jargon. Translators may be professionals but who are outsiders to the industry so ensuring all round understandings between parties becomes especially important. The use of multiple questions should be avoided, so do not ask someone more than one question at a time.

Other types of questions include closed questions. Closed questions present an interviewee with only a 'yes or no' answer and should generally be avoided. For example, 'is this your coat?' is a closed question. Leading questions provide the answer in the question and again may be answered 'yes or no'. Examples include 'is your address 22 Main Street?' Such questions mean that little information is actually gathered as the interviewer must ask the correct question only to get it affirmed or denied. Closed and leading questions are normally conversation killers, but they do have some advantages, as they can be used to put an interviewer in control of a situation, help to obtain specific facts quickly, or are useful for testing understanding and summarizing, or they may allow the interviewer to get an agreement. The closed questions also tie someone to a specific answer and questions such as 'did you steal the cash' require a person to lie if they did it but intend denying it. This form of blatant lie can be difficult for many people, so many people prefer to give qualified answers to questions. We will discuss these in more detail on detecting deception, but having to directly deny an accusation makes many people uncomfortable.

Presumptive questions are another tool in asking a question that assumes you know the answer to a fact that has not actually been asked. They may even include an implicit admission. So, a question such as 'did you use the money you stole to pay off your gambling debts?' for example assumes the theft is acknowledged and accepted, when it may be very much intended to be the subject of denial. It is a tactic that is commonly used in police interviewing and can be very effective as they move the interviewee to justifying their actions rather than continue denials. It is important to avoid backing a person into a corner by forcing them to deny repeatedly or say 'no' continuously as this makes constructive progress difficult because the lie is being reinforced and therefore easier to continue, a process known as psychological entrenchment, where the person becomes resistant to new ideas and cognitively inflexible.[12] Nevertheless, if you have evidence that shows the answer to be a lie, the person has anchored themselves to a difficult position, and this may serve a useful investigative purpose. Overall, closed questions limit the responses given and, moreover, can sound more like an interrogation, especially when accusations are made. Presumptive questions can also be confrontational. Normally, therefore, their use should be avoided as much as possible.

However, hypothetical questions are useful question types and very effective at exploring scenarios, for instance, 'what would happen if ...?' They may be a way of introducing presumptive-type questions or even closed questions in a less confrontational manner than a direct method. As always, language used, and how the question is framed, has a major impact on how the question is received. As a result, replacing the use of emotionally laden language such as 'theft' with questions about 'missing money' can have a major impact on cooperation. Even the word 'investigation' could be replaced with 'enquiry' or 'search for the truth' during an interview to maximize cooperation.

Whatever question types are used, allowing long pauses or silence is a critical technique, possibly one of the most important, in interviewing. Pauses can be used to encourage someone to keep talking, as emphasis, or to de-escalate an emotional situation. Pauses also give the interviewer an opportunity to process the information and formulate the next question while paying close attention to the interviewee. Pausing after asking a question also serves to create a form of psychological pressure on the other party to take the conventional turn in speaking. In addition, not taking this turn when someone has finished answering and expects you to then take the talking turn is very effective as people often find silence uncomfortable and may talk simply to fill the silence, which can lead to an uncontrolled word stream of consciousness with potentially useful information. When people fill the silence this way, they may also try to convince the interviewer of their sincerity or morality and in so doing may inadvertently make small admissions or use qualifying language that is unusual and possibly revealing in itself.

Listening

Listening is another critical skill to master to be a good interviewer. Listening involves paying attention to what the person says, using interpersonal adaptability through emotional intelligence, reading body language, and making the person feel listened to. Demonstrating an interest in the interviewee by listening to what they say is also an important step in establishing rapport and a good communication connection. It is essential to be interested in what the person is saying by genuinely listening as opposed to listening only for the information you want in answer to the question you asked. Spoken communication can be fraught with misunderstandings as people often find it difficult to say exactly what they mean, as thoughts must be—often imperfectly—encoded into words. As a result, a listener has to both accurately hear and decode the intended meaning in those words.[13] People use vague, ill-defined, or ambiguous terms that should be carefully defined to ensure understanding. Sometimes, a person will deliberately use such terms to hide behind the ambiguity. Careful listening can also pick up on many things that are left unsaid, either accidentally or deliberately in a conversation, that is, the thoughts that cross the interviewee's mind but are not verbalized or create gaps in a narrative. Careful attention to the vocal tone and energy of the interviewee will assist in this. Fundamentally, listening is probably the core skill of interviewing. The ability to have patience and diligence to carefully listen while being able to compare what is said from what may be known through other sources, such as other evidence gathered, is what separates a good interviewer from a bad one. The ability to pick up on body language is another vitally important skill. Both careful listening and close observation are thus necessarily used in combination.

Listening can be a difficult skill to master. Listening is not helped by filters in the listener that the message must pass through, such as culture, values, beliefs, attitudes, expectations, and intentions, all of which contribute to biases and are part of every individual's subjective reality. Other barriers to communication may include language fluency, and the meaning of phrases or words used, especially technical language, which may effectively block communication. Physical barriers, such as noise, may also obstruct communication. Equally important might be an uncooperative attitude in the interviewee including a refusal to communicate or even listen to the questions. To overcome these filters and biases, the interviewer needs to demonstrate patience and a desire to understand as well as showing respect to the interviewee throughout. Therefore, it is essential that the interviewer always remain calm and controlled, even when faced with provocation.

Listening should be an active process where one receives the message while paying attention to the person and then ask questions to deepen understanding. *Active listening* is the term given to this skill set that is essential to relaying to the other person that their words are important and, in turn, that they themselves are being treated respectfully. It takes normal listening skills to a higher level and can be very effective at getting into a person's emotional mindset. Active listening uses both nonverbal behavior and sounds to demonstrate interest. The interviewer uses positive body posture such as maintaining eye contact, leaning forward and nodding, or using encouraging words such as 'yes' or 'okay' (or affirmative sounds such as ah, hmm), which shows appreciation for the message.[14] Such actions are normal in most genuine conversations where there is rapport between the participants, and care should be taken to avoid any exaggeration that may have the opposite effect to the intended one. While people appreciate positive feedback, it is important to avoid overt praise or flattery. The skill is to listen to what is being said and avoid interrupting, disagreeing, or evaluating, while demonstrating to the speaker that you are treating what they have to say with respect.

The next step involves echoing back what the person has just said, either as a paraphrase or repeating some of his or her own critical words. Again, if this appears contrived or overdone, it is a dangerous technique so simply parroting back what was said should be avoided. Done correctly, it demonstrates a concerned and interested listener ensuring that the message has been correctly transmitted. It also helps to find common meaning in words or terms used, so timely feedback can be essential to avoid miscommunication and eliminate misunderstandings. At various stages, this technique is extended to summarizing back a relevant section of dialogue and sometimes an effort to interpret what has been said can be made, for example, 'I get the impression' or 'it sounds from what you said that …'.

This type of feedback helps open lines of communication. The interviewee may correct minor errors in the interpretation offered, but it often helps open the dialogue and demonstrates empathy on behalf of the interviewer. A closely allied skill is reflection; skillful reflection is not simply an echo but should move a little past what the person has said, although it is useful to understate the emotion displayed. Examples include statements such as: 'So this must make you feel …', 'you sound upset by that', or 'I would find that very frustrating if …'. Where emotions are displayed or an emotional 'energy' word used, it is important to reflect back and label those emotions. Emotional labeling has been shown to reduce confrontation, but the technique relies on recognizing emotions and commenting on them in a nonjudgmental manner.[15] It is also a method to reframe the narrative of the interviewee in more investigatively suitable terms. For instance, this may involve pointing out that the behavior that the interviewee is describing is criminal fraud, although they have avoided that word or anything as culpable. On the other hand, it may be useful to step the interviewee down from overdramatizing the situation they feel they are in.

Where the echo has a questioning intonation (voice raised at the end), the echo is converted to a question requiring clarification. If using reflection with an answer that contained both positive and negative characteristics, it is helpful to address the negative first and then reinforce the positive, even by just using voice tone. For instance, if someone has stated that he or she has useful information but is afraid of some potential consequences if they reveal it to you, then begin with the negative. Acknowledge that some challenges might arise as a consequence of disclosure but that the fact that he or she understands the importance of giving vital information is a reassuring sign of their honesty and integrity. Explain why the information the person has could be important, thereby focusing on the positives. Generally, be careful to avoid using negative emotionally laden language such as 'suspect' or 'crime' as any type of negative feedback is likely to simply increase resistance and reduce cooperation.[16] Focus instead on positive words such as 'help', 'assistance', or 'collaboration'.

Most interviewees respond well to this type of listening, but some may find it too like a therapy session. As always, every individual is different, but most people want an opportunity to be heard when they speak, so interpersonal adaptability is a key skill. Demonstrating interest in what the person said, respect for them, being nonjudgmental, and maintaining their dignity or self-esteem is what leads to a successful interview and the obtaining of the information needed. Research has established that people appreciate being listened to by persons in authority such as the police, even if the ultimate outcome is not favorable toward them, but being listened to was considered evidence of impartiality and objectivity, which enhanced perceived fairness.[17] Because of such active engagement, the interviewer may find interviewing both a physically and emotionally demanding task, particularly longer formal interviews. But it is critical that the interviewer pay close attention to what is being said rather than formulating the next question. This can be difficult to achieve, so the use of an aide memoire with relevant questions may be useful. The aide memoire should ideally only be consulted late in the interview to ensure any relevant questions have not been omitted, rather than at the beginning where it may seem more contrived.

Nonverbal Communication

Human communication uses nonverbal communication much more than verbal and can account for up to 65 percent of interpersonal communication.[18] Nonverbal behavior means anything involved in communication other than the spoken word. It includes the use of body language such as body posture, the use of the limbs, facial gestures, physical distance maintained, and emotions expressed. Being alert to emotion is important for the interviewer. The face, in particular, is usually the best reflection of internal emotions.[19] Emotion can also be gauged through the prosody of the voice which involves the tone and pitch of the voice that accompanies the spoken word and frequently becomes more animated the more emotional the content.

Nonverbal behavior is important in both transmitting messages and interpreting them to understand what message is being sent. Nonverbal behavior is also important in establishing the initial open communication. Indeed, we are evolutionary hardwired to size up an individual before he or she ever speaks as to whether they present a threat to us. As noted, social status and personality traits such as attractiveness, likeability, trustworthiness, competence, and aggressiveness are assessed by snap judgment within a 100-millisecond exposure to a new face.[20] Unfortunately, such rapid analysis will inevitably reflect biases, so making intuitive judgments about such things as other people's competence or trustworthiness within fractions of a second based on facial features is frequently inaccurate. Nonverbal behavior itself is inherently unreliable because of these biases and should rarely be relied on to make a definitive judgment.

Biases result from beliefs that create mental models about how the world works. Unfortunately, in the real world, beliefs are not always aligned and can even be contradictory. Because of a lack of logical coherence across all beliefs, people make decisions that can run counter to their own values and principles without even being consciously aware of it.[21] With nonverbal behavior, it is very easy to see what we expect to see and ignore contradictory information.

Nonetheless, nonverbal behavior is very helpful in creating rapport. Nonthreatening behaviors and gestures can reassure the interviewee and indicate friendliness. This is to emphasize the importance of first impressions in creating a conducive communication environment to begin to understand your interviewee and to begin to piece together different narratives and memories. The initial impression of a confident and competent investigator is vitally important to the perception formed by the other person. Of note here is the importance of dressing well; it is not necessary to be overkill but shabby clothes will give a poor message. Of equal importance is behavior that demonstrates an interest in the other person such as eye contact, nodding, looking interested, leaning forward, and (appropriate) touch that are all normal indicators that a person is interested in communicating. A good handshake provides important information also as it signifies confidence if done firmly but not overdone. Similarly, avoiding interrupting the person speaking and respecting personal space are also important nonverbal indicators that a person is nonthreatening.

Conclusion

An interview is a communication of information from one person to another. It happens in informal conversations every day. In a more formal setting, certain attributes are important in the interviewer to maximize cooperation. These include the open communication approach that a friendly person offers from the outset. There should be no contradiction between professionalism and friendliness. Using positive body language and conversation to make the interviewee at ease is building rapport. The better the rapport, the easier the verbal communication will be and the better the flow of information from the interviewee will be. Building rapport means being aware of your own communication style and being adaptable to respond to another person. It is about helping that person reduce their anxiety, showing them respect, and demonstrating impartiality. You want the interviewee to feel that you are fair and can be trusted to be impartial. This applies to any type of interview; Chapter 4 builds on this approach to discuss how to approach a more technically challenging forensic-type interview where deviance is being investigated.

Notes

1 Gudjonsson, G. H., "False Confessions and Correcting Injustices", *New England Law Review*, (2012), 46, pp 689–709; Kassin, S. M., Drizin, S. A., Grisso, T., Gudjonsson, G. H., Leo, R. A. and Redlich, A. D., "Police-Induced Confessions: Risk Factors and Recommendations", *Law and Human Behavior*, (2010), 34(1), pp 3–38; Kassin, S. M., "Confession Evidence: Commonsense Myths and Misconceptions", *Criminal Justice and Behavior*, (2008), 35(10), pp 1309–1322.

2 Cialdini, R. B. and Goldstein, N. J., "Social Influence: Compliance and Conformity", *Annual Review of Psychology*, (2004), 55(1), pp 591–621.

3 Cialdini, R. B., *Influence: The Psychology of Persuasion*, (HarperCollins, New York, 2007); Cialdini, R. B. and Goldstein, N. J., "Social Influence: Compliance and Conformity", *Annual Review of Psychology*, (2004).

4 De Waal, F., *Primates and Philosophers: How Morality Evolved*, (Princeton University Press, Princeton, 2006); Waal, F. D., "The Empathy Instinct", *Discover*, (2009), 30(9), pp 54–57.

5 Williamson, T. M., 'Towards Greater Professionalism: Minimizing Miscarriages of Justice', (ed) Williamson, in *Investigative Interviewing: Rights, Research, Regulation*, (Willan, Cullompton, 2006) pp 147–166; Alison, L. J., Alison, E., Noone, G., Elntib, S. and Christiansen, P., "Why Tough Tactics Fail and Rapport Gets Results: Observing Rapport-Based Interpersonal Techniques (ORBIT) to Generate Useful Information from Terrorists", *Psychology, Public Policy, and Law*, (2013), 19(4), pp 411–431.

6 Alison, L., Alison, E., Noone, G., Elntib, S., Waring, S. and Christiansen, P., "The Efficacy of Rapport-Based Techniques for Minimizing Counter-interrogation Tactics Amongst a Field Sample of Terrorists", *Psychology, Public Policy, and Law*, (2014), 20(4), pp 421–430: 422.

7 Willis, J. and Todorov, A., "First Impressions: Making Up Your Mind After a 100-Ms Exposure to a Face", *Psychological Science*, (2006), 17(7), pp 592–598.

8 Wells, S., 'Hostage Negotiation and Communication Skills in a Terrorist Environment', (ed) Pearse, in *Investigating Terrorism: Current Political, Legal and Psychological Issues*, (John Wiley, Chichester, 2015) pp 145–166: 152.

9 The rapport process is helped by following the original advice in the 1939 book, Carnegie, D., *How to Win Friends and Influence People*, (Ebury, London, 2006).

10 Langer, E., "The Mindlessness of Ostensibly Thoughtful Action. The Role of 'Placebic' Information in Interpersonal Interaction", *Journal of Personality and Social Psychology*, (1978), 36(6), pp 632–642.

11 Dando, C. J., Wilcock, R. and Milne, R., "The Cognitive Interview: Inexperienced Police Officers' Perceptions of Their Witness/Victim Interviewing Practices", *Legal & Criminological Psychology*, (2008), 13(1), pp 59–70: 60.

12 Dane, E., "Reconsidering the Trade-off between Expertise and Flexibility: A Cognitive Entrenchment Perspective", *The Academy of Management Review*, (2010), 35(4), pp 579–603.

13 Miller, W. R. and Rollnick, S., *Motivational Interviewing*, (Guilford Press, New York, 2002): 69; McMains, M. J. and Mullins, W. C., *Crisis Negotiations: Managing Critical Incidents and Hostage Situations in Law Enforcement and Corrections*, 4th ed., (Matthew Bender & Co, New Providence, NJ, 2010): 256.

14 Eric Shepherd (2010) has an acronym SOFTENS to cover these skills:

Signs—smile, open, and interested facial expressions
Open body posture—arms uncrossed
Forward leaning—toward interviewee to express interest
Touch—appropriate only; e.g., shaking hands
Eye contact—maintain eye contact but avoid staring
Nods—supportive nonverbal signs of interest in communication
Supportive sounds and noises—affirmative sounds of encouragement

15 Wells, S., 'Hostage Negotiation and Communication Skills in a Terrorist Environment', (ed) Pearse, in *Investigating Terrorism: Current Political, Legal and Psychological Issues*, (2015), p 156.

16 It is important to be open and honest with the interviewee. It is particularly important at the beginning to explain the reason for the interview. However, as the rapport builds, choosing careful framing of language can help rather than hinder the rapport process.

17 Tyler, T. R., "Enhancing Police Legitimacy", *The Annals of the American Academy of Political and Social Science*, (2004), 593(1), pp 84–99: 94.

18 Navarro, J., *What Every Body Is Saying*, (William Morrow, New York, 2008).

19 Ekman, P., *Emotions Revealed: Understanding Faces and Feelings*, (Weidenfeld and Nicolson, London, 2003); Ekman, P., Friesen, W.V. and Ellsworth, P., *Emotion in the Human Face: Guidelines for Research and an Integration of Findings*, (Pergamon Press, New York, 1972).

20 Willis, J. and Todorov, A., "First Impressions: Making Up Your Mind After a 100-Ms Exposure to a Face", *Psychological Science*, (2006).

21 Palazzo, G., Krings, F. and Hoffrage, U., "Ethical Blindness", *Journal of Business Ethics*, (2012), 109(3), pp 323–338: 324.

Bibliography

Alison, L., Alison, E., Noone, G., Elntib, S., Waring, S. and Christiansen, P., "The Efficacy of Rapport-Based Techniques for Minimizing Counter-Interrogation Tactics Amongst a Field Sample of Terrorists", *Psychology, Public Policy, and Law*, (2014), 20(4), pp 421–430.

Alison, L. J., Alison, E., Noone, G., Elntib, S. and Christiansen, P., "Why Tough Tactics Fail and Rapport Gets Results: Observing Rapport-Based Interpersonal Techniques (ORBIT) to Generate Useful Information from Terrorists", *Psychology, Public Policy, and Law*, (2013), 19(4), pp 411–431.

Ambady, N. and Rule, N. O., 'Thin Slices of Behaviour', (eds) Baumeister and Vohs, in *Encyclopedia of Social Psychology*, (Sage Publications, Thousand Oaks, CA, 2007) pp 990–992.

Bull, R., 'When in Interviews to Disclose Information to Suspects and to Challenge Them?', (ed) Bull, in *Investigative Interviewing*, (Springer, New York, 2014) pp 167–181.

Carnegie, D., *How to Win Friends and Influence People*, (Ebury, London, 2006).

Cialdini, R. B., *Influence: The Psychology of Persuasion*, (HarperCollins, New York, NY, 2007).

Cialdini, R. B. and Goldstein, N. J., "Social Influence: Compliance and Conformity", *Annual Review of Psychology*, (2004), 55(1), pp 591–621.

Dane, E., "Reconsidering the Trade-off between Expertise and Flexibility: A Cognitive Entrenchment Perspective", *The Academy of Management Review*, (2010), 35(4), pp 579–603.

De Waal, F., *Primates and Philosophers: How Morality Evolved*, (Princeton University Press, Princeton, 2006).

Ekman, P., "An Argument for Basic Emotions", *Cognition and Emotion*, (1992), 6(3/4), pp 169–200.

Ekman, P., *Emotions Revealed: Understanding Faces and Feelings*, (Weidenfeld and Nicolson, London, 2003).

Ekman, P., Friesen, W. V. and Ellsworth, P., *Emotion in the Human Face: Guidelines for Research and an Integration of Findings*, (Pergamon Press, New York, NY, 1972).

Gudjonsson, G. H., "False Confessions and Correcting Injustices", *New England Law Review*, (2012), 46, pp 689–709.

Houston, P., Floyd, M. and Carnicero, S., *Spy the Lie*, (St. Martins Press, New York, NY, 2012).

Kassin, S. M., "Confession Evidence: Commonsense Myths and Misconceptions", *Criminal Justice and Behavior*, (2008), 35(10), pp 1309–1322.

Kassin, S. M., Drizin, S. A., Grisso, T., Gudjonsson, G. H., Leo, R. A. and Redlich, A. D., "Police-Induced Confessions: Risk Factors and Recommendations", *Law and Human Behavior*, (2010), 34(1), pp 3–38.

Langer, E., "The Mindlessness of Ostensibly Thoughtful Action. The Role of 'Placebic' Information in Interpersonal Interaction", *Journal of Personality and Social Psychology*, (1978), 36(6), pp 632–642.

McMains, M. J. and Mullins, W. C., *Crisis Negotiations: Managing Critical Incidents and Hostage Situations in Law Enforcement and Corrections*, 4th ed., (Matthew Bender & Co, New Providence, NJ, 2010).

Miller, W. R. and Rollnick, S., *Motivational Interviewing*, (Guilford Press, New York, NY, 2002).

Navarro, J., *What Every Body Is Saying*, (William Morrow, New York, 2008).

Palazzo, G., Krings, F. and Hoffrage, U., "Ethical Blindness", *Journal of Business Ethics*, (2012), 109(3), pp 323–338.

St. Yves, M., 'The Psychology of Rapport: 5 Basic Rules', (ed) Williamson, in *Investigative Interviewing: Rights, Research, Regulation* (Willan, Cullompton, 2006) pp 87–106.

Tyler, T. R., "Enhancing Police Legitimacy", *The Annals of the American Academy of Political and Social Science*, (2004), 593(1), pp 84–99.

Waal, F. D., "The Empathy Instinct", *Discover*, (2009), 30(9), pp 54–57.

Wells, S., 'Hostage Negotiation and Communication Skills in a Terrorist Environment', (ed) Pearse, in *Investigating Terrorism: Current Political, Legal and Psychological Issues*, (John Wiley, Chichester, 2015) pp 145–166.

Williamson, T. M., 'Towards Greater Professionalism: Minimizing Miscarriages of Justice', (ed) Williamson, in *Investigative Interviewing: Rights, Research, Regulation*, (Willan, Cullompton, 2006) pp 147–166.

Willis, J. and Todorov, A., "First Impressions: Making Up Your Mind After a 100-Ms Exposure to a Face", *Psychological Science*, (2006), 17(7), pp 592–598.

Chapter 4

The Forensic Interview

Introduction

The previous chapter focused on the basic skills necessary to conduct an interview. Simply using skills such as building rapport and listening will enhance any type of communication exchange, whether in a customer setting, or HR situation, as well as in audit or forensic settings. However, forensic interviews are more complex than most other interviews and consequently require a deeper skill set. By using the term 'forensic', I am referring here to an interview that is investigating some specific deviance, with some potential for deception. It does not necessarily only mean criminal investigations or an interview of the person who is the likely culprit. Forensic interviews need to be properly prepared for and carefully planned and such interviews include witness interviews. The interview itself can be broken down into several distinct phases which include the initial engagement with the interviewee, seeking an account, and the closure phase of the interview.

The forensic investigative interview technique (FIIT) uses the investigative interviewing model, initially developed for British police officers, known by the acronym PEACE. The PEACE interview is used in all police forensic interview situations, from victim and witness to suspect. It is designed as a fact-finding, non-accusatorial exchange that remains orientated on building rapport and maintaining a level of cooperation from the subject. In the vast majority of police interviews, there is little difficulty in getting cooperation from interviewees, even crime suspects. Of course, there is always the potential that some people attend at an interview with the intention of being duplicitous and may even try to achieve this objective through a veneer of pleasantness and helpfulness. This can create some difficulties for an interviewing model that relies on engagement and cooperation. Consequently, it is necessary to be able to challenge accounts to ensure the veracity of the accounts given and the interviewer must remain cautious throughout the interview that he or she is obtaining a truthful account. It is therefore important to be suspicious; the deceptive person will not advertise their deception, so it is important to treat all persons with some skepticism. This does not mean that an interviewer

DOI: 10.4324/9781003269489-4

should openly express this suspicion, and doing so can usually be counter-productive, rather it's a matter of putting yourself in that mindset where you question everything, and you seek corroboration of any fact as much as possible. Attention to detail remains critical to ensuring information is accurate, and the interviewer must be alert to the smallest details. Therefore, while interviewing it is essential to maintain an open mind as an investigator should never prejudge any investigation. Such an attitude is ultimately the most productive method of fact-finding in any investigation.

Development of PEACE

Victims, witnesses, and suspects all have important information that an investigator needs to obtain. Yet, until the last few decades, police officers received little formal training in interviewing skills to obtain this information. The introduction of the Police and Criminal Evidence Act in 1984 in the United Kingdom provided for suspect and investigator interviews to be audio recorded, and a subsequent study of those recordings highlighted the ineffectiveness of many of the interviewers.[1] It was painfully apparent that many police officers lacked any skill or even confidence at interviewing suspects, with some terminating the interview at the slightest resistance from the interviewee.

Many reasons contributed to the poor standard of police interviewing, including the lack of training. It was usually considered an innate skill and that many suspects inevitably confessed anyway. Inevitably, this perspective and the fact that police interviews are often judged on their success at obtaining confessions from suspects create incentives and pressures for investigators to ignore protestations of innocence or exculpatory information and focus solely on indicators of guilt to push for a confession. Police therefore used whatever tactics necessary to get a confession. As a consequence, such practices lead to innocent people falsely confessing to crimes.[2] British police had their share of false confessions and miscarriages of justice and ultimately responded to the criticisms of the use of confrontational interrogation by developing the PEACE interview model in the early 1990s.[3] The acronym PEACE stands for the phases of the interview, consisting of:

- **P**—planning and preparation
- **E**—explain
- **A**—account
- **C**—closure
- **E**—evaluation of interview

The purpose of the PEACE model is to enhance interviewing effectiveness while minimizing false confessions by avoiding the confrontational style of an interrogation. It is orientated on an ethical questioning style with an emphasis on rapport and gathering facts rather than just confessions.[4] The model is built on treating the interviewee, whatever the circumstances, with respect as well as building a respectful relationship. This may be difficult to accomplish in all cases, at least initially, but there are skills to overcome initial resistance to successfully conduct an interview and even build rapport in trying circumstances. Training furthermore encourages police officers to dispel biases around guilt or innocence and focus on seeking an account.[5]

Following its introduction, it was found that the PEACE interview was somewhat too successful at eliminating confrontation from the interview. As a consequence, there was an identified need to add 'challenge and clarify' to the account stage as a persistent criticism was police officers were simply accepting any account given to them instead of testing it.[6] In other words, officers were not exercising any critical thinking skills or evaluating the information they were receiving. A more effective program was needed as ineffective training was identified as partly responsible.[7] Training is important, but regular practice is an important element to competence. Acquiring the technical interview skill as well as building the necessary confidence to challenge an account of an interviewee takes experience, and the role is ideally a specialist one, so an interviewer should be a regular practitioner.

Other types of police interview methods can be very confrontational as they tend to focus on the accusations and seeking admissions. Some accusatory interview models, such as the American Reid method, may have certain advantages in some circumstances. However, an in-depth understanding of the relevant criminal law is essential in their use, as some techniques advocated are considered oppressive in some jurisdictions. In such jurisdictions, there is then potential for the entire interview to be ruled inadmissible in any later court proceedings. These types of interview styles can also result in negative feedback in organizations as people can view the use of confrontational tactics as unfair.

The PEACE Interview Phases

The PEACE interview process is broken into various phases, which not only helps to conceptualize the process but also assists in setting out interview plans and objectives. In more detail, the acronym PEACE gives the interview phases of:

- **P**—planning and preparation
- **E**—explain; first contact, outline time frame, and ground rules
- **A**—account, clarify, corroborate, and challenge
- **C**—closure; review of the account given; next steps explained
- **E**—evaluation of interview, new actions to be taken

Because the model is designed for both witnesses and suspects, it includes elements of memory facilitation as gathering the most complete and accurate account of what was witnessed is a critical part of any account obtained from a witness. Memories are fallible, so obtaining a comprehensive account as early as possible is essential to the success of an investigation, and some potential witnesses may not even be aware of the vital information they hold. The different phases can be used in any type of interview but need not be adhered to rigidly, as they build a toolbox, and it is not always necessary to use all elements on every occasion. Circumstances will dictate how best to proceed, and an investigator needs to be adaptable to any situation and flexible enough to respond as circumstances change.

The PLANNING and PREPARATION Phase

Planning and preparation are the first phase of the interview process and critical to the overall success of any interview. Interviewing is a complex cognitive undertaking that requires high-order cognitive skills including the ability to manage conflict and assess new information input in real time.[8] Planning helps make this manageable. On occasion, it may be necessary to undertake interviewing with little prior information other than a short oral briefing, and indeed, sometimes there is an advantage to going into an interview with no preconceived ideas, thereby avoiding cross-contamination. As a fresh pair of eyes, as it were. Normally, however, the better prepared you are prior to an interview, the better. As an investigator gains experience, this phase is done almost reflexively, and in many incidences, it may be a short process. Nevertheless, it is an important process, and investigators need to understand the purpose it serves.

The planning and preparation stage is done before the interview to ensure the interviewer is as current and up to date on the progress of the investigation as possible and understands the significance of all available information or evidence. The strategic interview plan will be developed at this stage which should decide what purpose any interview is to serve. Interviews are time-consuming processes. The decision to undertake interviews will be evaluated against the potential for other methods of gathering evidence and what the interview topics need to cover. Each person will be selected for interview based on a belief that they can contribute something useful to the investigation. Any interview conducted as part of an investigation should add value to the investigation with preserving and strengthening any existing evidence a key objective. A familiarity with the existing evidence is therefore critical as well as its potential relevance. Every effort should have been made to gather as much potential evidence as possible prior and to carefully evaluate it to develop its usefulness to the interview process before making any interview arrangements.

Previous reports, investigations, or HR documents should be sought, if available. At the beginning of many investigations, there may often be little in the way of alternative evidence to consider, so early interviews may simply plan to obtain background on interviewees while maintaining an open mind. The strategic plan will then be broken into a tactical plan. The order of interviews, who is to be interviewed first, will be decided. This can vary; sometimes there is an advantage to talking to the alleged perpetrator early; alternatively, it can help to gather as much information from other interviewees as possible instead. In some investigations, a short interview where the perpetrator might be expected to make denials can be useful at the early stage, using a strategy where there is an intention to return to this person once more evidence has been gathered. Bear in mind that someone interviewed early on in an investigation as a witness may turn out to be the culpable offender at a later stage. Obviously, the interview of the culpable person at the end of an investigation process where there has been substantial evidence gathered will require extensive preparation work to properly prepare. All evidence gathered should be reviewed. Potential alternative explanations for the evidence should be explored and prepared before the interview. A needs analysis should formulate questions to cover gaps in knowledge or explanations sought. This will create the interview objectives that need to be attained and their likely place in the interview progression. The identifying of all objectives in an interview will help to inform the strategic interview plan as well as providing a measure by which to judge the success of the interview.

These objectives will include what needs to be proven through the interview and what other evidence exists to corroborate the allegations. In a criminal case, the allegation will be that someone broke a criminal law, such as theft, where the law might be written:

> A person is guilty of theft if he dishonestly appropriates property belonging to another with the intention of permanently depriving the other of it.[9]

Therefore, in a criminal allegation, there are various elements to be proved. As discussed in Chapter 2, these are known as *criminal proofs*, and in a theft or fraud allegation, they might include the different parts of the offense as above and include 'dishonestly appropriates', 'property of another', and 'intention to deprive the owner.' Theft only occurs where a person takes something with the intention of keeping it permanently, using it for his or her own purposes. Something borrowed and returned may not have been stolen unless it was taken to deprive the owner of its use. In most organizational investigations, it remains important to understand the specific definition of whatever you are investigating so that the various elements—the proofs—are covered adequately during the interview. These are the investigatively important matters. An interview may garner a lot of information, but if the interviewer fails to ask some seemingly pedantic questions, then these proofs have not been covered. It is pointless to spend two hours interviewing a subject and yet come away with an ambiguous statement where a witness fails even to disclose that any deviance occurred. In the case of theft, for example, the owner of the property should state that no one had any permission to take the property, together with the facts of its taking.

When interviewing the person suspected, it is perhaps better not to approach these proofs directly, at least not initially. It is better to examine the interviewee's guilty knowledge from different angles. For example, was there an effort to conceal the crime? Why was this so if nothing was done wrong? Did the person think the behavior was acceptable? Did they know it was wrong? Would they be proud if their parents/partner discovered what they had done? Did they turn a blind eye to the activity of others? Did they care if it was wrong/a crime? It may often be sufficient to show the person was reckless as to whether the activity was illegal or not. Recklessness or negligence can be approached through questioning about thoughts given to repercussions or actions taken to conceal the incident. What questions must be asked to cover any technical elements (depending on specific allegations) necessary will be prepared as part of the overall strategy. This approach should be adopted for investigating any type of deviance, the written policy that is alleged to have been breached should be carefully examined to ensure that its constituent elements are covered in the interview.

The strategic plan will be broken down to a tactical plan. Depending on the number of interviews planned with an individual, the tactical plan will consist of the order and progression of questions to be asked, the order in which topics are to be examined, the evidence to be presented, how it is to be presented, and at what stages. Most plans will begin with a rapport phase in the first interview or interview portion. This will normally be uncontentious, focusing on rapport-building questions, general information, and obtaining a baseline of behavior. A dedicated interview folder should be prepared to keep all the information in one location for review and might include an outline of the plan in a graphic at the front, together with relevant pieces of evidence, clearly marked, that may be used in the interview. This folder may be prepared from the investigation record but streamlined for use in the interview. Photos can be used instead of physical evidence, not just because the physical evidence is often cumbersome, and it is not possible to bring into the interview room, but as a matter of course. On occasions, it will be necessary to bring in the actual item to be identified by the interviewee, and when this is done, it should be planned, but showing a photo first can be effective and more tactically useful. It can be difficult to disguise a large piece of evidence in a small room, giving the interviewee time to prepare a response. The plan will consider gradually introducing any probing questions necessary after obtaining an account, depending on the investigation hypothesis built from acquired evidence.

The planning process means that a list of important questions is made before any interview. It is important that any prepared list of questions to be asked are used as a guide but not followed so slavishly as to miss opportunities that may arise in the interview. The list of questions should highlight any particular areas of concern as well as legal issues that need addressing at interview to ensure these are covered. I suggest keeping the list in the rear of interview folder so that it can be referred to periodically and especially toward the conclusion of the interview to ensure there are no topics left outstanding that should be covered. It is generally bad practice to simply read off prepared questions. The interviewers are normally unaware of what may be said in the initial account by the subject, so it is important to remain flexible and adaptable to the account and answers the interviewee provides, not simply following the investigation tactical plan regardless. It is only in totally uncooperative interviews that the only option is to follow the questions laid out in advance preparation. Therefore, the plan should prepare for both an uncooperative subject and a cooperative subject, unless that is known beforehand. This phase should also be used to tailor the interview to any particular individual characteristics of the interviewee. Any information, such as background material, available on the interviewee should be obtained to assist in this. Moreover, attention should also focus on factors that may inhibit cooperation such as previous interpersonal relationships or conflict in the organization.

Normally, it is sufficient to interview a person only once, but it is not uncommon to have several. This is especially so where matters are complex, or interviews open new enquiry lines. Nevertheless, there should not be an excess of interviews of the same person, there should always be a valid reason to reinterview. Long interviews should be avoided where possible, and regular breaks should be factored in, if considered likely. Ideally, every two hours or so, a bathroom break and an offer of refreshments should be made. If the interview extends to four hours, a substantial break should be included, and possibly that break should postpone the interview to another day. The length and conditions at interview are a major factor in any later examination of oppressiveness so are an important consideration in the planning process.

The EXPLAIN Phase

The 'explain or first contact' phase between the interviewer(s) and interviewee is the second phase. This phase is the beginning of the interview with an interview subject, when introductions are made, and where an explanation of the matter under investigation, what the interviewee's role is, the time frame involved, and the ground rules are all outlined. The interviewee will be told that he or she will be asked to try to provide as much detail about the matter being investigated, so he or she should 'report everything' they remember no matter how insignificant they think it is. The interviewee will be told that s/he has the information and will be given control of the interview to talk. It is also the time to provide the caution to the interviewee if it is a cautioned interview. Even if not a cautioned interview, it is advisable to inform the interviewee that the interview is being conducted as part of an investigation and that that information will be shared with their employers and may be passed to other parties, such as regulators or other state agencies, if appropriate.

As well as striving to remove uncertainty from the process for the interviewee, the explain phase serves to obtain a baseline of the interviewee in terms of abilities, level of understanding, and attitude. It also serves to provide a baseline of behavior and voice tone of the interviewee when being questioned. Changes in these may function later to indicate possible cues to deception or 'hot spots' that are seemingly touchy subjects. Bearing this in mind, rapport is still the essential element of this phase. While a distinct part at the beginning, care should also be taken to ensure rapport is nurtured throughout the interview. As previously noted, the purpose of rapport building is to create a nonjudgmental, noncoercive atmosphere conducive to disclosure in the interview. The presence of rapport is multifunctional as it encourages compliance, facilitates an account in response to questioning, reduces resistance, and also provides insight into the characteristics of the interviewee as well as abilities and possible motives. Be prepared to move on if initial efforts at rapport are unsuccessful, rapport can always be built slowly throughout an interview if not achieved early on. This is generally how many police suspect interviews progress, so do not waste excess time with small talk at the beginning. It may not be appreciated or effective, and in some interviews, it may not be necessary at all. For example, the interviewee may be anxious to provide a full account as soon as possible or make admissions immediately, or it may be an interview where only one question needs to be answered. Be responsive to the interviewee and their needs, not the interview formula and adjust your own behavior as necessary. Encourage them to ask questions at this stage and if appropriate answer them as honestly as possible. If you are asked something you do not want to discuss yet, just say that you will be discussing that subject in more detail later. Acknowledge any concerns or obvious emotion in the interviewee because as noted in the previous chapter, the identifying and reflecting back of any emotional indicators can save time and possible conflict later on. Make an effort to be empathetic and alleviate concerns, simply stating that you are only there to understand the truth of what happened can be a very powerful relaxing statement, if delivered compassionately.

The ACCOUNT Phase

Account of knowledge is the next phase and the important phase in obtaining a narrative from the interviewee. The aim is to elicit an account in the interviewee's own words and is based on a free narrative or a 'report everything' instruction given to the interviewee once you have explained what you are investigating. This usually begins with one of the TEDS acronym such as 'can you tell me what happened that day' or 'can you describe what you remember about the accident' and then you may mention some key components to obtaining an account, which are to tell the subject to: report everything; not to guess an answer, understand it is okay to say 'I don't know' in response to a question; and ask the witness to put effort into concentrating on their memory. Once the question is asked, it is important to allow the interviewee uninterrupted free recall. The subject should be relatively relaxed at this point, and he or she should understand that the interviewer wants them to control and direct the narrative while the interviewer simply listens. It may be necessary, on occasion, to gently guide the interviewee if they wander too far off topic, but generally, silence is the best method at this point, although continual nonverbal positive encouragement is good. With witnesses, it may be necessary to try to stimulate memories by doing memory recall in a variety of orders, asking the interviewee to imagine a changed perspective, or encouraging a mental reinstatement of context.

The initial account given by the interviewee might be very broad or even vague before it gradually becomes more focused as more open or probing questions are asked and answered. The interviewer's purpose is to encourage and guide through the account by a combination of active listening and skilled in-depth questioning. The vast majority of interviewees are not accustomed to telling their story from start to end in detail, so it is normal that there will be a need to respond occasionally with comments such as 'what happened then?' to keep the narrative moving. Where an interviewee moves off topic and veers into giving information that is not connected to the issue, then gently intervening by enquiring if that information is really relevant to the account may be necessary. This is a matter of professional experience as sometimes when someone is free talking, other relevant information comes out, so it can be beneficial to allow some latitude in allowing conversation flow before intervening. Nonetheless, if someone wants to talk about their pet, for instance, then relevance becomes pertinent.

In any interview situation, some type of note-taking is necessary, if only to occasionally jot down a note as a reminder during the narrative to probe later. In most interview situations, but particularly a formal interview, it is preferable if the interviewer refrains from writing immediately the witness starts recounting their account. There are a number of reasons for this including the fact that it can be very off-putting for the interviewee and damaging to the rapport. It also limits the interviewer's listening ability as it is not possible to write and listen. More importantly, most people are unused to describing an event in detail necessary for investigative purposes, and it may require time and some probing questions to get the necessary level of detail from the person. This requires active listening rather than transcribing. Even if two interviewers are present and one is tasked with transcribing, it may be better to develop the account in sufficient detail before moving to the transcription phase. The advantage of electronic recording here should be obvious. The objective of the account phase is to get a coherent and relatively comprehensive narrative around the issue under consideration from the interviewee. With the culpable interviewee, however, it is necessary to record everything they say; it may actually be useful to have different and contradictory accounts in such circumstances as it may indicate an effort to deceive. Almost inevitably, with any type of interviewee, there will be a need to expand some points mentioned and to ask for more information on some point. This leads to the clarify stage.

Clarify, Corroborate, and Challenge

The clarify stage involves the use of probing questions such as 'how, why, when, what, where, and who' to delve into the details of the account given. When an account has been given, it is usual practice to focus only on this account and probe it in considerable depth. Any other evidence is usually not mentioned until this probing is concluded. As noted, when the PEACE method was first taught, it focused on obtaining the free narrative account from the subject with no element of challenging the account included. This quickly changed following the realization that many police were blindly accepting the accounts given and failing to properly probe the accounts, even when they possessed evidence that contradicted those accounts. This is unsatisfactory as it fails to properly put contradictions to the interviewee which may invite an alternative explanation for the evidence, or it may encourage the subject to tell the truth. Obtaining a truthful account is the objective of an interview, not simply *any* account.

The introduction of a clarify, corroborate, and challenge (3Cs) element is to highlight to the interviewer the importance of probing the account and evaluating the narrative given by the interviewee, to clarify any ambiguities arising and corroborate the account from other existing evidence. If it is then necessary, any outstanding discrepancies should be challenged. Discrepancies may have simply resulted from a misunderstanding rather than an attempt at deception, and every effort must be made to resolve them satisfactorily. It is common for interviewers to be less concerned with checking the veracity of statements that are disclosing information they believe to be correct. As a result, it is often only contradictory disclosures that trigger challenges when in reality there is a need to be alert to all discrepancies. Therefore, it is important to corroborate all information, as much as it is possible to do so.

This 3Cs stage also allows any potential in the witness for bias or veracity to be fully explored as well as any limiting disabilities of the witness to be examined. Consequently, each individual topic should be comprehensively dealt with before moving on as topic skimming or allowing interruptions can result in failure to notice that only superficial information is being provided. It may seem that this part is really only for the perpetrator, but it's important to note that not every allegation made is genuine.[10] An investigator has to be very careful to treat every allegation as credible while also being sufficiently suspicious that it is probed in depth and challenged carefully. Disclosing information to an investigator can be a difficult process for some victims and must be handled delicately. The building of rapport and providing an explanation why the detailed probing is necessary is important to protect the victim as well as ensuring the investigator does his or her job.

Generally, it is best practice to get into the specific details of each individual topic before moving on, but sometimes allowing some issues to remain outstanding is a useful tactic. As an investigator gains confidence, a useful technique is to return to an outstanding topic after discussing something else for a while. This is a useful technique for disarming a subject who may then display some unusual nonverbal signaling. In other instances, moving on prevents a breakdown in rapport as the interviewee may be becoming distressed, agitated, or simply closing down. There is little point in heading down a conversational cul-de-sac, particularly very early in the interview, so generally cover the simpler, less contentious topics comprehensively before tackling the more contentious. It is better to move on and cover as much as possible in a cooperative manner before returning to the outstanding contentious topics. Sometimes, the disputed topic can be approached from a different angle that doesn't trigger the threat mechanism in the subject.

Note-taking can be useful at this stage to remind the interviewer of outstanding material. I use a mind-map or simple linear time map of events with different nodes of each of the topics needed to be covered. Much of this map can be made ahead in the preparation phase. Using a multicolored pen with different ink on this prepared graphic then allows new information to be incorporated and topics to be returned to highlighted. This type of graphic also allows available corroborating evidence to be readily visible during the interview.

Where challenges are considered necessary because the interviewee appears to be untruthful or inaccurate, then they should be characterized by both persistence and patience, combined with careful listening as well as a deep knowledge of the investigation file. The challenge should not be in a cross-examination manner or in any manner designed to oppress, intimidate, or humiliate. Rather, it should be in the manner of a problem-solving exercise. Such an approach might involve the interviewer blaming himself or herself for failing to understand. For example, 'I'm sorry, I must have misunderstood what you said earlier' could be the beginning of a challenge. Similarly, 'I hear what you are saying, however, this evidence seems to say something else, could you explain why this CCTV evidence is saying something different to you' is another challenge. The onus is then on the interviewee to explain to you to help resolve your misunderstanding. It is always better to be willing to appear foolish than to make the interviewee feel that way. Claiming a lack of knowledge or understanding can serve a useful tactical function and is usually a better approach than trying to appear omnipotent. It is vital though to be persistent with the questioning to resolve the matter, even if the interviewee keeps trying to close down the avenue of questioning.

Obviously, depending on the attitude of the interviewee, these challenges may have to be hardened. However, it is generally better to avoid calling the interviewee a liar, even when there is clear evidence of attempted deception, as this will close down cooperation. That is not to say that an interviewer should never say it. Sometimes, such straight talking can be effective, but generally, alluding to the possibility is preferable, and it offers an advantage of allowing the subject some room to maneuver from the impasse they may have created for themselves. Although saving face is a well-known cultural phenomenon in Asian societies, it remains relevant in every society and should always be borne in mind by the interviewer. Expressing humility is one thing, but demonstrating it by not taking advantage of an interviewee in a vulnerable position and displaying empathy is a more honorable professional approach. It is unnecessary to use shame or other strong negative emotions to force an interviewee into a vulnerable position. If you have prepared properly, it is both unnecessary and potentially unethical. As importantly, using such tactics generates negative fallout in organizations as people—including impartial observers—strongly value fairness and procedural justice.[11] Accordingly, the short-term gain of an admission is likely to be outweighed considerably by the long-term negative fallout in the organization.

The presentation of evidence will usually be done in this phase and is covered in more detail in Chapter 8. The clarify and challenge phase might be separated out in time from the account phase of an interview. So, for instance, the account might be taken as early as possible from the alleged perpetrator. It might be expected that this will consist of denials or some type of false account. In which case, a later date is set for a second interview, where the clarifications are sought, based on additional evidence gathered.

The CLOSURE Phase

Closure is the final interview phase. This can serve both a legal and psychological function. It involves a review of the account given, being read over from the notes if maintained, with any discrepancies that arose or remain outstanding mentioned, with the possible need to revert to a new mini-account. Once this has been done and there was a written account kept, the subject may be asked to sign the interview notes at the end and on each separate page of notes. The signing of any interview notes or a statement is a legal consideration. Most police interviews before electronic recording involved a culmination to a written confession which was a written narrative of admissions to committing the crime that was then signed by the interviewee and investigators and dated. This then became an incredibly valuable and powerful piece of evidence, which was why so many innocent people were convicted of crimes. Even if the person tried to withdraw the confession afterward, it remained potent as few understood how an innocent person could ever make such a detailed confession to begin with. Even professionals failed to understand the power of persuasive tactics, uncertainty, and the insertion of key crime details by investigators (sometimes subtly and unconsciously) that generated this strong evidence from whole cloth that was often insurmountable from a defense perspective.

Since the widespread adoption of electronic recording in police interview rooms, the written confession has receded in use, and most interviews are a series of question-and-answer sessions that may or may not be written down.

If admissions are written down, it is good practice to get the interviewee's signature on the written notes. These should also be dated and counter-signed by investigators present. If more than one page, then initials should be put on all other pages.

The interviewee should then be asked if they have any questions or concerns, which should be addressed. An explanation of what happens next should be provided as well as answering any questions from the interviewee. On many occasions, investigators assume that as they have repeated this process many times, that interviewees also understand what is involved. This is often not the case and interviewees may wish to have clarity brought to the process and, particularly, their own involvement.

As well as providing closure on this part of the investigation process, another objective of this phase is to leave the interviewee in a positive frame of mind and the door open for any future contact, especially if additional information later comes to mind. This is also an opportunity to throw out a final catchall question such as 'is there any other information that you know of that could help us in this investigation?' The interview was scheduled with this person because there was some compelling reason to believe this person had significant information, but it does not preclude the person having additional information that may be of use, in this investigation or something else. This question might be asked after the recording has been turned off as it is not unusual for people to be more reticent when anything they say is being recorded. If you offer someone anonymity to speak freely, and they do so, then that condition must be respected. What was said can be mentioned, but its source must be protected if it was given on condition that it was off the record. Even if the interviewee can think of no further information at the time, leaving him or her feeling positive about their interviewing experience and the investigators increases the chances of some follow-up contact.

The EVALUATION Phase

Evaluation of the interview outcomes is the final phase of the process. This involves reviewing the evidence that the interview has made available as well as explanations received for discrepancies. Any new physical evidence brought to light in interviews or other information gathered from the interview should be evaluated. If necessary, this leads to further investigation and begins the cycle again. It may be necessary to reevaluate the previously accepted investigation hypothesis, either adjusting or discarding it entirely. It may also be necessary to consider seeking some outside expertise or assistance in furthering the investigation. Perhaps, at this point, it may also be considered necessary to involve regulatory agencies or the police. If the interview has fulfilled its objectives and the interview is consistent with other available evidence, then the next aspect is preparing a report to outline the investigation process and its outcomes. This will be looked at in Chapter 7 in detail.

Conclusion

The fact-finding non-accusatory interview process involves using people skills to build a relationship between interviewer and interviewee. This relationship is leveraged to obtain an account, without judgment or criticism, from the interviewee. Any discrepancies that may arise should be worked through in a problem-solving approach to minimize negative feedback. The objective is to show respect and maintain the integrity of the interviewee throughout the process. The interviewer should always have this objective at the forefront of his or her actions. There may always be an innocent explanation for even the most apparently damning evidence. Furthermore, even where disciplinary or criminal action is warranted, the perceived fairness of the investigation process will be important to the entire organization. Therefore, fairness should always be an important guiding principle for any investigator. It is better to fail to resolve an investigation and learn from your mistakes than to take a shortcut to what you believe is the correct outcome. It is important as an investigator to value your integrity and to always act to the highest possible standards. The next chapter looks more in depth at the theoretical basis of forensic interviewing, including how to handle interviewees who refuse to cooperate.

Notes

1   Baldwin, J., "Police Interview Techniques–Establishing Truth or Proof", *British Journal of Criminology*, (1993), 33(3), pp 325–352.

2   Gudjonsson, G. H., "False Confessions and Correcting Injustices", *New England Law Review*, (2012), 46, pp 689–709, Gudjonsson, G. H. and Pearse, J., "Suspect Interviews and False Confessions", *Current Directions in Psychological Science*, (2011), 20(1), pp 33–37. Police interrogation techniques are an important contributor to the erroneous conviction of innocent people. Nevertheless, interrogation is not the sole factor involved, and many other problems including scientific errors are also involved. However, investigator's bias is significant, and the use of interrogation methods in such circumstances is fraught with risk. Unfortunately, most of the other criminal justice actors are no less imperfect.

3   Bull, R. and Milne, B., 'Attempts to Improve the Police Interviewing of Suspects', (ed) Lassiter, in *Interrrogations, Confessions, and Entrapment*, (Springer, New York, 2004) pp 181–198, Pearse, J. and Gudjonsson, G. H., "Police Interviewing Techniques at Two South London Police Stations", *Psychology, Crime & Law*, (1997), 3(1), pp 63–74.

4   Shepherd, E., *Investigative Interviewing*, (Oxford University Press, Oxford, 2010); Walsh, D. and Bull, R., "What Really Is Effective in Interviews with Suspects? A Study Comparing Interviewing Skills Against Interviewing Outcomes", *Legal & Criminological Psychology*, (2010), 15(2), pp 305–321; Walsh, D. W. and Milne, R., "Keeping the PEACE? A Study of Investigative Interviewing Practices in the Public Sector", *Legal & Criminological Psychology*, (2008), 13(1), pp 39–57; Fahsing, I. and Rachlew, A., 'Investigative Interviewing in the Nordic Region', (eds) Williamson, Milne and Savage, in *International Developments in Investigative Interviewing*, (Willan, Cullompton, 2009) pp 39–64; Oxburgh, G., Walsh, D. and Milne, B., "The Importance

of Applied Research in Investigative Interviewing: A Real-life Perspective", *Journal of Investigative Psychology & Offender Profiling*, (2011), 8, pp 105–109.

5 Milne, R. and Griffiths, A., 'Will It All End in Tiers? Police Interviews with Suspects in Britain', (ed) Williamson, in *Investigative Interviewing: Rights, Research, Regulation*, (Willan, Cullompton, 2006) pp 167–188: 174; Oxburgh, G., Walsh, D. and Milne, B., "The Importance of Applied Research in Investigative Interviewing: A Real-life Perspective", *Journal of Investigative Psychology & Offender Profiling*, (2011).

6 Walsh, D. and Bull, R., "What Really Is Effective in Interviews with Suspects? A Study Comparing Interviewing Skills Against Interviewing Outcomes", *Legal & Criminological Psychology*, (2010), p 306, Milne, R. and Griffiths, A., 'Will It All End in Tiers? Police Interviews with Suspects in Britain', (ed) Williamson, in *Investigative Interviewing: Rights, Research, Regulation* (Willan, Cullompton, 2006) pp 167–188.

7 Clarke, C. and Milne, R., *The National Evaluation of the PEACE Investigative Interviewing Course*, (Institute of Criminal Justice Studies, Report No. PRAS/149, Portsmouth University, 2001).

8 Shepherd, E., *Investigative Interviewing*, (2010).

9 Theft Act 1968, United Kingdom.

10 Unfortunately, the criminal justice system pendulum often swings between one of two extremes. For many years, allegations made by both women and girls about sexual abuse were disregarded, which allowed the abuse to continue. Indeed, it is still a valid argument that in many such cases that the trial process only compounds the trauma, for instance, see Walklate, S., *Victimology: The Victim and the Criminal Justice Process*, (Routledge, Oxon, 2013). On the other hand, in the 1990s, the criminal justice system was swept up with allegations of incest and sexual abuse that women claimed to have repressed only to have recovered the memories in therapy, often through hypnosis. Unfortunately, the methods of recovery had more to do with the malleability of memory and the power of suggestion than accurate recall, see Loftus, E. F., "Creating False Memories", *Scientific American*, (1997), 277, pp 70–75; Loftus, E. F. and Palmer, J. C., "Reconstruction of Automobile Destruction: An Example of the Interaction Between Language and Memory", *Journal of Verbal Learning & Verbal Behavior*, (1974), 13(5), pp 585–589.

11 Tyler, T. R., "Enhancing Police Legitimacy", *The Annals of the American Academy of Political and Social Science*, (2004), 593(1), pp 84–99.

Bibliography

Baldwin, J., "Police Interview Techniques–Establishing Truth or Proof", *British Journal of Criminology*, (1993), 33(3), pp 325–352.

Bull, R. and Milne, B., 'Attempts to Improve the Police Interviewing of Suspects', (ed) Lassiter, in *Interrogations, Confessions, and Entrapment*, (Springer, New York, NY, 2004) pp 181–198.

Clarke, C. and Milne, R., *The National Evaluation of the PEACE Investigative Interviewing Course*, (Institute of Criminal Justice Studies, Report No. PRAS/149, Portsmouth University, 2001).

Fahsing, I. and Rachlew, A., 'Investigative Interviewing in the Nordic Region', (eds) Williamson, Milne and Savage, in *International Developments in Investigative Interviewing*, (Willan, Cullompton, 2009) pp 39–64.

Gudjonsson, G. H., "False Confessions and Correcting Injustices", *New England Law Review*, (2012), 46, pp 689–709.

Gudjonsson, G. H. and Pearse, J., "Suspect Interviews and False Confessions", *Current Directions in Psychological Science*, (2011), 20(1), pp 33–37.

Loftus, E. F., "Creating False Memories", *Scientific American*, (1997), 277, pp 70–75.

Loftus, E. F. and Palmer, J. C., "Reconstruction of Automobile Destruction: An Example of the Interaction Between Language and Memory", *Journal of Verbal Learning & Verbal Behavior*, (1974), 13(5), pp 585–589.

Milne, R. and Griffiths, A., 'Will It All End in Tiers? Police Interviews with Suspects in Britain', (ed) Williamson, in *Investigative Interviewing: Rights, Research, Regulation*, (Willan, Cullompton, 2006) pp 167–188.

Oxburgh, G., Walsh, D. and Milne, B., "The Importance of Applied Research in Investigative Interviewing: A Real-life Perspective", *Journal of Investigative Psychology & Offender Profiling*, (2011), 8, pp 105–109.

Pearse, J. and Gudjonsson, G. H., "Police Interviewing Techniques at Two South London Police Stations", *Psychology, Crime & Law*, (1997), 3(1), pp 63–74.

Shepherd, E., *Investigative Interviewing*, (Oxford University Press, Oxford, 2010).

Tyler, T. R., "Enhancing Police Legitimacy", *The Annals of the American Academy of Political and Social Science*, (2004), 593(1), pp 84–99.

Walklate, S., *Victimology: The Victim and the Criminal Justice Process*, (Routledge, Oxon, 2013).

Walsh, D. and Bull, R., "What Really Is Effective in Interviews with Suspects? A Study Comparing Interviewing Skills Against Interviewing Outcomes", *Legal & Criminological Psychology*, (2010), 15(2), pp 305–321.

Walsh, D.W. and Milne, R., "Keeping the PEACE? A Study of Investigative Interviewing Practices in the Public Sector", *Legal & Criminological Psychology*, (2008), 13(1), pp 39–57.

Chapter 5

Forensic Interviewing Concepts

Introduction

In any interview, obtaining an account of the information that the interviewee possesses is the fundamental reason that you are there. Developing rapport and getting the cooperation of the interviewee is to facilitate the information exchange as smoothly as possible. Usually, this is achievable without difficulty as most interviewees are cooperative. Nevertheless, even where cooperation is absent, the interviewer still must endeavor to obtain the information needed. This chapter focuses on techniques to obtain the account stage in more depth. The PEACE model uses two theoretical models to obtain an account: the cognitive interview (CI) and the conversation management (CM) interview concepts. Based on my own experience, I include the motivational interviewing (MI) model as I found it to be more applicable to the corporate investigative environment. Used together, these concepts allow any interview situation to be planned for and responded to, whether a fully cooperative or resistant interviewee. The fundamental approach of professionalism, ethical behavior, and respect for the interviewee does not change, but the ability to interview persons who are reluctant or resistant is essential, and together, these approaches offer an escalating response to even the most challenging interviewees.

The CI was developed in response to concerns about the quality and paucity of information obtained by police interviewers. This remains a gold standard in open questioning and is used even when interviewing children in criminal investigations—such as sexual abuse and assault cases—where all suggestive or closed questioning need to be eliminated.[1] This is because in some jurisdictions, the video recording of the questioning can be given evidence to a court in criminal prosecutions in lieu of direct testimony from the victim. The MI model was developed by therapists seeking to change self-destructive behavior such as alcoholism and does so by careful questioning to have the person arrive at the desired conclusions rather than telling them what to do. The final technique, CM, can be used in any type of interview situation, but its ability to respond to uncooperative interviewees is essential to developing a rounded ability to undertake all types of interviews, including the most challenging. It

DOI: 10.4324/9781003269489-5

can move closer to an interrogation in terms of tone as it strives to get answers to questions from uncooperative interviewees to achieve interview objectives. It continues to try to build rapport, if possible, but this model acknowledges that rapport is not always possible, but answers to questions can still be obtained. It is important to emphasize that one should not move through the models as if they were an escalation policy. It is usual to move up and down through the models, depending on the engagement style of the interviewee, so that they are generally seamlessly interwoven. Therefore, it is about flexibility, adaptability, and utilizing the correct tools to perform the role as efficiently as possible.

The CI

Psychologists Ronald Fisher and Edward Geiselman studied police witness interviewing techniques and discovered that many police officers were simply interviewing witnesses for their department report-filing purposes and thereby missing out on a lot of the information that witnesses potentially had. Police were not trained in any interview techniques and simply obtained the minimum information needed to populate the relevant form.[2] Officers often made no effort to probe the memories of witnesses any further, thereby potentially losing investigatively important material. As a result, Fisher and Geiselman developed the CI method as a comprehensive tool to assist police in obtaining information. The CI focuses on improving communication between the witness and interviewer, as well as improving memory recall with the minimum of interference.[3] The CI is considered a major success from both a psychological and legal perspective.[4] It uses memory retrieval and communication techniques to maximize information obtained. Communication focuses on efforts to maximize rapport and shared understandings between the interviewer and interviewee at the introduction stage and throughout. The CI was initially designed for witness interviewing, but it can be used in most suspect questioning contexts. It is particularly suited to serious financial crime investigation.[5] It does require cooperation from the interviewee, however, as a level of active involvement is necessary in offering a free narrative and accepting the memory enhancement techniques. Three key pillars are central to the CI:

- Knowledge representation/memory retrieval processes;
- Social dynamics, developing rapport; and
- Communication skills.

All of these are contained within a structured, phased model, which compounds the effectiveness of the process as it progresses. The important aspects of the CI-phased model as previously discussed are:

- Developing a rapport with the witness;
- Asking open-ended questions primarily;

- Asking neutral questions and avoiding leading or suggestive questions;
- Funneling the interview, beginning with broader questions, and narrowing down to more specific questions.[6]

The major difference in CI from normal police-type interviews is the transference of control to the interviewee instead of the police officer controlling the conversation. This is to emphasize that the witness has all the information so is the important person in the interaction, while the officer has little. The officer's function is to obtain as much of this information as possible by appropriate questioning. CI therefore uses a 'report everything' instruction to the interviewee, emphasizing the need for witness compatible questions, and where necessary guided imagery questioning, as well as the use of reverse order recall to probe memory for detail.[7] Guided imagery involves asking the interviewee to imagine themselves back in the scene and visualizing the event. Reverse order asks a witness to work backward in chronology of the event, beginning at the end and asking what happened just before.

Trust and confidence in the interviewer by the interviewee together with a private and (relatively) comfortable setting are essential. Leading questions should always be avoided as much as possible, with open questions the preferred approach. Leading questions increase the risk that an interviewee will simply affirm the suggestion made by the interviewer rather than provide accurate information, but this risk is particularly pronounced in the case of vulnerable interviewees such as children or when probing memories. In order to be fully effective, CI needs a friendly tone and a relaxed and almost conversational approach. The questioning method may not suit every interviewee. There may be some persons who may find taking control of the conversation difficult, for example, those who are socially anxious, so an ability to understand this and accommodate accordingly is essential. Occasionally, with some witnesses, it may be easier to ask then to recreate any actions done rather than asking for a verbal description. So, the instruction might be 'show me what happened then' as putting the situation into words may be difficult. The CI structure is guidance and not a recipe. Therefore, while it is important to understand the progression that is to be achieved, it is also important to tailor it to the individual interviewee and not follow slavishly.

CI was developed to assist police investigators gather information, sometimes with a significant time lag after the event so that it uses memory prompts to help access information that the witness may not immediately recall. Minor details that might prove to be vital may be forgotten or are often omitted as witnesses consider them irrelevant. A witness may be anxious to assist police but often feel the need to edit information and not waste time as the witness does not understand the relevance of that fragment of information. The importance of the instruction to 'report everything' to a witness is designed to minimize such editing. Other witnesses may simply have forgotten some details as they were not considered important at the time. Therefore, where considered necessary, the CI uses various memory techniques designed specifically to stimulate the memory. In general, such techniques are unnecessary in the corporate investigation scenario. However, the reverse order questioning technique, where one works chronologically backward, is a valuable technique when a witness or alleged perpetrator appears to be using a prepared script to answer questions.

One major criticism of cognitive interviewing is that it can be time-consuming, especially with witnesses who are investigatively important. However, the technique need not always be used in full. The CI interview is designed for the interviewee to take control of the interview, as it is they who have the knowledge. Where rapport is quickly established, there is no point in wasting further time on additional small talk to establish it. Move to quickly allow the interviewee to control the interview, with the interviewer simply guiding the conversation with appropriate open or probing questions. With some witnesses, one simple point is all that may need to be addressed. For instance, someone in appropriate authority may have to state that he or she gave no one permission to take or use property that has been stolen. Tailor the interview accordingly. However, bear in mind that you are not always aware of what information a witness has, so never assume even with an authority witness as above that they have no further information. Therefore, toward the end of every interview, it is a good idea to ask the open question: 'do you have any other information that you think I might be interested in?'

The closing remarks are also an especially important element. Witnesses should be made to feel that their contribution was important. This, of course, is polite, but more importantly, if a witness later remembers something he or she forgot to mention, then if a positive closing has been achieved, he or she will be more likely to communicate the additional information to the investigator. It is a feature of human nature that the closing impression is often the lasting one. Therefore, if the interview was somewhat difficult, the closing stage is even more important, and particular emphasis should be placed taking the time to thank the interviewee. Leaving a positive impression at this point may go some way to smooth over any earlier negative feelings.

Motivational Interviewing

The CI requires a significant interaction and positive contribution on the part of the interviewee, and as a consequence, on its own it can be ineffective with reluctant interviewees. An interviewee may be reluctant for any number of reasons, including shyness, uncertainty, or nervousness about the process. It is the responsibility of the interviewer to adapt and conduct the interview, whatever the circumstances. MI techniques can be of benefit with reluctant interviewees. Psychologists and therapists William Miller and Stephen Rollnick developed the MI approach as a therapeutic intervention in their work in addiction counseling.[8] Many clients of these services are themselves reluctant, even if they recognize the need for intervention or a change of behavior. The MI therapeutic technique is a form of intervention to change entrenched behavior and strives to create an environment that is collaborative rather than confrontational. It is an effective technique that helps develop rapport and reduce maladaptive behaviors in resistant subjects. There is increasing awareness of the value and other potential uses of MI. For example, MI is now being used as a contributory model in areas such as business coaching and employee mentoring as well as in helping criminal offenders reintegrate into society. Researchers have identified key parallels between therapeutic and investigative interviewing, as in that both strive to establish an empathetic, respectful, and nonjudgmental atmosphere for communication.[9] The technique's nonconfrontational approach, use of active listening techniques, empathy, and respect for the interviewee makes it a suitable technique in the organizational interviewing context. Denial can often be another characteristic shared between interviewees who have substance abuse issues and those encountered in investigations. From the therapist's perspective, the technique utilizes careful questioning and active listening to encourage the interviewee to define the negative elements of their own behavior and also to find more constructive ways forward. The MI technique is divided into two different phases. The first phase is to define the problem, while the second phase helps to promote and encourage change. The investigative interview is not really concerned with the second phase, so the first phase is the important phase from an investigation standpoint. The active listening technique is the central important aspect of MI. This is the ability to listen and then reframe the interviewee's own words back to him or her to probe further into the account. Expressing empathy is an important part of the model and understanding the perspective of the interviewee, as well as getting information. The technique is to identify the conflicting emotions in the interviewee, express empathy for that situation, and encourage the interviewee to identify the divergence between actual behavior and underlying values and beliefs. Ideally, the interviewee will gradually become more relaxed, and the CI technique will become more applicable. However, there are no distinct boundaries as to when you stop using one technique and replace it with another, as there is considerable overlap. The ability to combine the CI with MI allows information to be gathered from even initially difficult interviewees.

The Principles of MI

Express Empathy

Empathy is of particular importance in MI. Empathy is an element of rapport but a very specific part. Empathy is about having the ability to understand the perspective of another person, particularly the interviewee. It is the skill of being able to appreciate his or her emotions and distress and to communicate that you understand directly or indirectly to the interviewee. The first principle, therefore, is to understand the feelings and emotions that the interviewee is experiencing and to let the interviewee know that you know. The attitude is one of acceptance and a willingness to listen without judging or criticizing. It is important not to overdo the emotional empathy, as a patronizing approach would be highly offensive. It is also important not to try to equate a similar experience that you may have had as each person processes events differently. The aim is to understand the interviewee's perspectives as comprehensible, at least within his or her worldview or cognitive framework and to communicate that you are willing to listen without judging.

Develop Discrepancy

Draw out the inconsistencies in the different accounts the interviewee has given, or in the evidence available, or in the emotions expressed. MI assumes that the interviewee will experience equivocation during the process where he or she will hold two opposite views at the same time, which can result in uncertainty, confusion, and discomfort. The interviewer's task is then to tip the motivational balance in favor of compliance. There are different types of ambivalence—choosing between two good things, choosing between two bad outcomes, or losing something while gaining something useful or keep something valued while losing something needed. It is important to raise awareness of consequences and create and amplify any discrepancy between behavior and broader values and goals. In effect, attempt to create cognitive dissonance in the interviewee. Help the subject present rationale for a change of opinion or perspective: The concept is to skillfully change the person's perceptions of the discrepancy highlighted without creating any sense of being pressured or coerced.[10]

Probably, one of the most useful discrepancies to focus on and one that is used to generate cognitive dissonance is the discrepancy between deeply held values and beliefs contrasted with actual behavior. For instance, an alcoholic would be led to explore his stated love for his family and his desire to nurture and protect them with his alcoholism and its actual effects on his family. In the forensic interview, the discrepancy can be developed between values and behavior with the evidence of actual behavior presented. The need for a truthful account can be built from a core value of honesty, for example. A useful tool to use to develop discrepancy is reflection. For example, when you believe someone is lying to you about a specific incident, then it might be useful to approach it along the lines of: 'you have previously told me how important honesty and integrity is to you and how these are core values for you, do you think you are living up to those values at the moment?' The idea is to point out the discrepancy between core values and behavior but without directly referring to the mendacity. It rarely helps a relationship to refer to efforts at deception or to otherwise accuse a person of lying.

Avoid Arguments

This segues to the next point. It is never productive to get into an argument. Calling someone a liar directly usually elicits a defensive response which is most likely going to be verbal aggressiveness. Verbal aggressiveness leads to raised voices as one person struggles to be heard over another. Shouting is not productive and is unprofessional from an interviewer. It is also unprofessional for an interviewer to have an interview deteriorate into a situation where the interviewee is angry and shouting. It does happen, and sometimes is unavoidable, but if a lot of your interviews go this way, it's time to reconsider your career choice.

It's also a waste of time to argue with someone over a difference of opinion or belief. In fact, it is counterproductive because having someone defend their behavior or values only tends to encourage defensiveness on his or her part and makes the person more attached to their beliefs. Therefore, using arguments or logic to challenge the beliefs of an interviewee is more likely to strengthen those beliefs and unlikely to ever be successful at changing their mind.[11] Therefore, avoid taking any high moral ground, giving the impression that you as the interviewer know better, overtly contradicting the interviewee beliefs, or appearing condescending.

People seek to avoid having to change their beliefs, particularly core beliefs, to as great an extent as possible. It is a profound shift for many people and most people resist it as much as possible. The easiest and most likely defensive method for an interviewee when under such an attack is to attack the source of the unwelcome information, which means the interviewer. Such behavior is not conducive to rapport or a productive interview. Act with humility and an awareness that even when you have contradicting information to that being presented, it could be in error, or your interpretation may be mistaken.

Beware Resistance

Resistance is when the interviewee appears to close down, not engage any further, or when the tone becomes aggressive. When someone is under stress, fight or flight is a common response, but when physical action is not possible, people tend to use avoidant and psychological fleeing mechanisms instead, that are dissociative.[12] This may appear in nonverbal behavior, often fight is seen in clenching fists, facial muscles, and general signs of anger. Flight can be more subtle with a closing down of posture, making oneself appear smaller, or covering the face or eyes with the hands.[13] Resistance is a signal to change interview strategies, so an interviewer needs to be alert to nonverbal signals of resistance such as body posture and facial expressions. High levels of anger or frustration can bring dissonance to the interview process from the outset of the process and needs to be addressed before any productive interviewing can begin.

Listening carefully is also vital as misunderstandings that arise can likewise bring dissonance to the process. Miller and Rollnick list 12 behaviors that in therapeutic interview situation are so maladaptive that they will function to act as roadblocks to a positive relationship between client and the therapist: These include directing or commanding; giving warnings or threats; giving advice or solutions; moralizing; trying to persuade with logic, arguing, or lecturing; and blaming, shaming, or labeling.

A forensic interview is a different situation, in that its purpose is to ask questions so that it is the expectation people have at the outset. Nonetheless, understand that people may get defensive about certain questions as they consider them off-limits in a professional setting or find them threatening. That is why the rapport stage at the beginning is important, if someone is reluctant to volunteer some personal details, perhaps about family, the interviewer should recognize this reluctance.

Nonetheless, interviewing is a dynamic process, and if a mistake is made and, for example, the interviewer tries to persuade the interviewee with logic which causes the interviewee to close down, it is possible to recover and bring the interviewee back on track. While one should avoid patronizing behavior such as lavish praise, or approval and flattery, some subtle encouragement to keep talking is important. Nodding the head may be sufficient. Similarly, avoid any personal analysis. This is not the same as trying to interpret what a person has just said as in active listening. This is trying to interpret the root cause or context of a person's environment or behavior. Analysis is a role for a psychiatrist, psychologist, or therapist. Generally, avoid giving personal advice. The purpose of the interview is to get information, not solve anyone's personal problems.

Roll with Resistance

There are four common types of resistant behavior that an interviewee may use: arguing, interrupting, negating, and ignoring. The energy of this resistance can be used to change perceptions and assumptions. Reluctance and ambivalence are rational and understandable in an interviewee. Resistance can be reframed to create a new momentum in changing perceptions. New perceptions can be invited from the interviewee and the interviewee can be used as a resource to find solutions. Invite the subject to consider new information and offer a new perspective on the events under investigation. Sometimes, rolling with resistance can be about allowing the interviewee to vent his or her frustration while you remain calm. The interviewee may be very anxious and emotional; once he or she has calmed down, the interview may proceed if you have remained calm and in control. It is important to be proactive and demonstrate a high level of confidence by using a good interview strategy. Have questions prepared; know the objectives to be achieved. Silence is a really powerful tool after asking a difficult question.

Support Self-Responsibility

Keep the interviewee responsible for choices and choosing. Turn questions or problems back on the interviewee. Help the interviewee to identify the range of options available and affirm positive statements. Always remain aware of the interviewee's rights and feelings. It is paramount that the interview overall be seen as fair, even if some of the questioning has to be difficult.

The MI approach is a very subtle but powerful technique. It developed in therapy, and as a result, the tone is less a conversation and more a therapy session approach. The interviewer should be talking softly and have moved to be physically closer to the interviewee, simply leaning in toward the interviewee is usually sufficient. Everything the interviewee says is taken as important, and occasionally, interpretations are offered. It is important not to overdo the technique as to do so will create a patronizing environment, which may create hostility in the interviewee. Therefore, it may be better to gently introduce the technique. Allow the interviewee to struggle with answers for a little time before slowly introducing active listening. If it is accepted, then more of the technique is slowly introduced. The objective is to help the interviewee disclose his or her account in an ethical but in a complete manner as possible by offering understanding that ambivalence is normal, and the person is grappling with telling the truth while trying to protect themselves or someone else as much as possible.

Conversation Management

The CI approach and the MI approach both require some active cooperation of the interviewee. This unfortunately is not always present. Therefore, for more uncooperative or resistant interviewees, the CM technique is an alternative option for obtaining information.[14] Eric Shepherd developed this approach to cover both cooperative and uncooperative interviewees, and with uncooperative interviewees, it comes closer to a traditional police interrogation-type interview, but it continues to respect the interviewee. It may resemble an interrogation in the sense that the tone can be more formal and business-like, but no accusations are made, and abusive language or trickery is not used. However, the interviewee will be in no doubt, when this approach is used, that he or she is expected to answer the questions that are being asked. Efforts to distract by giving vague or long-winded answers to questions are not tolerated, and the interviewer is much more in control of the dialogue in this model. Again, it may not be necessary to use this approach throughout the entire interview and having the adaptability to change between models during the interview is essential. The interviewer needs to have the flexibility to move seamlessly between the different styles and the skill to know when to apply pressure and when to back off. An interviewer may move between the therapist-style interview of MI to the police interrogator of CM and possibly repeat this cycle a number of times throughout the interview. Where interviewees are unco-operative or are not even engaging, communication can become difficult. It is important to always avoid trying to become the alpha debater or not to react to efforts by the interviewee to become one or to use *ad hominem* rhetoric which is attacking the person rather than the argument itself, or otherwise trying to make the person look weak or foolish. As always, tone can be communicated by either party through nonverbal communication such as a peremptory tone, a cold stare, constant interruptions, or just a defensive posture.

The CM model likewise emphasizes the importance of rapport as well as being mindful of the other person and their sense of esteem and self-respect. The model encourages adopting the interviewee's perspective and being empathetic toward their situation.[15] The interviewer strives to be honest and open, encouraging equals talking with each other, with a reciprocal relationship being developed through good manners and open communication.

However, the most important advantage of the CM model is its ability to facilitate an interview with a noncooperative interviewee. The reality in conducting investigative interviews is that rapport is not always possible, and interviewees may often be resistant to being interviewed. The reasons may or may not concern guilt or innocence. Interviewees may simply be shy or of a nervous disposition. The interviewee may be an introverted personality type who finds talking to strangers, especially in these types of stressful situations, dif-ficult. There may be fear of consequences involved, either for themselves or for someone else. Many people would prefer to avoid being responsible for getting someone else into trouble or giving evidence against them, especially in what may be considered noncriminal relatively trivial matters. The other models can respond to these situations usually. However, some other interviewees may be hostile simply because they are busy and regard the interview as a burden-some meaningless imposition. Senior executives can be particularly frustrating to interview as many are inclined to look at the whole process as beneath them in some way. But, of course, some interviewees do not want to cooperate to protect themselves and believe frustrating the interview is a useful strategy.

The interview must be completed whether rapport is possible or not, and it is important to be able to move the interview forward. For uncooperative persons, the CM is more suitable as it puts the interviewer in control after the first free account is given, if an account is even given. In some interviews, the initial account and rapport phases are concluded without difficulty, but when the interviewer begins the challenging phase, then the interviewee turns less cooperative if not hostile. Some interviewees may be reluctant from the very beginning and may not even engage in a free narrative. The interviewer will probably notice immediately that the interviewee is reluctant, and rapport questions may get only short replies if not simply a shrug. The interviewee may be sitting in a closed posture with his arms crossed and barely answering questions and avoiding eye contact or staring intently into the interviewer's eyes. At this point, it is useful to point out the obvious reluctance to cooperate to the interviewee. You can describe what you perceive as a very defensive posture and nonverbal behavior as well as the fact that all questions are being answered with unusually brief answers. This serves two purposes, it provides an account for the recording, and it lets the person know that you are paying attention to his behavior, in all forms. A simple question such as: 'you do not seem happy to be here, is there a reason for that?' may often be sufficient to get the person talking, and once this happens, the rapport builds, and the interview proceeds normally. Sometimes, the person is simply overworked and not happy to be dragged into something that takes from their day. However, it is more often likely that the most reluctant interviewees are the persons responsible or culpable for the deviance. Be aware also that if the interview is only being audio recorded, then it is useful to describe the nonverbal language you are witnessing for the purpose of the record.

It is important that the interviewer has control in these situations and appears confident. The interviewer should be in total control, and this should equally be obvious to the interviewee. The impression given is that we will be as pleasant as possible in the circumstances, but I am here to ask you questions, one way or another. The CM technique suggests setting out the ground rules as well as the investigative purposes of the interview from the beginning. The purpose of the interview should be explained in some detail, especially if this person may be culpable. The expectations for cooperation from the organization should be laid out. How and why the investigation started should be explained. The expectation that the person will do their best to cooperate should be emphasized. There is an ongoing investigation, and it is expected that everyone will assist in resolving the issue. It will be explained that this is an opportunity for them to provide their account of events and that it is important to obtain that. This should be done slowly and deliberately; the person should be asked if they have any questions or comments to make at the conclusion of this explanation. Long pauses should be used, and the pace overall is much slower than a normal interview with silence a major tactical advantage for the interviewer.

Initially, the interviewee is asked to provide an account of events through an open question as normal, even though rapport is absent. The account given by the interviewee may be reluctant or not as complete and comprehensive as possible. The interviewee is obviously reluctant to answer, and the normal subtle cues of encouragement are ineffective. Sometimes, it is useful to continue to use them; at other times, rapt, focused, and silent attention is better. The interviewer needs to use more questions to get the information out than other approaches, but questioning still begins focusing only on the account given, no matter how short. The answers may continue to be very short, incomplete, vague, or even absent. Again, this behavior should be noted by the interviewer. Probing questions such as 'Can you elaborate some more on that answer?' or 'can you repeat what you just said?' should be asked. Once questioning based on the open account finishes, questioning around the available evidence begins. The interviewer decides what other areas to focus on, and in what order, asking the usual broad questions first and progressively more focused, probing questions. As noted, it is usual to exhaust a topic before moving on because detailed questioning is more likely to turn up discrepancies than 'topic skimming', but sometimes staying unpredictable has advantages. This incongruity in a logical progression of topics can be useful in detecting deceit 'hotspots' in interviewees as they may be mentally preparing for the next expected question and be caught off guard by the sudden topic change. Once asked, the interviewer should observe the interviewee closely for nonverbal responses and wait until the interviewee has responded before speaking again unless it's to point out that he or she is either failing or refusing to answer the question. Asking unanticipated questions or asking for answers in an unexpected format, such as by drawing, is also a useful technique when examining for deceit.[16]

It is important to allow long pauses even after answers during this technique to encourage the interviewee to talk. In this way, an interviewee may disclose information as they struggle to fill the silences. A very hostile interviewee will probably not fill the silence in this way, but the silences ensure the interviewer has control of the conversation. Using the evidence skillfully is one way to move the conversation forward. Indeed, it is essential to have evidence gathered when dealing with a resistant interviewee. Evidence gathered is how questions are formulated as this is what the interviewee has to provide an explanation for. Pointing out what the evidence is suggesting while the interviewee has not offered any alternative suggestion, followed by silence, can be a powerful technique. It is important to be persistent even in the face of resistance. Being assertive and persistent in seeking answers, but this is not the same thing as being aggressive. It remains important to avoid aggression or to use any type of threat of violence. Be aware of your own body language and remain respectful, honest, and professional. You may point out the interviewee's employment obligation to assist investigations and that currently you do not feel that he or she is fulfilling this obligation.

Use phrases such as 'I noticed', 'I feel', and 'I observed' to make comments about the interviewee's behavior, as this is not an accusation, and the interviewee can correct your erroneous perception. It is important to feel comfortable with or at least, accepting of, a little conflict at times throughout the interview. An interviewer has to develop an ability to handle conflict as some interviewees can be hostile. Always remain calm and composed. It is probable that even an initially very reluctant and uncooperative interviewee will develop some type of rapport with you as the interview progresses. Encourage this by occasionally reassuring the person of your independence, integrity, and desire only to establish the truth. As the interview progresses, in an ideal world, this should be obvious to the interviewee. The working relationship is fostered by an awareness of potential barriers to disclosure, realistic expectations about memory abilities, and an explanation to ensure shared understanding and rapport. The interviewer should continue to display relationship-building behaviors as well as genuine regard and respect for the interviewees' rights whatever the allegation is.

The DEAL Technique

Nevertheless, despite the interviewer's best efforts, the interviewee may try to disrupt the interview by being uncooperative, dissembling, evasive, overly emotional, or even aggressive. The person may simply make denials rather than answer questions or the person may even try to denigrate or insult the interviewer. Disruptive behavior may vary from reticent or incomplete answers to outright refusal to talk or even abusive behavior. As mentioned, sometimes allowing a person to vent can be a useful technique; however, this is a matter of judgment. It is unlikely there is a situation where such behavior should be tolerated when an interviewee has been hostile from the beginning. If you permit a venting of emotion, it is important to regain control immediately. Acknowledge the interviewees emotion, ask them if they require a drink of water, a short break, or if they are ready to resume the interview. In other situations, it is necessary to do more to counter the interviewee's inappropriate or disruptive behavior and CM uses the DEAL technique.[17] The DEAL acronym is:

- **D**escribe the problem behavior;
- **E**xplain why the behavior is an issue and the actual or potential effects of the behavior;
- **A**ction required to correct behavior is outlined; and
- **L**ikely consequences if corrective action is not taken.

The DEAL technique may be used only in part; that is, it may often be sufficient to draw the interviewee's attention to behavior that is disrupting the interview to allow him or her to change that behavior. Shepherd suggests ignoring disruptive behavior on the first and probably second occasion it is used. Ignoring it first, perhaps with a long pause, may be sufficient to get the message to the interviewee that you are in control and will not be deterred. If this is unsuccessful, then the problem is highlighted by specifically referring to it, and an explanation provided why it is a problem. It is then explained to the interviewee what needs to be done to remedy the behavior. No mention is made of likely consequences at this point. If the disruptive behavior happens again, the full explanation should be given again together with the likely consequences, which may involve termination of the interview. Where behavior is particularly egregious, DEAL can be used but immediately rather than incrementally. The interviewer should never accept abusive bad behavior in an interview situation and should show a willingness to terminate the interview immediately as a consequence of such behavior. This, together with a report of the behavior to the relevant management, should be the implementation of the likely consequences outlined to the interviewee. Once again, however, an ability to handle conflict is a tremendous asset in such a situation. Sometimes, being willing and able to stay calm, composed, and in control will allow a good interviewer to regain control even in such situations, especially if the person has overreacted. It is a judgment call for the interviewer and will vary from situation to situation. There is little to be gained to have a situation escalate to physical violence. Fortunately, this should be an unusual occurrence in this type of interviewing environment. Electronic recording is again tremendously useful in both countering and dealing with the consequences of disruptive behavior.

Conclusion

To sum up, the three models outlined will allow an interviewer to obtain an account from subjects ranging on the spectrum of cooperativeness. They may be used interchangeably, although in some interviews, the interviewer may find one technique is solely used, particularly the CI model. In other interviews, especially where the interviewee experiences a broad range of emotions, the three techniques may be used in an alternating manner. The object is to obtain information from the interview subject, so how best to handle the subject during this process is a dynamic process. Even when mistakes are made, it is possible to recover and succeed in getting the information. Therefore, know the tools but use them in a manner that best suits your own personality and communication style. It is the interaction between interviewer and interviewee that leads to success, and having flexibility and adaptability is critical to the process. Use the toolkit with your own judgment and reflect on the results. As in everything, the timing is critical. Knowing when to switch from a soft approach to applying some pressure varies from person to person. Practice and experience will help to develop this, but there is the element of an 'art' to it. Nevertheless, an interview does not have to be perfect, just effective enough at getting the questions answered or otherwise obtaining information. The interview is a critical part of the process, but gathering evidence through other means is another vital aspect of an investigation. Chapter 6 looks at how to do this.

Notes

1   As mentioned in Chapter 4, suggestibility is a major issue in the criminal justice system. Some people are very prone to suggestibility and inclined to take information provided through questions and incorporate them into their own memories, thereby contaminating the memory irrevocably. The importance of avoiding any suggestive questioning in any investigation but particularly in cases of sexual assault/ abuse cases cannot be overstated. Beginning in the late 1980s, a movement began that claimed that repressed memories of sexual abuse were resulting in physical and psychiatric ailments in adults. Books such as *Courage to Heal: A Guide for Women Survivors*

of Child Sex Abuse by Bass and Davies in 1988 encouraged women to undergo hypnosis to recover these repressed memories and confront their abusers. Therapists helped hundreds of thousands of women to recover such repressed memories and to confront their abusers who were often family members. Thousands of families were destroyed by such recovered memories that were bogus. These 'memories' were often brought forth by suggestive and leading questioning of therapists who believed that such incidents must have happened and worked until their patients had found the memory or constructed it. This is not to say memories of traumatic incidents cannot be repressed, rather that careful questioning is vital to avoid contaminating an individual's memory.

2   Fisher, R. P., Geiselman, R. E. and Raymond, D. S., "Enhancing Enhanced Eyewitness Memory: Refining the Cognitive Interview", *Journal of Police Science & Administration*, (1987), 15, pp 291–297; Fisher, R. P. and Geiselman, E., *Memory-Enhancing Techniques for Investigative Interviewing. The Cognitive Interview*, (Charles C. Thomas, Illinois, 1992); Fisher, R. P., "Interviewing Cooperative Witnesses", *Legal & Criminological Psychology*, (2010), 15(1), pp 25–38.

3   Later changes to enhance social exchange led to the model being developed as the enhanced cognitive interview (ECI).

4   Memon, A., Meissner, C. A. and Fraser, J., "The Cognitive Interview: A Meta-analytic Review and Study Space Analysis of the Past 25 Years", *Psychology, Public Policy, and Law*, (2010), 16(4), pp 340–372.

5   Lokanan, M. E., "The Application of Cognitive Interviews to Financial Crimes", *Journal of Financial Crime*, (2018), 25(3), pp 882–890.

6   Fisher, R. P., "Interviewing Cooperative Witnesses", *Legal & Criminological Psychology*, (2010), p 26.

7   Fisher, R. P., Geiselman, R. E. and Raymond, D. S., "Enhancing Enhanced Eyewitness Memory: Refining the Cognitive Interview", *Journal of Police Science & Administration*, (1987); Milne, R. and Bull, R., "Does the Cognitive Interview Help Children to Resist the Effects of Suggestive Questioning?", *Legal & Criminological Psychology*, (2003), 8(1), pp 21–39.

8   Miller, W. R. and Rollnick, S., *Motivational Interviewing*, (Guilford Press, New York, 2002).

9   Alison, L. J., Alison, E., Noone, G., Elntib, S. and Christiansen, P., "Why Tough Tactics Fail and Rapport Gets Results: Observing Rapport-Based Interpersonal Techniques (ORBIT) to Generate Useful Information from Terrorists", *Psychology, Public Policy, and Law*, (2013), 19(4), pp 411–431.

10 Miller, W. R. and Rollnick, S., *Motivational Interviewing*, (2002): 39.

11 Roberts, K., 'Social Psychology and the Investigation of Terrorism', (ed) Pearse, in *Investigating Terrorism: Current Political, Legal and Psychological Issues*, (John Wiley, Chichester, 2015) pp 202–213; Ross, L. and Anderson, C. A., 'Shortcomings in the Attribution Process: On the Origins and Maintenance of Erroneous Social Assessments', (eds) Kahneman, Slovic and Tversksy, in *Judgement Under Uncertainty: Heuristics and Biases*, 2008 ed., (Cambridge University Press, Cambridge, 1982) pp 129–152.

12 Perry, B. D., "Fear and Learning: Trauma-Related Factors in the Adult Education Process", *New Directions for Adult and Continuing Education*, (2006), 110, pp 21–27: 24.

13 Navarro, J., *What Every Body Is Saying*, (William Morrow, New York, 2008).

14 Shepherd, E., 'Developing Interview Skills', (ed) Southgate, in *New Directions in Police Training*, (HMSO, London, 1988) pp 170–188; Shepherd, E., *Investigative Interviewing*, (Oxford University Press, Oxford, 2010).

15 A reminder that Shepherd uses the SOFTENS acronym:

Signs—smile, open facial expression
Open posture—arms uncrossed
Forward leaning
Touch—shaking hands only
Eye contact—not staring
Nods—supportive nonverbal signs
Supportive sounds and noises

16 Vrij, A., Granhag, P. A. and Porter, S., "Pitfalls and Opportunities in Nonverbal and Verbal Lie Detection", *Psychological Science in the Public Interest*, (2010), 11(3), pp 89–121.

17 Shepherd, E., *Investigative Interviewing*, (2010): 239.

Bibliography

Alison, L. J., Alison, E., Noone, G., Elntib, S. and Christiansen, P., "Why Tough Tactics Fail and Rapport Gets Results: Observing Rapport-Based Interpersonal Techniques (ORBIT) to Generate Useful Information from Terrorists", *Psychology, Public Policy, and Law*, (2013), 19(4), pp 411–431.

Fisher, R. P., "Interviewing Cooperative Witnesses", *Legal & Criminological Psychology*, (2010), 15(1), pp 25–38.

Fisher, R. P. and Geiselman, E., *Memory-Enhancing Techniques for Investigative Interviewing. The Cognitive Interview*, (Charles C. Thomas, Springfield, IL, 1992).

Fisher, R. P., Geiselman, R. E. and Raymond, D. S., "Enhancing Enhanced Eyewitness Memory: Refining the Cognitive Interview", *Journal of Police Science & Administration*, (1987), 15, pp 291–297.

Lokanan, M. E., "The Application of Cognitive Interviews to Financial Crimes", *Journal of Financial Crime*, (2018), 25(3), pp 882–890.

Memon, A., Meissner, C. A. and Fraser, J., "The Cognitive Interview: A Meta-analytic Review and Study Space Analysis of the Past 25 Years", *Psychology, Public Policy, and Law*, (2010), 16(4), pp 340–372.

Miller, W. R. and Rollnick, S., *Motivational Interviewing*, (Guilford Press, New York, NY, 2002).

Milne, R. and Bull, R., "Does the Cognitive Interview Help Children to Resist the Effects of Suggestive Questioning?", *Legal & Criminological Psychology*, (2003), 8(1), p 21.

Navarro, J., *What Every Body Is Saying*, (William Morrow, New York, NY, 2008).

Perry, B. D., "Fear and Learning: Trauma-Related Factors in the Adult Education Process", *New Directions for Adult and Continuing Education*, (2006), 110, pp 21–27.

Roberts, K., 'Social Psychology and the Investigation of Terrorism', (ed) Pearse, in *Investigating Terrorism: Current Political, Legal and Psychological Issues*, (John Wiley, Chichester, 2015) pp 202–213.

Ross, L. and Anderson, C. A., 'Shortcomings in the Attribution Process: On the Origins and Maintenance of Erroneous Social Assessments', (eds) Kahneman, Slovic and Tversksy, in *Judgement Under Uncertainty: Heuristics and Biases*, 2008 ed., (Cambridge University Press, Cambridge, 1982) pp 129–152.

Shepherd, E., 'Developing Interview Skills', (ed) Southgate, in *New Directions in Police Training*, (HMSO, London, 1988) pp 170–188.

Shepherd, E., *Investigative Interviewing*, (Oxford University Press, Oxford, 2010).

Vrij, A., Granhag, P. A. and Porter, S., "Pitfalls and Opportunities in Nonverbal and Verbal Lie Detection", *Psychological Science in the Public Interest*, (2010), 11(3), pp 89–121.

Chapter 6

Gathering Evidence

Introduction

This chapter will examine how to gather evidence and will generally discuss evidence from a forensic perspective where the chain of custody is paramount. Generally, police or regulatory investigators will seize evidence—any material that they believe is relevant to the case under investigation (or any other suspected offense)—with the intention of examining it, and if relevant producing it before a court as proof when the matter is at trial. The chain of custody refers to the ability of the prosecution to establish that the evidence is the same as it was when it was first seized, that it has not been interfered with or anyway changed in nature for some unaccountable reason other than because of some forensic examination when warranted.

The situation from a private investigation may be different as when investigators are called in to an organization, there may be no intention to make a criminal complaint. Moreover, the organization will generally retain the bulk of the relevant evidence as it was material produced in the course of normal business, such as production records, invoices, etc. In the vast majority of cases, this information cannot simply be seized and stored somewhere else, the volume of data may be immense, and the storage security of the organization will oftentimes exceed the capabilities of most private investigators. Additionally, in most private investigations, it is unnecessary to seize the information as it is perfectly useful in its normal form, and obtaining copies as warranted is sufficient from an investigative standpoint.

Nonetheless, even though an organization declines to make a criminal complaint meaning that the police may not become involved, any investigation may ultimately end up in some type of court setting or tribunal. Employees who are disciplined or dismissed will have rights to appeal this decision through a number of mechanisms depending on the jurisdiction; the issue may be of concern to a regulatory body, such as the Food and Drug Administration (FDA) or a financial regulator, who may decide to conduct their own investigations or take punitive actions; even a small-scale private investigation may subsequently uncover more serious deviance, including serious criminal matters that may tip

DOI: 10.4324/9781003269489-6

the balance toward making a formal police complaint after the private investigation has begun.

If an investigation ends up before a tribunal or court of some type, the investigation will need to be recreated for the purpose of such a hearing as well as withstanding the scrutiny of cross-examination. While it may be possible to reinterview subjects (within reason), physical and forensic evidence has to be gathered correctly the first time, as there will be no second opportunity. If evidence becomes contaminated because of a bad process collecting it, then it is useless or worse, counterproductive. If an internal investigator uncovers sufficient evidence of serious fraud to warrant an outside investigation whatever evidence initially gathered by the internal investigator must be passed to the police or regulatory body. If the custody chain of evidence is later not capable of being proved as secure, the case cannot succeed in court. Therefore, only competent persons should be involved in the evidence-gathering process. There may be other reasons why what appeared simple becomes complex, and therefore, this chapter tries to provide some broad outlines about the seriousness of the evidence-gathering process. Once gathered, the available evidence usually needs to be evaluated to provide a hypothesis as to the occurrence under investigation and to guide future investigatory actions. The proper use of evidence is a fundamental part of the interview process as evidence is the critical tool in obtaining the truth from individuals. This chapter will also discuss some techniques for tracking evidence as well as report writing, which is the essential skill in bringing the results from the investigation together for the purpose of delivering it to the commissioning clients.

Gathering Evidence

In a perfect world, crime scenes would be preserved immediately, and vital trace evidence and forensics protected until they were gathered by experts, who securely and safely stored them until they were expertly examined. The expert analysis would be in controlled laboratory environments where all tests and results were diligently and carefully conducted through validated means. Evidence of innocence would be treated as importantly as evidence of guilt. In reality, various pressures such as time constraints interfere with the collection of evidence. While it is a general rule that all evidence should not be considered the sole property of the prosecution, but that all evidence should be made available to the other side, unfortunately, even in high-profile criminal cases, this does not always happen. Evidence is not only treated as exclusive property of the prosecution, but more nefarious misuses or abuses include the exaggeration of forensic evidence, findings are inadequately supported, the result of shoddy analysis, impacted by bias, or a product of unvalidated scientific methods with insufficient foundation.[1] The issues are not confined to forensic evidence, and bias can cause all types of evidence to be misinterpreted, with an overly heavy focus on conviction seeking rather than truth seeking. There are many reasons for these problems, but the principle of neutrality or objectivity in an investigator is essential to avoid such problems in misinterpreting or misusing evidence.

Unlike investigating agencies such as the police, corporate investigators derive much of the access to information from the rights of the organization as employer and owner of data.[2] Clarissa Meerts argues that investigators in the private sphere have an advantage over police in gathering information as internal communications systems such as phone records, emails, personnel records, and internal financing records are readily available, and the gathering of them rarely moves out of the private sphere, so most norm violations can be dealt with autonomously from the criminal justice system.[3] It is important to give employees some notice of a forthcoming investigation, especially prior to a formal interview. This permits them an opportunity to seek legal advice if applicable. Lawyers who act as investigation counsel may serve a formal notice of investigation on any employees who may possess relevant information as normal practice in corporate investigations. Whatever type of notice, it should be vague enough that the integrity of the investigation is not compromised but provide sufficient details to cover the scope of the investigation. This can be accompanied by a document preservation notice instructing personnel not to alter, delete, destroy, or otherwise interfere with any potential evidence.[4] However, it may be prudent to begin an investigation before issuing such notices as it is difficult to conceal the true nature of an investigation, and notwithstanding instructions not to destroy evidence, it is often the first response of perpetrators.

Public sources of information should not be neglected. Open-source intelligence (OSINT) is an important investigation tool in its own right. Examples of OSINT include newspapers and broadcast media and other public sources of information such as company registration offices or land registry offices.[5] For a fee, it is possible to obtain past company filings and other useful information. Sites such as *WhoIs* may yield information about Internet domain owners, while *Maltego* is a tool that can link other domains listed at an Internet protocol (IP) address or domain name to email addresses, phone numbers, and people. Even phonebooks or reverse directories are useful sources. OSINT will invariably include social media platforms such as *LinkedIn*, *Twitter*, and *Facebook*. For example, where someone has public access on their social media, then gathering information may be allowed. It is important to understand that intelligence is not evidence. Such an approach as OSINT may allow background information to be gathered and that may lead to investigatively important sources of evidence. Photographs uploaded and friends connected are all useful sources of intelligence. It may provide corroboration of other evidence but may never be disclosed at interview. As noted, many investigations are more employee relations issues and dealt with as such, even when fraud or other criminal matters are concerned. Nonetheless, it remains pertinent to be alert to good forensic evidence-gathering practice.

Analyzing Evidence Needs

An investigator should maintain a record of the investigation. At its simplest, this can be a notebook where all actions taken are recorded, as well as times and dates. This record is the original record of the investigation and should be retained safely.[6] In many investigations, the investigator may combine the investigation record and the investigation report that the investigator writes as he or she progresses, often on a laptop. This is perfectly acceptable in many minor investigations, but as with all electronic records and data, it should be backed up securely on multiple locations to prevent accidental loss. The final report may ultimately be edited for clarity and final submission, so the original record with all information gathered should be retained safely. To clarify, the original record may contain unused material that may become relevant, possibly to the alleged perpetrator for defense purposes, and must be securely retained.

It is usual to begin at the end event and work backward to identify areas where evidence can be gathered. The intention is to have a chain of relevant evidence linking all parts of the event from beginning to the end. This evidence is to corroborate any facts alleged or otherwise support or refute any investigative hypotheses. It helps to understand that all evidence is not equal, and some evidence carries more weight and is more useful. For instance, how do you prove a person's name is what he claims? Obviously, forms of identification he produces will verify it; different forms carry greater weight, a passport is better than a library card. But it may be necessary to go back further, to examine birth and school records, social services, and work history, perhaps even social media to fully confirm a person's identity. Similarly, how do you prove a person has been on a foreign trip recently, without having to travel there to interview staff or view CCTV? Statements from coworkers will help but may only prove the person's absence. Travel agency bookings may only prove an intention to travel. Boarding cards for aircraft and credit card receipts/bills from the location are good. Airline manifests or passport entry and exit stamps are probably the most definitive. Certain photographs of the person taken there might help. Ordinary photographs alone may not be useful as they could be from anywhere or at any time, but if digital, embedded geolocation data provide coordinates with date/time and are excellent corroboration.

In many situations, there may be no *smoking gun* piece of evidence, that is, evidence that is clear and unambiguous, and proves the matter one way or another unequivocally. Documents may often be ambiguous or limited in what they actually prove and may be open to various interpretations. Data found on electronic devices may appear incriminating, but it must be established that the person was aware of the presence of these data. Therefore, questioning may be needed to clarify evidence found. Likewise, witnesses may provide testimony open to different interpretations. If the evidence does not directly relate to the matter at hand, it may be useful as *circumstantial evidence*. It is important for the investigators to understand precisely what it is that needs to be proved and then evaluate the evidence for relevance and to see what the evidence actually shows or any alternative explanations that might account for the evidence. If necessary, additional evidence may have to be sought to bring clarity. One should also be conscious of the missing evidence. What Sherlock Holmes referred to as 'the dog that didn't bark'. For example, if someone claims to have been in holiday to Australia recently, then it would be unusual and probably suspicious if not a single piece of corroborating evidence could be found to support the claim.[7] In addition, beware that the *absence of evidence* does not equate to the *evidence of absence*, so just because you cannot find evidence does not mean it does not exist. Bear in mind that circumstantial evidence can accumulate in probative value as inferences can be drawn from it. In other words, the more strands of evidence, even if they are individually tenuous, may come together to form a strong rope of linkage, corroborating the investigation hypothesis. Such situations might also arise in a bullying case, for instance, where one uncorroborated incident is unlikely to be sufficient to make a determination. However, other incidents, involving the same victim or another, may allow a pattern of behavior to be established in relation to the alleged perpetrator. A single incident may be insufficient, but a number of similar or linked incidents may shift the balance of probability toward guilt. It is normal to give a subject an opportunity to respond to allegations and to evidence gathered; indeed, this is one important purpose of the interview. This is in fairness to anyone accused as not all allegations made are made in good faith, or there may be an alternative explanation other than the one alleged. This is also an opportunity to seek an account of evidence gathered. Therefore, putting the evidence to a person at interview will be required, but as will be discussed in the how to use evidence section in Chapter 7, this should be done in a tactical way.

Jobs Book

Throughout the investigation, identifying gaps in knowledge and making efforts to obtain the missing information is essential. It is important to keep a track of tasks that are identified as requiring attention and any outcomes, particularly in complex investigations. For smaller investigations involving a sole investigator maintaining the investigation record is sufficient. Tasks or jobs may include interviews to be done, inquiries to be made, searches made to find evidence, or forensic examinations required. When a number of investigators are involved, the most basic method is to keep a separate book known as the *Jobs Book*; it outlines the job to be done, by whom and date of issue of the job. The date of completion and result of the job are also entered. Investigative software is now available that fulfills this function.[8] The use of paper still has some advantages; first, it is not subject to computer viruses or malware. Second, courts still prefer original paper; changes or alterations are easier to spot, so paper records can be authenticated easier.

Where the task assigned has generated evidence, then a *catalog* or *exhibit number* for each piece of evidence should be entered in the jobs book. The original number may or may not continue to be used throughout the report or in court proceedings. Normally, the member of the investigative team who first handles the evidence creates the catalog number. This may simply be his or her initials combined with a sequential number. For example, investigator James Gomez will mark the first item he seizes as JG 1 and so on. If a large folder or box of documents is seized which cannot be gone through on-site, then it should be sealed and marked with a catalog number. Later, any items discovered in the box or folder can be marked with a number that includes the original number, for example, JG 1(i) or JG 1(a). The catalog or exhibit number should be referenced in any statement made where it is relevant. If an additional job is then generated from the discovery of the item of evidential value, that should also be noted in the jobs book. The idea is that every job created is closed with a result, and no gaps are left unpursued in the investigation, even if not always successfully.

As noted, in many private investigations in organizations, there may not be a lot of original evidence seized. Most companies do not want to release information, especially if proprietary, and it may be part of critical infrastructure that cannot be obtained without incurring significant costs. In such cases, a printout, a photocopy or picture of the documents, or even a picture of the computer screen may suffice. Normally, the original business information will probably be retained for some considerable time and securely as part of the normal evidence-gathering procedure. Although that should not be assumed, and it may be necessary to ensure that routine destruction policies do not delete the information. If the original data are usually destroyed quickly as normal practice, then it is wiser to retain the original if practicable. This action is done more covertly and is important in the preservation of information and evidence in some cases. If copies are used, it is important to record all these copies of the original records accurately. It is also important to understand what you are obtaining. Taking a photograph of a document without understanding its relevance may result in a lot of data uploaded but confusion within days as the investigator struggles to decipher it all.[9] Therefore, take time when taking photographs or receiving other copies of documents to label them properly and comprehensively and record any explanation you receive for its relevance in the investigation record. Obviously, the explanation received may not be sufficient or it's possible there may be some hidden relevance that becomes apparent later—but at the initial point, the principle is not to simply take a mass of photos that overwhelms the investigator at a later stage. It is also wise when receiving copies of electronic data to immediately ensure that it is usable and readable. Take heed from the mistake of the investigators and prosecutors in the fraud case against Elizabeth Holmes, former CEO of Theranos, who discovered when they got around to review the large data cache that they had received from Theranos, that it was encrypted, and no key had been given. To make matters worse was the fact that the servers with the original data had been destroyed in the interim.

Searching for Evidence

In most cases, it is not legally permissible to enter into areas considered private to obtain evidence unless a search warrant from a court or judge is obtained. For instance, in many jurisdictions, a person's home is legally protected from unauthorized entry. An entry into an individual's home without a warrant may not only see any evidence obtained rendered unusable, but the aggrieved householder may be entitled to seek civil damage for trespass. Moreover, search warrants are usually only issued to law enforcement agencies (LEAs) such as the police or other regulatory enforcement agencies. Most warrants, however, do permit the LEA personnel to bring specialists on the search. It is important that a private investigator does not use illegal methods of obtaining evidence such as an illegal search or wiretap.[10] Utilizing such methods is illegal, unethical, and possibly a criminal offense in itself. Any evidence obtained by such methods is unusable in a court and taints any good evidence and the investigator as well.

Electronic data are an important component of any investigation. While ownership of data on company devices usually remains with the company, compliance with the requirements of data privacy is always a consideration. In Europe, the General Data Protection Regulations (GDPR) provides limits on the processing of personal data that can be used to identify a person. Article 6 provides for the processing of personal data in a number of situations including having a legitimate interest to process someone's personal data, processing is necessary to satisfy a contract to which the data subject is a party, and it is necessary to process the data to comply with a legal obligation. Processing in the public interest or for an official function is also legitimate.

CCTV evidence provides an important example of evidence collection. While different jurisdictions naturally have different principles and legislation, in Europe, at least, CCTV is considered data from a GDPR perspective. This means that it should only be gathered for a specified purpose and retained only as long as necessary. This normally means that CCTV data are automatically overwritten every 28–30 days. It can be retained for longer and downloaded if it is likely to be evidence of any criminal wrongdoing or for health and safety purposes, but because of the automatic deletion, it is necessary to be alert to its presence early. This is not always possible as investigators may not be brought in until some time has passed. Where CCTV does exist, it can provide critical information to an investigation. However, CCTV is not simply evidence for the prosecution, and CCTV needs to be made available to the defense also. From a human rights perspective, the principle is that the defense should be entitled to inspect any evidence with a view to establishing any additional information pertinent to their case. Therefore, it is insufficient to simply have watched CCTV footage before it was deleted. It must be downloaded and available to the defense, if required, in a readable format with its provenance assured.[11] Therefore, time and date stamps should be displayed and accurate (or adjusted correctly).

Jurisdictions vary in the legality of searching employee's lockers or desks at work. Generally, employees may have a reasonable expectation of privacy in certain aspects, such as not being physically searched, but not in relation to work-related activities or property. Expectations about cooperation and expectations of privacy may be specified in an employment contract, but where a credible reason exists, then a search may be reasonable. This particularly applies to regulated industries where employees generally have a lower expectation of privacy in relation to work practices. As noted, however, a private organizational investigation has advantages as it generally retains ownership and access rights to all hardware, software, and company documents. Many company policies will explicitly state that company computers or electronic devices offer no expectation of privacy and could therefore be a ready source of evidence. Desktops can be accessed in offices, and it may be advisable to secure offices to prevent access while an investigation is ongoing. Laptops or other personal electronic devices that belong to the company can also be seized and forensically imaged. It is normally good practice to secure access to an employee's company email account and other messaging or communication systems, including any on a company cell phone. Such messaging may provide valuable information that is both contemporaneous and goes to the state of mind of the person.[12] Relevant documents can be requested from employees, and usually, an organization provides a liaison person who can coordinate such collection. In all cases, consideration and respect should be shown to employees when collecting evidence.

Few modern organizations retain pen and paper records, with electronic data being the default option. This generally means lots of relevant information, sometimes vast amounts, that needs to be captured and analyzed for its relevance. After forensic imaging or seizure, this has to be searched and evaluated. Running a program to filter based on identified parameters can help make evaluation manageable by eliminating unwanted or uninteresting files,[13] but it can still be a major undertaking to examine gigabits of data. Digital evidence gathering can be complex, but once familiar with the procedures, other types of evidence such as documents can be dealt with similarly.

The Capture of Digital Evidence

The capture of digital information including, computers, CCTV, mobile phones and other forms of digital media must be accomplished in the same way as any other evidence, they must be handled and seized appropriately and should be treated with as much care as any other item that is to be forensically examined. Electronic data, however, can be extremely fragile and require particular care. As a result, two considerations are important: first, the protection of the fragile information from accidental loss or damage through incorrect storage or through exposure to contamination such as water or electromagnetic influence; second, the protection of the evidence from unauthorized access to prevent alterations. With electronic equipment, bear in mind the possibilities for remote access to equipment such as laptops that may permit someone to access data even if the equipment is stored securely.

It is essential that any investigator who seeks to capture electronic data are competent to do so. In the vast majority of organizational investigations, where the matter is noncriminal, someone in the organization can assist and download the relevant items while also providing an explanation for the data; however, few companies have technical experts qualified to collect forensic evidence correctly or indeed have the necessary forensic imaging equipment. Where the forensic seizure of digital evidence is necessary, it is essential that only a competent person retrieves the data who is subsequently able to give evidence to a court of law of any such access and skill to do so.[14] There is furthermore a need to ensure all forensic methods used have been validated such that any tools, techniques, and methods used to obtain electronic evidence are fit for purpose.[15] The forensic obtaining of a bit-by-bit image of a 2-TB hard drive currently takes approximately 10 hours to image.[16] Therefore, whether to bring in such outside expertise is an important consideration depending on matters under investigation.

Before seizing any item, consider whether the item is likely to hold evidence. It is important to bear in mind that items may be needed for the manufacturing or other essential operational processes in an organization, and its removal may create difficulties in the organization fulfilling its core mission. Even in a police investigation, the person in charge of the investigation must have reasonable grounds to remove property, and there must be justifiable reasons for doing so. Digital devices and media should not be seized just because they are there, they should be considered to hold relevant information before doing so.[17] An alternative solution may have to be explored, such as obtaining a forensic imaging software in situ. Ensure that the details of where the item was found are recorded as this could assist in prioritizing items for examination at a later stage.

Principles of Digital Evidence

Once found, the security of evidence is particularly important so that no one interferes with it in any unauthorized way. This is a particular risk with digital evidence as even turning on a device generates changes and accordingly a number of specific principles apply to digital evidence, but which also apply as best practice policy with any type of evidence. The following is guidance to British police. This advice has also been adopted by a number of other European agencies.[18]

> **Principle 1**: No action taken by LEAs, or persons employed by those
> agencies, should change data, which may later be relied upon in court.

Principle 2: Where a person finds it necessary to access original data, that person must be competent to do so and should be able to give evidence explaining the relevance and the implications of their actions.

Principle 3: An audit trail or other record of all processes should be created and preserved. Any independent third party should later be able to examine those processes and achieve the same result.

Principle 4: The person in charge of the investigation has overall responsibility for ensuring that the law and these principles are complied with.[19]

Computer operating systems and other programs frequently alter, add, and delete the contents of electronic storage. This is a normal ongoing that happens automatically without the user necessarily being aware that the data have been changed. The best forensic practice is, wherever practicable, proportionate, and relevant, to make an image of the device after first inserting a write blocker to prevent any further alterations before any imaging is done. This will ensure that the original data are preserved and will enable an independent third party to re-examine it and achieve the same result in accordance with the third principle. This may be a physical/logical block image of the entire device or a logical file image containing partial or selective data (which may be captured as a result of a triage process). Investigators should use their professional judgment to endeavor to capture all relevant evidence if this approach is adopted. Once a cloned copy is obtained, only the cloned copy or image of the evidential device should be examined, and the original should be stored securely.

In cases dealing with data that are not stored locally but stored at a remote, possibly inaccessible location, it may not be possible to obtain an image. It may become necessary for the original data to be directly accessed to recover the data. Due consideration must also be given to applicable legislation if data are retrieved which exist in storage in another jurisdiction, which may include cloud storage. Many sources of electronic data will be unavailable to a private investigator, such as records from telephone companies, social media sites, and Internet service providers as only court warrants will provide the relevant access. This may become an issue with cloud storage of data, where little is maintained on the devices hard drive. An alternative to telephone company records is the call logs from the phone itself. These can be easy to clear, however, so a forensic examination of cell phones may be necessary. Likewise, with computers, there may be an effort to delete files. A cursory examination may reveal little, while a forensic examination may find both useful evidence and the deletion effort.

It is essential for investigators or technicians to display objectivity in a court of law, as well as ensuring the continuity and integrity of evidence. Experts will need to demonstrate how evidence has been recovered, showing each step of the evidence-gathering process. It should be noted that the application of the above principles does not preclude a proportionate approach to the examination of digital evidence. Those making decisions about the conduct of a digital investigation must often make judgments about the focus and scope of an investigation, taking into account available intelligence and investigative resources. This will often include a risk assessment based on technical and non-technical factors, for example, the potential evidence which may be held by a particular type of device, the type of offense being investigated, or the reliance of the company on the device. Such decisions should be justifiable, with actions being transparent and the rationale recorded. From the first arrival on scene careful recording is essential.

Arrival at Scene

The Association of Chief Police Officers (ACPO) guide suggests that on first arrival to the location of evidence, it is important to secure and take control of the area containing the equipment. Move people away from any computers and power supplies. In order to comply with Principle 3, records must be kept of all actions taken in relation to digital evidence, which could include photographs/diagrams of equipment locations, details of any information provided by persons present, and records of any actions taken at the scene. Once the scene is secured where equipment is *off*:

- Photograph or video the scene.
- Allow printers to finish printing.
- Do not, under any circumstances, switch the computer on.
- Make sure that the computer is switched off—some screen savers can give the appearance that the computer is switched off, but hard drive and monitor activity lights may indicate that the machine is switched on.
- Be aware that some laptop computers may power on by opening the cover.
- If possible, remove the main power source battery from laptop computers. However, prior to doing so, consider if the machine is in standby mode. In such circumstances, battery removal could result in avoidable data loss. Many modern laptops make battery removal difficult. The objective is that it is not accidentally turned on, so in such cases, it should be secured, by being placed in an evidence bag, for example.
- Unplug the power and other devices from sockets on the computer itself (i.e., not the wall socket). A computer that is apparently switched off may be in sleep mode and may be accessed remotely, allowing the alteration or deletion of files.
- Label all of the ports and cables so that the computer may be reconstructed at a later date.
- Ensure that all items have signed and completed exhibit labels attached to them. Failure to do so may create difficulties with continuity and cause the equipment to be rejected by forensic examiners.

- Search the area for notebooks or pieces of paper with passwords on which are often attached or close to the computer.
- Consider asking the user about the setup of the system, including any passwords, if circumstances dictate. If these are given, ensure to record them accurately.

Where an electronic system is powered on (running), it needs to be handled with particular care, as there is the potential to make unwanted changes to the evidence if these are not dealt with correctly. In addition, volatile data of evidential value may be lost. It is particularly important not to manually close down the system or open any files on a computer. If the power is removed from a running system, any evidence stored in encrypted volumes will be lost, unless the relevant key is obtained. Also, note that potentially valuable live business data could be lost, leading to damage claims, for example, because of missing corporate or manufacturing data. Of course, this concern needs to be balanced with the possibility that the computer may be accessed remotely and evidence compromised. However, a private investigator has potentially more responsibility to minimize additional damage or loss to the organization he is employed by than do police agents. Forensic collection software is available for use in such circumstances. Also be aware of networked systems and cloud storage, as information may not be actually stored on the individual device. Cloud storage presents a particular challenge for forensic collection because of the dynamic nature of the storage.[20]

Where the electronic device is still *running*, then it is important to record what is on the screen by photographing and by making a written note of the content of the screen. If the screen is blank or a screen saver is present, a short movement of the mouse should restore the screen or reveal that the screen saver is password protected. If the screen restores, photograph or video it and note its content. If password protection is shown, continue as below, without any further touching of the mouse. Record the time and activity of the use of the mouse in these circumstances.

- Where possible, collect data that would otherwise be lost by removing the power supply, e.g., such as running processes and information about the state of network ports at that time. Ensure that for any actions performed, all changes made to the system are understood and recorded.
- If no specialist advice is available, remove the power supply from the back of the computer without closing down any programs. When removing the power supply cable, always remove the end attached to the computer and not attached to the socket. This will avoid any data being written to the hard drive if an uninterruptible power protection device is fitted.
- Remove all other connection cables leading from the computer to other walls or other sockets or devices.
- Proceed then as with off section.[21]

In reality, it may not be possible to remove a computer involved in most manufacturing and business processes as it may be built into integrated systems. Other items that should be retrieved include external hard drives, any memory or storage devices, modems and routers, and any other electronic devices with memories. For instance, modern photocopiers are also potential useful sources of information as many have hard drives and store a lot of information. Such a copier may store copy jobs, items photocopied, job logs, and things such as email addresses that offer useful investigative information. It is important to always label the bags containing these items, not the items themselves. The label should contain the catalog number, date and time, and investigating person. Notes made should include location found, make and model numbers, and any comments made by persons there.

Custody Chain

Electronic data and documentation that is taken into an investigator's possession must be secured, and any unauthorized interference with it must be prevented. Any authorized interference, such as tests, must be recorded. It is important that the investigation itself is conducted impartially and objectively. The onus is always on the investigator and prosecutor (if a criminal court is involved) to prove that the evidence that is presented in court is the evidence in the original condition as it was when it was first discovered and taken possession of. Therefore, a detailed record of the investigation should be maintained which may be subject to judicial review in any court case.

So, in addition to listing all persons who had access to the evidence, it must be shown why they had access, how long they had access, and what they did while having access. It must also be shown that other than those authorized persons, no one else could have had access. In other words, the evidence was stored securely and protected from interference other than as detailed in the custody chain. Documentary evidence such as reports, charts, or other documents should not be written on or tampered with and should ideally be stored in plastic wallets to protect them. In many cases, making a working copy of the document may allow it to be used in inquiries without risk to the original. Copies are preferable to use in interviews to avoid loss or damage of originals.

A separate file or master file should be kept with all originals, including statements taken, to ensure their security and protection from accidental tampering or loss. Any other items or equipment relevant to the investigation that is considered as potential evidence must also be safeguarded and stored securely without any alteration to their original condition, for example, personal computers and any records thereon. Items of evidence marked with a catalog number when gathered should be recorded along with a description of the evidence. For this purpose, it may be useful to use an *evidence book* to record all evidence, to include any movement of the evidence, for example, when moved for examination or otherwise used. Original documents should have the catalog or exhibit number put on the protective wallet rather than the document itself. It is therefore vital that the evidence is described alongside the exhibit number when entered into the evidence book, to permit verification and reconciliation of exhibit numbers with the correct evidence. The book should record the time, date, place, and person who recovered the material as well as any movements. Documents should be cross-referenced with use in interviews.

In general, it is preferable that the same team member should control and move the items wherever they need to be moved. For instance, if evidence is being taken for forensic testing such as handwriting analysis, fingermark examination, or Electrostatic Detection Apparatus Analysis (ESDA), then the same person should take it to and receive it from testing. Evidence should ideally never be posted; where it is necessary, registered post is essential. The person who brings the evidence should obtain a receipt for the items on handing them over with an appropriate description to identify the items on the receipt. This person's written statement should then reference this movement and transfer of the items, with dates and times and reasons. Anyone taking possession of such evidence should make and keep a full record of all actions taken and make a statement, if necessary, of all actions taken with any results. This statement should also contain the qualifications or expertise of the person forensically examining items. These must be disclosed to the defense, who may subsequently cause a further examination to be conducted. A significant part of such an examination will be to validate the actions and results of the original examination.

Investigation Record

The movements of items of evidence will form part of the detailed record of the investigation. This record should be maintained and constantly updated. This record should include a chronological file recording details of telephone conversations, discussions, meetings and interviews, details of documents reviewed, items taken possession of, and details of any tests and analyses undertaken. Any notes taken in notebooks or in such records should be made contemporaneously, that is, at the time or immediately after the interaction or event. These notes and records should also be kept, as they could be vital evidence later in court in relation to matters that were said or done.

Report Writing

Such notes and records will form the basis of any written statements made by investigators for a court or report purpose, as well as the investigation report itself. The report describes the investigators findings based on the evidence gathered, including the interviews. It is the final deliverable from the investigation, and it is important that it looks professional, precise, and meets the client's requirements. There may be occasions when a client may prefer an oral report rather than a written report. A written report may contain potential embarrassing findings if made public, information that regulators may use against the company, or provide information to potential litigants who are made aware of issues under investigation.[22] However, regulators will look dimly on any internal investigation conducted in a regulated industry that was concealed from them.

The finished written report may vary in exact format as some clients will have specific requirements or require a comprehensive criminal investigation-type format, while others require the minimum to address the issue that concerns them. For instance, in cases of complex corporate and financial crime interviews, a high level of technical detail will be expected in the report and accompanying statements.[23] So, the first rule is to understand who the reader may be and the purpose of the report. It is also important to think like a lawyer and use logic to interpret the evidence gathered to construct a plausible narrative of the events at issue, and the report is the place to communicate this narrative.

The investigator's report should be clear what the purpose of the investigation was and should address the specific allegations. Normally, the report begins with the background to the investigation and the mandate to undertake the investigation. This should outline the scope of the investigation as to what exactly the investigators were tasked with, and any limitations imposed, or other difficulties encountered. It is vital that the investigator clearly lay out in detail what is being investigated or has been uncovered. In even simple cases such as bullying, for instance, the term will be defined in legislation or regulations. It is important that this definition is used, and the various elements of the definition are covered in the investigation. As noted, in a criminal matter, these are known as the proofs. This is usually part of the executive summary part and should cover whether evidence exists to support the proofs necessary for the allegations. This generally depends on the type of investigation, and some clients want the most substantive parts disclosed as quickly as possible in a report. Then the report proper begins with a description of the investigation, followed by findings. The final section is the conclusion.

In terms of layout, a report should be presented to begin with a clear cover page with title, dates, and names of the investigators. A content page should also be included, either on the cover page or on the next page. This should list all statement and exhibit/appendix numbers together with a brief description of these items. It may also include a dramatis personae list, if necessary. I usually use an appendix number in the report instead of exhibit number as it avoids criminal justice connotations. The appendices are at the rear of the report sequentially and contain copies of all statements, expert reports, documentary evidence, photographs, or CCTV stills, etc. Statements are numbered sequentially, and this number should be referenced whenever the person who made it is referred to in the report. In the case of large binder reports, colored tabs can be used to identify the different sections linked to the content page. If the report is electronic, then either a PDF or Word document may be used. PDF is preferable with hyperlinks from the contents page to that part. As much as possible, keep the writing and language clear, simple, and concise. A glossary of terms may be necessary. Use good spacing, justified text, and clear space between paragraphs and sections. A cluttered report is off-putting to readers.

Executive Summary

The executive summary provides the synopsis of the principal issues as succinctly as possible. There is no element of suspense required. This is where the findings are clearly laid out. The findings should be based on what was uncovered in the investigation as measured against whatever guideline or regulation that is being used to define the investigation. If an organization is being investigated, the relevant guideline document is used to define the findings. In such a case, each finding should cite the applicable regulation or guideline. If an individual was under investigation, state the allegations that were being investigated, who is involved, if evidence of deviance has been uncovered, and if the evidence supports further action and whether it is warranted. This is not to say that the sanctions should be recommended. Sanctions are not within the purview of the investigator; however, the investigator is entitled to comment on the level of cooperation or hostility encountered during the investigation. The summary forms a stand-alone section that should provide all readers with the essential elements of the investigation. The summary may also include recommendations such as the need for an HR follow-up on some issues identified. For many organizations, the final report will essentially be an executive summary with an appropriate introduction and conclusion, as that is sufficient without the addition of a more detailed report. In either case, the executive summary will provide the essential elements while the body of the report will provide the detail necessary if the reader wishes to read it.

Report Body

It is important for an investigator to avoid bias and attempt to be as impartial and fair as possible in his or her report. Alternative explanations should be explored whether these have come from interviewees or based on the investigator's own experience. This document may be reviewed at some point in a court and any obvious bias or unfairness will attract criticism.[24] A report that tries to explore other explanations is a fairer report than one that goes straight for the jugular.

After the executive summary, the next section has the full report, and the exact format of the report can vary substantially. It goes into details on the allegations being investigated. What the issue is, how did it come to notice, who was the first to become aware and how. This may follow a simple timeline.

Any initial actions taken or enquiries made will also be included here. Then the detailed progression of the investigation is laid out. Normally, it is broken into relevant sections and, in large reports, chapters. Breaking a report down to its basic components helps both with the writing and reading of a report. Its principal purpose is to systematically lay out what the investigation has uncovered. It should describe what offenses or breaches, if any, were uncovered and what supporting evidence has been gathered, to support further action. The report stays focused on relevant matters, but if other useful information was gathered, it may be briefly mentioned.

The findings outline in detail what the investigation has found. It is usually necessary to refer to the source of any information used, or factual finding made, so the evidence for the finding is clear. This means that in many reports, the testimony of witnesses and any other evidence is referenced. The critical information or salient points that a witness has given in a statement should be referred to when elaborating on the findings. The statement of the person is available in the appendix if the reader wishes to refer to that document or any other mentioned in the report. The investigator should be careful not to extrapolate from facts but rather stick to what the facts say in an impartial manner. The danger here is that an investigator may allow their bias to interpret facts in an excessively inculpatory light which is beyond that supported by the facts. If evidence contradicts between witnesses or other sources, this should be highlighted. Inability to find evidence or to be able to prove any issue should also be noted and explained. Where a statement or exhibit is mentioned in the body of the report, its reference number should accompany it in brackets. The activities cataloged in the report should be referenced and outlined through the evidence gathered. For example:

> Security guard John Wallace (s.15) states that only Donald Cruz (apx.1a) entered the premises between 9 pm and 9.30 pm. The digital entry card readout (apx.26) assigned to Donald Cruz has the time of entry at 9.26 pm. CCTV footage (apx.25) confirms this and shows Donald Cruz entering with the time of entry as 9.22pm. When verified the CCTV clock was found to be 4 minutes slow. The correct time should then read 9.26 pm.

The evidence should be interpreted cautiously, and other potential alternative explanations for its presence should be carefully explored. For larger investigations, I write a different section for each piece of evidence with a PDF image of the evidence in the body and an explanation of what the evidence purports to show. The number used here to identify the evidence should be consistent throughout the report. If the import of the evidence is unambiguous that should be stated, if other alternative explanations are possible, then what needs to be done to follow up, if possible, should be stated. In small-scale investigations, the PDF image in the body of the report may suffice without a need for a separate copy in the appendix. This is normally the case for most of my current corporate investigations; the company retains the original evidence, and I use my phone to take a photo or scan of the document. This I convert to a PDF for inclusion in my report. In other words, I find it not necessary to seize the original data for many corporate investigations.

In the case of the account of a witness or another interview, this is usually given in a memo form. In my own case, I no longer take a traditional full written witness statement. Rather I tape record the interview and take some written notes. Then afterward, I use both to generate a written memo or outline of information given by the witness. As I write each witness's account, I use direct quotes from this memo. The memo itself may be included in the appendix although it may be used in the main body of the report also. The tape recording is available to be fully transcribed if necessary, and for HR purposes, this is the normal procedure. However, using the full transcribed interview in the report can be burdensome. Most interviews are lots of 'ums' and 'ahs' with a great deal of nonverbal that does not come across in transcripts. Therefore, I find it more convenient to include the shorter memo which has all the pertinent information without any loss of critical data. The memo should lay out the account given, the reaction to evidence presented, and any explanations the witness offered. I also include in the memo the level of cooperation from the witness, as this is an important context in which the interview occurred. Other important aspects such as hostility or refusal to answer certain questions should also be outlined. However, the investigator should be careful to not limit the memo to inculpatory evidence only. Investigators have a duty to discover truth and that includes exculpatory evidence, and this should be given equal prominence in the memo, where such evidence has been offered.

The tape recording remains available, if necessary. All such evidence should be retained. I would suggest for a minimum of two years, but it can depend on the time available to take court actions in different jurisdictions. On a further note, I prefer to keep the investigation separate from any disciplinary process. Therefore, I suggest to clients that while my transcripts can be used in any disciplinary process investigation, the disciplinary process should be done as a stand-alone process with additional statements taken by HR as per usual procedure. This ensures fairness to all concerned by separating the investigation and potential disciplinary process. In many investigations, of course, the interviews are an integral part of the HR process.

Where a gap exists in the evidence, it should be clearly stated that the investigation failed to uncover the evidence, a reasonable opinion or probability may be inserted, however, based on the investigator's knowledge and judgment. This is speculation, however, and should be clearly stated as such. The purpose of this is to help rectify potential reoccurrences of similar incidents, not simply present the evidence gathered. Naturally, a criminal prosecution file does not usually have such speculation. Nonetheless, most clients want expert opinion, not simply to resolve current issues but to design out and prevent future ones.

It is also good practice to avoid definitive language; the investigator was not actually present and can never state anything with absolute certainty, simply evidence that supports his or her theory. Therefore, use phraseology such as 'it appears' or 'the probability is' in the report. This demonstrates a willingness to accept ambiguity where evidence is inconclusive and re-evaluate if other information comes to light; in other words, it demonstrates fairness as opposed to dogmatic adherence to guilt or any rigid opinion. Furthermore, few investigators have absolute certainty on any event and should openly acknowledge this.

Conclusion and Recommendations

The conclusion should explore what the findings might mean for the organization from a legal or regulatory perspective. This may have been mentioned in the executive summary, but more detail can be given here as well as expert opinion. The conclusion may offer other opinions or recommendations but needs to be consistent and impartial. While the purpose of the report is to lay out the findings and not to recommend sanctions against anyone, recommendations are important. These recommendations may also extend beyond the investigation matter, *per se*, and as such combine the expertise of the investigator with other potential problems identified. Recommendations also provide options to the client about how to handle the problem. Systemic problems and recommended structural changes can also be included as recommendations. Such recommendations can easily include the need for extra training, which is always the low-hanging fruit. If issues with a culture of noncompliance have been identified, however, extra training is unlikely to be successful. People who do want to comply with policies are unlikely to be swayed by additional compliance training. Another frequently used recommendation is the need for additional rules/policy/regulation. Sometimes, this is necessary, but when overused, it merely increases complexity and actually encourages employees to develop methods to work around to ease their workload. It might just be feasible, on occasions, to consider streamlining rules already in place, to make them more effective and easier to understand.

Unlike a criminal justice situation, professional opinion and expertise can be used to reach conclusions depending on what the client's requirements were, and these will dictate what is to be in report. It should be appreciated that in some cases, this report might be presented to regulators or state investigators as evidence of action undertaken to respond to problems. If regulators regard the investigation as thorough and comprehensive, it may be sufficient to avoid an audit. On the other hand, if it shows systemic issues that were not dealt with over time, it may instead provoke aggressive intervention from them. In some circumstances, it has been noted that a shortage of suitable resources in police departments can mean that police sometimes do not want to take on a full new investigation, in which case, a comprehensive investigation done privately may be repurposed with some minor alterations to satisfy the relevant prosecution service.[25] In some jurisdictions, this may be the only realistic way that a criminal case comes before the courts.

Other evidential items gathered but not used remain recorded in the investigation file. Such records may form part of the unused material for the case under investigation but which the defense may request. The principle is that evidence discovered that would support innocence should be made available to the defense. Remember, it is not evidence of guilt that is sought but the facts, and it is important to be perceived as impartial and fair. Nevertheless, any apparent evidence of innocence should always be probed sufficiently to account for its presence. This highlights the importance of analysis. The outcome of an investigation is unknown at the beginning, especially whether a court case will be later involved. Therefore, it is better to always maintain the same high standards as such standards will be able to withstand the rigors of a cross-examination in court. Poor custody management and record keeping can have disastrous results for a prosecution.[26]

Conclusion

The gathering of evidence is a critical part of an investigation. Many investigations are relatively straightforward and minor with little need for various records of different exhibits. Nonetheless, investigations can become complex quickly, and there is no greater sin for an investigator than to corrupt the evidence chain. This is critical in a criminal court, but grievous errors in procedures will not be forgiven in any type of tribunal. Therefore, prepare and operate as if every investigation is a potential court case and act accordingly.

Evidence is also the key to successful interviewing, and the interview is often guided by the evidence gathered and explanations sought from different interviewees for its presence and significance. The investigator should try to seek unbiased guidance about the relevance of evidence where its significance is poorly understood. Assuming the evidence means what you hope it means can lead to losing the initiative at the interview as the interviewee patiently schools you on your ignorance. The understanding and analysis of evidence is therefore the next step in preparing for an interview and the subject of Chapter 7.

Notes

1   PCAST, *Report to the President: Forensic Science in Criminal Courts: Ensuring Scientific Validity of Feature-Comparison Methods*, (2016).
2   Williams, J. W., 'The Private Eyes of Corporate Culture: The Forensic Accounting and Corporate Investigation Industry and the Production of Corporate Financial Security', (eds) Walby and Lippert, in *Corporate Security in the 21st Century: Theory and Practice in International Perspective*, (Palgrave Macmillan UK, London, 2014), pp 56–77.

3 Meerts, C., "Corporate Investigations: Beyond Notions of Public–Private Relations", *Journal of Contemporary Criminal Justice*, (2020), 36(1), pp 86–100.

4 Missal, M., Fishman, E., Ochs, B. and Kline Dubill, R., "Conducting Corporate Internal Investigations", *International Journal of Disclosure and Governance*, (2007), 4(4), pp 297–308.

5 OSINT is an important tool in an investigator's toolbox. The Bellingcat website offers some basic and more advanced techniques in using OSINT, establishing the veracity of videos and photos and countering disinformation generally. Available at www.bellingcat.com/

6 I would recommend a minimum of two years and longer if litigation is known to be involved or expected.

7 The classic example to consider the missing evidence is the story of how Abraham Wald, a mathematician working for the US military during World War II, identified where to put armour on aircraft to maximize protection but minimize weight. Reasoning that it was irrelevant to examine damage to aircraft that returned to base, even if badly damaged as these were an example of 'survivor bias' and therefore revealed little about aircraft vulnerability. Instead, aircraft that had failed to return must have been damaged in places where survivor aircraft had not and thereby destroyed. Thus, it was this damage that was the most relevant. Statistically analysing this unseen damage led to the placement of armour that increased aircraft and crew survivability. See also Taleb, N., *Fooled by Randomness*, (Penguin, London, 2004) for more on missing evidence.

8 If software or electronic recordings are used, ensure regular backup and consider printing off a copy regularly that is signed and dated.

   An example of an electronic investigation system is the Home Office Large Major Enquiry System (HOLMES) used by British police in major investigations, which was developed after a serial murderer named Peter Sutcliffe (the Yorkshire Ripper) killed 13 women between 1975 and 1980. In total, 250,000 people were interviewed, 32,000 written statements taken, and 5.2 million car registrations checked. Sutcliffe was interviewed himself nine times, but the manual card index system in use in the incident room was not fit for purpose for the enquiry and was overwhelmed, meaning Sutcliffe slipped through time after time.

9 Gathering electronic data is especially challenging because of its volume. This needs to be searched for relevant information to the investigators. Tools such as Nuix (see www.nuix.com) are available to assist with this.

10 Williams, J. W., "Governability Matters: The Private Policing of Economic Crime and the Challenge of Democratic Governance", *Policing and Society*, (2005), 15(2), pp 187–211: 199.

11 CCTV downloads are particularly susceptible to issues with usability. Many providers use proprietary software that must be converted to another format to be usable generally. Therefore, ensure any download of CCTV data is in a readable or viewable format. There is software available that converts most proprietary software into common viewing platforms, but ideally getting the installation company to download also provides the expert evidence of downloading.

12 Missal, M., Fishman, E., Ochs, B. and Kline Dubill, R., "Conducting Corporate Internal Investigations", *International Journal of Disclosure and Governance*, (2007).

13 Joseph, P. and Norman, J., "Forensic Corpus Data Reduction Techniques for Faster Analysis by Eliminating Tedious Files", *Information Security Journal: A Global Perspective*, (2019), 28(4/5), pp 136–147.

14 Acceptance of expert evidence in a US court is governed by the Daubert standard to assess the scientific validity of the expert's testimony and the technique used. This determines if the technique can be and has been tested, if it has been subjected to peer review and publication. It has a known or potential error rate, if there are standards controlling its operation in existence and, finally, its widespread acceptance in the scientific community. See Daubert v Merrill Dow Pharma, 509 U.S. 579 (1993). European courts have adopted similar criteria.

15 Horsman, G., "ACPO Principles for Digital Evidence: Time for an Update?", *Forensic Science International: Reports*, (2020), 2(100076), pp 1–6.

16 Joseph, P. and Norman, J., "Forensic Corpus Data Reduction Techniques for Faster Analysis by Eliminating Tedious Files", *Information Security Journal: A Global Perspective*, (2019).

17 The Association of Chief Police Officers (ACPO) in the United Kingdom was part of a network of agencies that formerly undertook research and determined best policy for police actions. The digital evidence principles and actions to be taken are from their 2012 best practice guides on Gathering Digital Evidence and Good Practice Guide for Computer-based Electronic Evidence. Version 5 is available here: www.digital-detective.net/digital-forensics-documents/ACPO_Good_Practice_Guide_for_Digital_Evidence_v5.pdf. [Accessed December 5, 2021].

18 Horsman, G., "ACPO Principles for Digital Evidence: Time for an Update?", *Forensic Science International: Reports*, (2020).

19 ACPO Good Practice Guide: 6.

20 Hemdan, E. E.-D. and Manjaiah, D. H., "An Efficient Digital Forensic Model for Cybercrimes Investigation in Cloud Computing", *Multimedia Tools and Applications*, (2021), 80(9), pp 14255–14282.

21 ACPO Good Practice Guide v.4.

22 Missal, M., Fishman, E., Ochs, B. and Kline Dubill, R., "Conducting Corporate Internal Investigations", *International Journal of Disclosure and Governance*, (2007).

23 Lokanan, M. E., "The Application of Cognitive Interviews to Financial Crimes", *Journal of Financial Crime*, (2018), 25(3), pp 882–890.

24 For examples, see Williams, J. W., "Governability Matters: The Private Policing of Economic Crime and the Challenge of Democratic Governance", *Policing and Society*, (2005), p 199.

25 Williams, J. W., "Governability Matters: The Private Policing of Economic Crime and the Challenge of Democratic Governance", *Policing and Society*, (2005), p 197.

26 Countless cases have been lost because of such mistakes. For an example of such an event, in May 2017, the (second) high-profile Irish criminal trial (lasting 126 days) of banker Sean Fitzpatrick collapsed. Fitzpatrick was being prosecuted for providing unlawful financial assistance to ten individuals, in July 2008, so that they could buy shares in another bank and allegedly misleading the bank's auditors about millions of euros in loans between 2002 and 2007, among other things. However, legal counsel as investigators had failed to keep proper records of their activities and evidence causing the prosecution to collapse. Report available at www.thejournal.ie/sean-fitzpatrick-not-guilty-3404388-May2017/

Bibliography

Hemdan, E. E.-D. and Manjaiah, D. H., "An Efficient Digital Forensic Model for Cybercrimes Investigation in Cloud Computing", *Multimedia Tools and Applications*, (2021), 80(9), pp 14255–14282.

Horsman, G., "ACPO Principles for Digital Evidence: Time for an Update?", *Forensic Science International: Reports*, (2020), 2(100076), pp 1–6.

Joseph, P. and Norman, J., "Forensic Corpus Data Reduction Techniques for Faster Analysis by Eliminating Tedious Files", *Information Security Journal: A Global Perspective*, (2019), 28(4/5), pp 136–147.

Lokanan, M. E., "The Application of Cognitive Interviews to Financial Crimes", *Journal of Financial Crime*, (2018), 25(3), pp 882–890.

Meerts, C., "Corporate Investigations: Beyond Notions of Public–Private Relations", *Journal of Contemporary Criminal Justice*, (2020), 36(1), pp 86–100.

Missal, M., Fishman, E., Ochs, B. and Kline Dubill, R., "Conducting Corporate Internal Investigations", *International Journal of Disclosure and Governance*, (2007), 4(4), pp 297–308.

PCAST, *Report to the President: Forensic Science in Criminal Courts: Ensuring Scientific Validity of Feature-Comparison Methods*, (2016).

Taleb, N., *Fooled by Randomness*, (Penguin, London, 2004).

Williams, J. W., "Governability Matters: The Private Policing of Economic Crime and the Challenge of Democratic Governance", *Policing and Society*, (2005), 15(2), pp 187–211.

Williams, J. W., 'The Private Eyes of Corporate Culture: The Forensic Accounting and Corporate Investigation Industry and the Production of Corporate Financial Security', (eds) Walby and Lippert, in *Corporate Security in the 21st Century: Theory and Practice in International Perspective*, (Palgrave Macmillan UK, London, 2014) pp 56–77.

Chapter 7

Evaluation and Analysis of Information

Introduction

The incorporation of an evaluation step is essential to the forensic investigative interview technique (FIIT). It is vital that evidence is understood correctly to inform an investigation. Evaluation is an ongoing process throughout the investigation and should particularly occur before interviews because it is necessary to understand what the purpose of any interview is. Interviewers need flexibility to adapt to unexpected revelations during an interview, but the planning and preparation stage is about evaluating all known information ahead of an interview. Acquiring information, analysis, and evaluation of that information, and subsequently making decisions and judgments based on that information are therefore critical investigation skills. Developing an attitude of questioning information and careful analysis before drawing conclusions is developing the scientific method of critical thinking.

The theory of the event should encompass who, what, when, where, why, and finally, how. Usually, in a post-event investigation, it is sufficient to establish what happened, when did it happen, who did it, and how did it happen. Nevertheless, uncovering why something happened is essential to understanding how to prevent future reoccurrences as well as understanding motivations. A comprehensive understanding of the causes may facilitate the development of corrective and preventive actions including new policies, remedying systemic issues, and training. Too often, investigators are satisfied to find the person responsible for a deviant behavior but fail to probe any deeper to find underlying systemic issues. Where systemic issues exist, they will manifest themselves repeatedly and probably become exacerbated. This is a critical difference between a police-style investigation and a private investigation—prevention is always better than cure, especially in an organization. An investigation may uncover causes that range from accidental to deliberate. Accidental causes may include systemic, cultural, factual misunderstandings, ignorance of policies/rules, or negligence causes; deliberate causes include selfish or malicious motivations. Indeed, there may often be no single motive but what may become apparent to the investigators is a history or pattern of frustration, aggrandizement, or sense of entitlement

DOI: 10.4324/9781003269489-7

that has developed over time and which may involve more than those directly involved in the specific incident. Therefore, the potential exists to build a systemic understanding of an organization when called upon to investigate an issue. This can provide the necessary understanding to prevent repetitions or even greater deviance if left uncorrected. Issues to be examined include culture, compliance to policies, the attitude of management, and whether cultural norms conflict with written policies. This needs to be achieved as impartially and free from biases as possible. This can be difficult to do as often our biases are unconscious, and effort must be made to make them explicit. Motivated reasoning means everyone is inclined to reach the conclusions each individual wants to reach, which creates obvious risks when trying to evaluate information impartially. This chapter explains some methods to help in evaluating information and building understanding in as unbiased manner as possible to ensure fairness to all involved and consistency across investigations.

Although the interview itself creates evidence, as the testimony of a witness is now available to inform the investigation, the reliability of witnesses is always an unknown. Sometimes, this is because the credibility of the witness is poor; it does not necessarily involve conscious deceit, but witnesses can be subject to biases and may unconsciously believe something that is not completely accurate. Accordingly, evidence from witnesses need to be as corroborated as much as possible. Physical evidence and other witness testimony can do this to support proofs but only when the evidence is examined thoroughly and fairly.

Judgment and Decision-Making

To understand interviewing, and obtaining information generally from people, my argument is that people use their feelings to make judgments about cooperation. Likewise, investigators use feelings as the base for decisions they make, which can create problems. We all recognize that it is difficult to reach a rational decision when we are angry or otherwise highly emotionally aroused, as experiencing intense primary emotions impairs higher cognitive functioning,[1] but emotion is more important than that. Antonio Damassio argues that emotion is central to all our decision-making; in fact, he demonstrates that patients who are clinically unable to access their feelings find it impossible to make any decisions.[2]

This is not the dominant paradigm of human behavior, and one alternative and probably the dominant theory of human behavior, Rational Choice Theory, tries to argue people process information and execute behaviors in a way calculated to maximize their expected utility, and that decisions therefore result from a calculated cost–benefit analysis.[3] This theory has been represented in some form in many disciplines, despite its obvious limitations. Such limitations include the fact that human cognition has limited processing capacity with some information being prioritized over other. As a result, people often behave sub-optimally. For example, people demonstrate incomplete and sometimes even incoherent choice preferences; often miscalculate risks and discount the future excessively; are vulnerable to framing, anchoring, priming, and other biases or effects; and often behave in ways that are difficult to interpret as being exclusively motivated by self-interest.[4] This lack of self-interest means that oftentimes people often behave altruistically toward others and will sacrifice their own self-interest out of a moral sense of fairness.[5] This may even extend to self-sacrifice for a nation or cause.[6]

Humans are intelligent animals but that does not mean that every decision is intentional and considered. Evolution permits habits to develop that allow routine tasks to be rapidly responded to without needing to consider every action thereby saving time. Humans do not even consider all the information available to them in the world, as to do so would be an enormous cognitive burden. Instead, our perception filters the available information through our cognitive mental models to evaluate what information is important, and what can be ignored. These mental models use our deep underlying assumptions and beliefs about our world to build our worldview. These beliefs may be inaccurate, and even a reasonably held belief can be false. Moreover, the fact that many of our deepest assumptions and beliefs actually contradict each other indicates that at least some must be false.

Understanding motivated reasoning means understanding that we tend to believe what we want to believe, readily seek out confirming information, are inclined to reject or discount disconfirming evidence, and avoid hard cognitive and emotional work.[7] When faced with a decision, instead of thinking hard, people are happy to trust a plausible judgment that comes quickly to mind.[8] As a result, humans are *cognitive misers*, and to avoid cognitive effort, we are inclined to use mental shortcuts, or *heuristics*, to solve many cognitive tasks such as decision-making or making judgments.[9]

Heuristics allow many decisions to be made on the basis of simple cues or pattern recognition that activate a quick or even automatic behavioral response, almost like a behavioral habit. This type of cognitive processing is referred as system one processing; system one processing is autonomous and rapid with an almost automatic engagement on presentation of the triggering stimuli. It can operate in parallel, without interference with other cognitive processing, so multiple tasks can be accomplished simultaneously.[10] System one processing includes behavioral regulation by emotions and the processes of implicit learning and conditioning through the emotional learning mechanisms.[11] As a consequence, a great deal of decision-making is practiced to the point of habit.[12] Over repeated iterations, automatic responses create scripts for behavior, which confer the advantage of a quick response on the presentation of a stimulus, but they also tend to overgeneralize, and therefore, granular detail is lost. As a result, many everyday decisions ignore the substantive details of the informative environment.[13] Issues include individuals not properly calibrating degrees of belief or allowing their choices to be affected by irrelevant context. Therefore, our actions can be determined by those—such as advertisers and marketeers—who create the stimuli that best trigger our shallow automatic processing.[14]

In contrast to system one, system two processing is a more recently evolved cognitive ability that performs better at analytical behavior and is responsible for high-level cognitive control.[15] System two processing can, if properly engaged, override system one. System two processing is slower and more computationally expensive; it is also a serial process, so conscious effort is necessary to avoid interference in its operation. One difficulty is that humans may believe that they are using system two, when in fact, they are using system one. The cognitive miser will tend to avoid type two processing, if at all possible, and especially in situations of high emotional arousal where the default response will be an emotional reaction.[16] In such situations, the analytical system may then be called upon to simply produce a post hoc rationalization that provides sufficient justification for the decision.[17] Thus, humans may not always make rational decisions, but they are incredibly adept at rationalizing any decisions they do make. Moreover, a type two override response is not possible if the most appropriate response has never been learned or if incorrect information forms the basis of beliefs.[18] It takes considerable conscious effort to keep system two engaged, especially when evaluating evidence with high emotional valence and your emotional brain is screaming at you.

The consequences of using heuristics are biases in cognitive processing and decision-making because cognitive attention is easily shifted to anything that is focal, perhaps because of vividness, salience, availability, or recentness, which generates primary association in our memory generating one or several biases. As a result of our experiences and associated memories, we tend to perceive what we expect to perceive. The tendency of people to perceive what they *expect* to perceive is more important than any tendency to perceive what they *want* to perceive. Our five senses do not operate and record events passively; rather they operate to *construct* a subjective and acceptable reality for us. Indeed, the evidence supporting the claim that people tend to perceive what they want to perceive can generally be explained equally well by this *expectancy* thesis.[19]

Biases may consequently influence how we evaluate information from the very beginning. One study found that when it came to a deeply held belief and evaluating evidence that contradicted it, students were more likely to be critical and dismissing of the information.[20] On the other hand, they enthusiastically endorsed supporting information. Even professionals are unaware of their own biases, and research with opposing lawyers have found that even with the same information, each side tended to believe the judge would favor their side more.[21] While participants could readily identify the effect of bias in others, they felt personally immune to such effects. As a result, it appears that our biases distort the way we interpret information from the outset to suit our own positions or perspectives. This is important to emphasize: it is not just the pernicious effects of misinformation, two individuals can literally look at the same facts, but each can interpret the facts differently to best suit themselves and their personal beliefs yet remain ignorant of that distortion. The more personally invested in a position, the more difficult it is to objectively evaluate information.[22] In some cases, there appears to be a state of denial about contradictory information to protect self-esteem when we have committed to a position.[23]

There is a long list of biases, and the list keeps growing. One of the most well-known biases is *anchoring*, which is ignoring base rate information and substituting instead some other attribute with which to make the estimate, even if totally unconnected.[24] Once a number is put into someone's mind, it retains powerful influence; hence, its importance in negotiations where the first offer made can serve as the anchor. One bias in particular that can affect investigators is *hindsight bias*. For instance, following the 9/11 attacks in New York, great emphasis was placed on the failings in the intelligence community to spot, what appeared in hindsight, to be obvious indicators of threat. Typically, a conclusion post-event can involve hindsight bias as we tend to evaluate decisions made through their known outcome. When the outcome is negative, we may be unable to understand how the decision was made or evaluate it from the perspective of the past when the future outcome was unknown. Such hindsight bias fails to evaluate the predictability of such cues beforehand when a great deal of noise interfered with those cues; all such noise might or might not have been cues to other threats or to false leads that amounted to nothing, which is a regular part of intelligence work. Furthermore, memories are seldom reassessed or reorganized retroactively in response to new information. For example, information that is dismissed as unimportant or irrelevant because it did not fit a person's expectations does not become more memorable even if the person later changes his or her thinking. Nassim Taleb has named a very similar phenomenon the narrative fallacy, where people are biased toward generating a plausible causal narrative for events that have happened.[25] This often uses the minimum amount of data points to preserve coherence, rather than deal with complexity and disconfirming data in the narrative to maintain simplicity. Such biases highlight the importance of using a method of structured thinking when evaluating information. This can be called critical thinking, but that term is somewhat vague, and despite great efforts to teach it, evidence from the world in a time of Covid is that it is more notable for its absence than use.[26] It seems that the ability to regulate emotion and incorporate it into the decision-making process is more effective at making good decisions than vainly striving for a rationality-only input by excluding emotional input.[27]

Cognitive Tools

This section explores some tools that can be used to help analyze information uncovered during an investigation. It applies to an active investigation or to any process of strategic planning. Unfortunately, simply knowing the tools does not guarantee success, and real learning comes from practice. Indeed, although the heuristics and biases literature continue to expand, it has not improved the quality of critical thinking. Rather people assume if they are aware of the existence of biases that they are somehow immunized against their effects. Sadly, it does not. Biases are automatic and unconscious processes. Learning how to overcome preexisting biases means both unlearning old habits and supplanting them with new ones that can be used effectively. That is enormously challenging but achievable. Instead, we often see an example of the Dunning–Kruger effect where people who are terrible at a particular task think they are much better than they are, while people who are very good at it tend to underestimate their competence.[28] Nevertheless, there are approaches that can help, and I discuss some here. In short, all rely on situational awareness, an open mind, humility, and curiosity. Also necessary is a willingness to ask questions and learn from mistakes as a reflective learning process because it is only by making mistakes and recognizing that fact that improvement occurs, although such an approach is indicative of humility.

The first step is to clarify the problem and understand what you are trying to achieve. Then the problem can be broken down into the 4Ws, who, what, when, where. These questions are the most important initially. Then set targets as to other information needed and avenues to achieve them. Another important aspect to evaluation of information is to examine the context it occurs in. Derek and Laura Cabrera argue that communication and many information modeling techniques (such as mind-maps) place an overreliance on the information but often fail to examine the structure that includes the hidden contextual structure that contributes to meaning. This means the structure of the mental model is overlooked, and the full meaning can be the resultant casualty.[29] They suggest that visualization maps or such diagrams should give equal weight to relationship structure as they do to information.

Deductive Reasoning

Dealing with highly ambiguous situations on the basis of information that is processed incrementally while under pressure for an early judgment is a recipe for inaccurate understanding and poor decisions. New information may not sufficiently be factored in to re-evaluate the image already formed, as in the anchoring heuristic. In particular, new information, particularly when it arrives incrementally, often fails to cause a re-evaluation of old analysis; rather it is downgraded as it arrives or even ignored altogether rather than risk a good theory.

Deductive reasoning is one method to try to prevent the misrepresentation of information. People use formal knowledge, formal rules, or mental models to evaluate information.[30] Formal knowledge and rules are usually acquired through a method such as education or training where explicit information is shared. In education, the knowledge shared is based on theories that have been supported by research; examples would be mathematics, science, and history. Using this acquired knowledge, deductive reasoning therefore is drawing conclusions from a logical chain of reasoning in which each step follows necessarily.[31]

Deductive reasoning compares to the alternative type of reasoning, which is inductive; knowledge is gained from personal experiences, and a general rule is established from those particular instances of experience. Mental models are problematic (discussed in more detail in Chapter 9) partly because they are heavily influenced by inductive reasoning. Inductive reasoning provides learning opportunities throughout life as we personally have experiences that we draw lessons from. Information acquired through our own experiences principally consists of a pattern recognition system that looks for cause and effect and searches memories for previous instances or categories. It is a strategy that we continue to use throughout life. Many decisions can thus be made almost automatic through heuristics or conditioning that tends to look for the commonalities in circumstances and react according to past behaviors.

Unfortunately, using inductive reasoning based on personal experiences may create potential negative results. People are ready to extrapolate a great deal from their personal experiences and make assumptions accordingly. As Nisbett and Borgdia note, people show a willingness to infer the general from the particular matched only by their unwillingness to deduce the particular from the general.[32] Another issue is that we are inclined to use past experiences as a guide for future behavior; because something has happened every day for a year does not necessarily mean it will happen tomorrow.[33] Thus, it appears that we are quick to invoke personal experience or a companion's personal experience over deductive inferences as the cause of an event. For instance, many of us will dispense with a statistically accurate survey on the reliability of a prospective new purchase of a motor car if our neighbor offers an alternative opinion. We prefer a vivid emotionally salient personal anecdote to boring abstract statistics. This condition is particularly important with risk where people react strongly to concrete and visible risks but not to abstract risks. It was noted that as Americans declined to fly after 9/11, there was a serious increase in road fatalities as a result of the increased traffic.[34] The tragedy of 9/11 was vivid, while road usage risk was abstract. Similarly, people can be more willing to purchase life insurance that specifically states cover in the event of a terrorist attack over a full life insurance policy that covers in all circumstances, including in the event of terrorism.[35] This problem generalizes to people's sensitivity to small sample sizes, the *law of small numbers* when making decisions. For example, witnessing a particular class or race of person commit a criminal act can lead to the very broad inference that this person is representative of an entire race of people.

Deductive reasoning is the type of learning used in formal education where concepts and theories provide the knowledge that can be applied in novel circumstances. It can involve forming a theory from the available evidence and knowledge and then testing the theory as to its reliability. Testing a case theory is a critical part of the process. Simply because a conclusion may be obvious is no reason not to consider possible alternatives. A theory may never be capable of being proven right. It may be impossible to confirm a theory as every incidence of confirmation only agrees with your initial assumption and no matter how many confirmatory instances you produce; one single contradictory instance is all that is necessary to disconfirm the theory. Using the concept of falsification, a case theory should be examined from the intention of disproving it.[36]

How does one disprove a case theory? Questions about alternatives may be asked such as why or what are the alternative explanations for events or behavior? Every conceivable alternative explanation should be explored for the evidence at hand before an interview takes place. Doing this also helps to minimize the tendency of confirmation bias. Unfortunately, *satisficing*— selecting the first identified alternative that appears 'good enough' is often chosen rather than examining all alternatives to determine which is 'best'.[37] It may not be possible to examine every alternative explanation for the presence of the evidence, and despite the best efforts, in a subsequent interview, the subject may present an unimagined explanation. However, the point remains valid about keeping an open mind and examining the evidence critically instead of accepting the most obvious conclusion immediately. Those evaluating and analyzing evidence or information should be self-conscious about their reasoning processes and rather than trying to eliminate biases should instead try to identify what biases are creeping into their reasoning and make them explicit.[38]

It is important for investigators to try to identify alternative models, conceptual frameworks, or interpretations of the data, perhaps by seeking out individuals who disagree with them rather than those who agree. It is more comfortable to talk with like-minded colleagues who share the same basic worldview, but the more diverse the background of the investigative team, the more valuable the insights each team member may bring. Consequently, external investigators bring experiences and skill sets to the investigation that an internal team cannot, as they may simply be too close to the situation. Externals may also be in a position to criticize organizational policies or culture that an internal may not be able to.

Judgment Tools

An investigator will rarely have all the information available and must at some point move into uncertainty. Judgment is what investigators or analysts must use to fill in the gaps in their knowledge.[39] As the aphorism notes: *good judgment comes from experience, and experience comes from bad judgment,* and it is certainly true that experience is an important element in analyzing information. Unfortunately, investigators rarely get the opportunity to review their bad judgments, and many can continue to believe they are endowed with good judgment. Over time, police have recognized this and developed investigative methodologies rather than rely on personal skills to ensure investigation gaps were filled, particularly in the cases of serious crimes with unknown suspects.[40]

Fortunately, the corporate environment is likely to have a narrow pool of potential suspects and often there is little dispute over who is the likely culprit.

R.J. Heuer suggests using the twin techniques of decomposition and externalization to assist analysis.[41] Decomposition means breaking a problem down into its component parts. Externalization means getting the problem out of our heads and into some visible form that we can work with. Tools for structuring a problem include outlines, tables, diagrams, trees, and matrices, with many subspecies of each. For example, diagrams include causal diagrams, influence diagrams, flow charts, and cognitive maps.[42] Doing this allows assumptions to be made explicit. Diagrams are also helpful in identifying gaps in knowledge and developing tasks to be done.

One useful visualization method is root cause analysis (RCA) which is a process for identifying the multiple causes of problems or events. RCA is a process to identify the ultimate causes of an issue identified and is largely based on evidence of causal relationships through interviews and analyzing data. RCA can also be a means of identifying good practice as part of continuous improvement. It is based on the idea that effective management requires more than putting out fires for problems that develop but finding a way to prevent them. The identification of root causes is often a matter of judgment and is an iterative process, and it may result in a number of causes being identified for a particular issue. The *Ishikawa Diagram*, a.k.a. the *fishbone method*, is the tool used where the problem or overall effect is analyzed through the various contributing factors.

For instance, these factors might include people, process, equipment, materials, environment, and management. All these factors are individually examined to understand each component's part in the problem. Each component may consist of subcomponents that contribute to each, although to

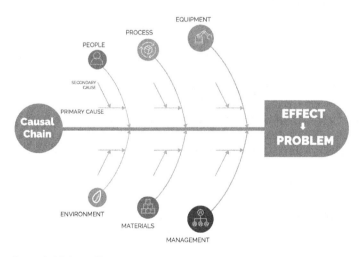

Figure 1 Ishikawa Diagram.

varying degrees. This method takes a multifaceted approach to understanding how the problem arose. It is not enough to examine each aspect or factor in isolation; frequently, it may be the interaction between the various factors that might lead to issues. Hence, using a systems thinking approach to examine relationships and various perspectives is key to successfully using fishbone analysis.[43] It is only through obtaining a deep understanding of the components, including the structural context, and the interaction influences that a meaningful analysis will be achieved. For instance, interpersonal conflict may be a primary driver of behavior even though proxies are used to fight the battles. Therefore, it may be necessary to move beyond the immediate and more visible or proximate causes to find the deeper or ultimate causes of the problem.

Systems Thinking

Systems thinking is a method of analyzing a problem that uses multivalent (many states) logic rather than simply bivalent (two states), but it is also possible to use in combination with other techniques. Multivalent state means rather than examining the problem in a binary, black or white, manner, there is an effort to understand the gray through examining different dimensions. Systems thinking is about approaching thinking in a holistic manner, understanding mental models and how they are often skewed from reality, and how systems adapt. Of particular importance is putting equal focus on the structural context as well as the raw information. This is achieved through a simple model Distinctions, Systems, Relationships, Perspective, or acronym DSRP.[44] Distinctions is about making boundaries between ideas or things, defining what is inside or outside the boundary. This creates two fundamental elements: the *thing* inside and the *other* outside. Systems organizes the ideas into *parts* or a *whole* and is part of deconstructing or creating meaning. The next step is to identify the relationships between ideas and things. At the basic level, all relationships are about *action* and *reaction*. Concepts such as correlation, causal, feedback, inputs/outputs, and influence, etc. are all examples of action/reaction. Perspectives involve trying to evaluate the ideas and relationships from different *points* and *views*. It involves trying to examine biases and using different lenses to adopt a different perspective. Derek and Laura Cabrera use this simple model and its associated rules to understand complex wicked problems which they define as problems where there is a mismatch between reality (how a real-world system actually works) and mental models (how we think they work). There are inherent links between the different elements, so an idea or thing may have each of the four elements. Real-world problems are complex networks of many interacting variables that are nonlinear and do not correspond to our desires for simplistic, hierarchical, and linear explanations.[45] Accordingly, there is a need to go beyond simple tools such as org charts in companies to establish true relationships between individuals, for example, romantic relationships or friendships, that may matter more in terms of relationship than the official positions. Cabrera and Cabrera also recommend using visualization tools to trace the DSRP in problems.

Analysis of Competing Hypotheses

Another useful tool to use as a lens through which to examine information is the Analysis of Competing Hypotheses (ACH) method. Former Central Intelligence Agency (CIA) analyst Richards J. Heuer developed ACH as an essential tool for intelligence analysis.[46] It is also probably the most useful in corporate investigations as it was developed to work with intelligence to minimize biases. Heuer suggests that the first step in evaluating information is to (1) define the problem, understand what you are being asked to do, so that you are asking the right questions and being asked the right questions. The next step is to (2) generate a number of hypotheses that are plausible and that need to be tested. The list of hypotheses is generated by discussing with other team members. Then set objectives and attempt to collect further information; use what is given to you but set forth a number of additional tasks to gather more. Collect information to evaluate all the reasonable hypotheses, not just the one that seems most likely. Then (3) begin the evaluation of the hypotheses. Do not be misled by the fact that so much evidence supports your preconceived idea of which is the most likely hypothesis. The same evidence may be consistent with several different hypotheses, so it is important to stay open-minded. Focus on (4) developing arguments *against* each hypothesis rather than trying to confirm hypotheses.[47] Recognize that your conclusions may be driven by assumptions that determine how you interpret the evidence rather than by the evidence itself. (5) Proceed by trying to reject hypotheses rather than confirm them.

The methodology is designed to overcome analytical and cognitive pitfalls. A matrix of hypotheses (e.g., the persons of interest) by arguments (pieces of evidence) can be constructed. Heuer describes how the inconsistencies between the hypotheses and pieces of evidence should be scored, interpreted, and how conclusions should be reported. The analysis can use a number of simple techniques: data immersion, the use of situational logic, the application of theory, and comparison.

Data Immersion

Data Immersion is the simplest method of analysis and is the method most commonly used in investigations. The available data are examined objectively until an answer comes spontaneously. The investigator uses his or her experience and general knowledge as a guide. Normally, most investigations are relatively straightforward, and evidence is found to corroborate the most likely hypothesis, while there is no contradictory evidence. The issue with this method is that this type of analysis overlooks the fact that information cannot speak for itself. Humans favor information that has coherence and provides a causal narrative, so it is easy to be misled by prior beliefs. One particular feature of the human psyche is known as the *fundamental attribution error* where we tend to regard others as intending their actions based on personal dispositions and often ignore the importance of the situation that such actors found themselves in.[48] Furthermore, this method only considers the available information, and the information that is not known cannot be factored in. As noted, there is a default position for the imagination to construct a coherent narrative out of fragments of data. The significance of information is always a joint function of the nature of the information and the context in which it is interpreted. The context may be provided by the investigator in the form of his or her worldview, set of assumptions, and expectations concerning human and organizational behavior.

Situational Logic

In situational logic, the incident is treated as a one-of-a-kind incident, and therefore, it must be understood in terms of its own unique logic. The generation and analysis of hypotheses start with a consideration of the concrete elements of the current situation, rather than with any broad generalizations that encompass many similar cases. Starting with the known facts of the current situation and an understanding of the unique forces at work at that particular time and place, the objective is to identify the logical antecedents or consequences of this situation. A scenario is developed that hangs together as a plausible narrative. It may be usual to work backward to explain the origins or causes of the current situation or forward to estimate the future outcome.

Situational logic commonly focuses on tracing cause–effect relationships, and any situation, however unique, may be evaluated in this manner. The strength of situational logic is its wide applicability and ability to integrate a large volume of relevant detail. Its weaknesses, on the other hand, include the possibility that the investigator may project his or her own values, prejudices, or worldview to other actors and fail to judge the situation from the perspective of the actors involved. This *mirror imaging* tends to assume everyone else thinks as I do, when in reality, people have diverse worldviews and motivations.[49]

Application of Theory

Both data immersion and situational logic have the pitfalls of human decision-making to contend with. The application of theory is another model of interpretation of information, although rarely used. A theory is a generalization based on the study of many examples of some phenomenon, so permits deductive reasoning. It specifies that when a given set of conditions arises, certain other conditions will follow either with certainty or with some degree of probability. For example, concepts such as the *Five Dysfunctions of a Team* from management theory or *Situational Action Theory* from criminology may all offer insights.[50] Psychological theories, particularly from social psychology, such as *Social Identity Theory* (SIT), explain why group dynamics has the influence over individual behavior to the extent it does.[51] Therefore, rather than basing evaluations and assumptions arising from the data on personal experiences, the data may suggest a comparison to a theoretical model and provide applicable frameworks with which to interpret the available data. Such an approach avoids, at least to some extent, personal biases or a lack of experience. While theories can provide insight, it is also important not to force data to fit the theory.

I personally find this method theory application of significant use. Two theories that I have found particularly useful are the *Nut Island Effect* and *Performance-enhancing Risks* and the insights and predictive value they both afford have been invaluable as well as illustrating the power of group dynamics through SIT.

Nut Island Effect

Developed by Paul Levy, the Nut Island Effect is a classic management concept that was developed to explain one particular type of situation.[52] The Nut Island Effect was never really developed into a theory as such, but the process of slow incremental decline of highly competent and dedicated workers who were passionate about their role into a dysfunctional group is replicated on a regular basis both in my experience and through analysis of other organizational decline. The concept also dovetails with other established academic theories that highlight the importance of small group dynamics on personal behavior that recognizes the primal need people have to belong to a group. Psychological traits are important, of course, but over the longer term, group dynamics define the rules of the game.

The Nut Island concept does not have to involve financial gain, and usually doesn't, although eventually it may become about financial malpractice. Initially, the problem is that a group of individuals who are skilled and even highly valued by the organization may become toxic to the organization and its mission. Because of their self-reliance and invisibility, the team becomes a serious liability to the organization with the potential for catastrophic consequences, but management ignores them while being oblivious to the risks.

As is usual, the dynamic develops over time, culture is not stable, and various events all impact either positively or negatively, sometimes with cumulative effects. The initial factor is an important task given to a core group of responsible and capable individuals. This task is a behind-the-scenes task and is completed quietly, or in some way, that casual scrutiny or oversight is difficult. The team works well together and self-organizes. Management is happy because the job is done efficiently with little fuss, and the team basically runs itself. The team begins to self-select for membership and share similar values, taken-for-granted assumptions, and a common cause, with any dissenters weeded out, often simply through attrition. This is part of a process of *social validation*, where certain beliefs and values are promoted by the shared social experience of a group.[53] Some dissenters may simply leave, whereas those who try to openly disagree or contest group values risk 'excommunication' from the group. Dissension is usually difficult in groups, and depending on the importance of the group to the individual, exclusion can be a literally painful experience. Most opt to change their values to conform to the group in preference to exclusion. As a result, the group is more harmonious internally, even at the risk of groupthink.[54] All of these steps are pathway dependent. In other words, at any point along the path, another decision can put the group onto another path either avoiding the Nut Island outcome or, perhaps, exacerbating the adverse outcome. Sometimes, this is down to a single highly influential individual, and at other times, it may be a consequence of a particular circumstance or event that unfolds.

At this point, the group performs its role and meets or exceeds expectations, and there are no performance issues. Unfortunately, at some stage, the group will need assistance and may request additional resources or some type of extra support, but management may not heed the warnings or requests for assistance because it has come to regard the team as self-sufficient and capable of resolving any issues that arises. Levy notes that this can breed a sense of resentment in the team as they feel treated unfairly. In my experience, other reasons can breed resentment in the team. It may be a belief that management are not treating the team fairly or are expecting too much from the team, with expectations that are escalating constantly, perhaps being too ambitious and beyond reach. It may be that the team is not rewarded as well as others for their effort. What is important at this point is a perception of some unfairness felt by team members. In an individual, this may result in simple disgruntlement, but when the entire team comes to feel the same way, it breeds resentment. A sense of grievance, real or perceived, can be a powerful motivator of behavior. One can imagine how the internal conversation of the group becomes fixated on the unfairness of their treatment and how, over time, their beliefs alter, and resentment becomes a dominating assumption in their worldview. This in turn may become the lens through which all further interactions are viewed.

What follows may be the next step in the spiral with the development of a sense of isolation and the development of an us–against–them mentality with the team determined to stay out of management's way and do their work while now minimizing or even denying that any issues exist. The team grows skillful at disguising any problems and presenting a unified response to any queries.[55] This lack of engagement with management further encourages a sense of resentment in the team and reinforces the isolation but heightens the comradeship of the group as a band of heroic outcasts. Management, meanwhile, hears only what they want to hear, and as the team never complains, it reinforces management's perception that all is well. Management, in effect, has abandoned the team and fails to do any deep examination or checks on the reality of the situation. Management makes no effort to connect the team's mission to any sense of the greater purpose. The team starts to develop its own rules of operation and ways of working. Although Levy, in his original article, stated that the Nut Island team continued to focus on their core mission, it is possible that, at this stage, many teams will develop rules more orientated toward enhancing the team's comfort and reducing work burdens while continuing to appear to perform their role.

Over time, this leads to the final stage, that of deviance. The team comes to believe that only they truly understand the work and close their ears to alternative viewpoints. They generally ignore management or go over their heads to higher authorities if any attempt to interfere with their operations is made. This sense of invincibility emboldens the team. They have already taken small steps toward deviance that becomes normalized over time, and through a combination of groupthink and cognitive dissonance, the team practices self-deception and rejects any alternative information that clashes with their view of reality. Eventually, there is an adverse outcome. In many cases, over enough time, the deviance can lead to fraudulent or otherwise criminal behavior. This is what Diane Vaughan explains as *normalization of deviance* process in action; that given sufficient time, very small incremental steps begin to accumulate, leading to disaster.[56]

This consequence can easily be blamed entirely on the team, but, on the other hand, management, busy with more pressing and obvious matters, continued to ignore the team and their task. It is not just that management are misled; often management choose to be misled as they have many other important issues. Too often, the adage *no news is good news* is an easy option for managers to take advantage of. It will then usually take a sudden crisis to dispel this complacency. The unfortunate end result is a failure to fulfill the mission brief, even though the task was assigned to a dedicated and capable team of good people. What is important to note is that this type of deviance does not have to personally benefit the group at all, and they may genuinely have had the best motivations or intentions, as they saw it, despite the adverse outcome.

Performance-Enhancing Risks

If the Nut Island situation is a bottom-up process, then performance-enhancing risks is a top-down one. As noted by Edwin Sutherland, the line between sharp business practice and illegality can often be blurry.[57] Sometimes, it is simply taking advantage of regulatory loopholes; sometimes, it is what Robert Shiller calls disingenuity—where businesses take advantage of a boom, staying within the law but exploiting it beyond where the owners themselves believe in it.[58] Sometimes, organizations adopt their own rules and norms through which they simultaneously resist and oppose legislative rules.[59] In these cases, it is the tone at top of the organization that is root cause of subsequent issues. As Malcolm Sparrow notes, every organization needs and develops processes as these are how things get done, and making these as efficient as possible is key to improvement.[60]

Often management set clearly identifiable metrics to improve processes and become very focused about the achievement of these metrics. In some organizations, risks can be taken as methods to speed up operational processes and meeting the metrics. Potential risks and pitfalls are ignored as metrics are being met, so the threat does not originate in individuals or isolated groups, but instead, it is derived from the organization itself.[61] Potential risks may include safety hazards.[62] The risks may be invisible and not easily apparent. Perhaps, the best-case scenario is used as justification as the most likely scenario. Hidden or ignored risks include the use of *creative compliance*.[63] Creative compliance is the use of technical experts such as lawyers or accountants to manage the appearance of the structuring, practices, and transactions of the company so that they can claim that they fall on the legal side of the boundary between lawfulness and illegality. Enron, for instance, used legal complexities to obscure dubious dealings. In Enron's case, Doreen McBarnet argues that an expectation developed that any deal, no matter how duplicitous or even fraudulent, could be repackaged as lawful. Any deal that was not expressly illegitimate was by definition legal, and this was seen as clever rather than deviant. This playing up to the borderline of illegality has become normalized in many organizations.

Rule by metrics can become dogma. In cases where the metrics are considered vital, management can become willing to tolerate certain behaviors if the results that flow from it are beneficial to the organization. Individuals throughout the management hierarchy may also be benefiting personally as targets or metrics are being met which means that kudos, including bonuses and recognition, are awarded while everyone is content to turn a blind eye to how they are actually achieved. For employees on the frontline, there is no indication of engaging in any form of deviant behavior as there is constant management support for the prevailing cultural norms, even if often delivered unofficially; official policies may diverge sharply. As a consequence, sometimes even recognizing that there is an ethical conflict in the first place is not always easy. First, one must be morally aware of a dilemma to evaluate any information from a normative perspective.[64] If the dilemma is recognized, then one may be minded to reach an ethical decision. If one does not recognize the dilemma in the first place, then no further action can be taken. And if everyone in the group is doing it, this indicates social proof, suggesting there is no dilemma and conformity means just going along. This leads to a neutralization of morals where unethical behavior can be simply overlooked because of identification with the group.[65] Even where a dilemma is recognized, an employee's moral choice is about whether to go along with the group behaviors that are normalized or to resist. Resistance is difficult as the individuals have become socialized into the group norms by their peers.[66] Moreover, those willing to step up to do the behaviors are often celebrated as heroes willing to do what needs to be done to succeed. This, as we have seen, is the process of social validation, which is very difficult to resist, especially if the group is an important part of one's identity. Thus, organizational toxicity arises not only when cultural norms are opposed to legal norms but also when an organization condones, tolerates, or enables rule-breaking, neutralizes or obstructs compliance, or creates actual practices that conflict with expressed values.[67]

Sparrow emphasizes, however, that high-risk means of achieving metrics need not only be illegal to create potential problems. For instance, underestimating a safety risk is not unlawful. Moreover, sometimes the choice might not clearly be about means versus ends but may be about balancing two different kinds of risks. One risk may be tied to a visible performance metric, or it may involve choosing efficiency over accuracy in operations, while the other risk may be more long term, ambiguous, or just not available to be measured accurately.

Accordingly, Sparrow lists operational environments with the following elements as inadvertently at risk of using deviant means:

• A core, imperative performance task that is considered essential; is unambiguous, tangible, and usually made highly visible; and is seen as critical to organizational success by management.
• Metrics to measure core performance are objective metrics, which are both numerical and easily available to everyone. Meeting these metrics is everybody's focus.
• A reward system that recognizes the contribution of individuals for meeting the metrics incentivizes and encourages them to optimize performance.
• A set of behaviors which are perceived as enhancing a contribution to the core requirement.
• The possibility of ancillary risks, such as legal or regulatory exposure, being produced by these behaviors, with potential harm to organization.
• These ancillary risks have uncertain, indirect, or long-term consequences. This permits the discounting of danger, with the ability to hide behind ambiguity about the rules, while being safe in the knowledge that the organization itself does not want to know. The longer it continues, the less the organization even considers the risks as they become normalized.
• There are inadequate countervailing pressures to control the ancillary risks or the behaviors of employees who expose the organization to them.[68]

Sparrow notes how the meeting of metrics becomes the imperative that is a subtle but unmistakable signal to all employees, sometimes with the message to achieve those metrics, by whatever means necessary. When the cultural norms and social context in any organization come to place greater emphasis on achieving targets but much less emphasis is placed on the norms regulating the means, these norms tend to lose their power to regulate employees' behaviors.[69]

In effect, the behaviors to achieve the imperative are tolerated although there is a danger that if you get caught, you will be disavowed. As a result, the message that employees receive is 'do what is necessary but don't get caught', with any subsequent punishment meted out being seen as not so much for the deviant behavior as for getting caught. Consequently, an important element throughout is that management can maintain plausible deniability. Management can point to official policies if any of the ancillary risks associated with meeting the metrics occur. In many cases, even a criminal investigation would find linking the behavior to meet the metrics and the risks that eventually blew up to any knowing management decision difficult, if not impossible. Intent will be difficult to establish. Management can produce official guidance, policies, and procedures and deny any knowledge, instead blaming rogue elements. Management thus both retain the long-term advantage of the risky behaviors while remaining protected from any negative consequences. Management may even calculate the risky practices into the business plan. For example, in the case of the Volkswagen emission scandal and the infamous case of the Ford Pinto, evidence has emerged that senior executives calculated the likely legal costs to be incurred on discovery against the benefits of continuing malpractice.[70]

Naturally, the level of management's awareness will differ in each organization as well as one's place in the hierarchy. In the case of Wells Fargo Bank, a combination of the bank's aggressive selling culture and a highly competitive performance management system put pressure on employees to engage in unlawful practices.[71] Senior management took the option of setting ambitious metrics while closing down any channel of communication that was sending back signals it did not want to hear. Such a strategy was able to generate willful blindness to how the overly ambitious metrics were actually being achieved. Other tactics used to encourage selling included the setting of aggressive targets by local managers and intrusive micromanagement by senior management to follow up on meeting metrics. As in the Nut Island example, senior management can always claim plausible deniability as they were busily focused on strategic goals and did not have time to actually understand local business practices and how employees met metrics imposed.

Both Nut Island and performance-enhancing risks are systemic problems, beyond any individual behavior. Even in circumstances where insufficient resources are available to employees, but outputs are still expected, there is a performance-enhancing risk created. Both indicate issues that require remedial action as more deviance will inevitably arise if there is no intervention. The investigator can evaluate any organization from these concepts how far along the deviance spectrum the organization actually is.

Comparison

Comparison is the final method from Heuer and involves comparison with similar previous events or drawing analogies from historical data. Investigators use their understanding of the historical precedent to fill gaps in their understanding of the current situation. Drawing analogies is one type of comparative methodology. Drawing analogies can be dangerous however, especially if data are forced to fit or cherry-picked. Comparison differs from situational logic in that the present situation is interpreted in the light of a more or less explicit conceptual model that is created by looking at similar situations in other times or places. It differs from theoretical analysis in that this conceptual model is based on a single case or only a few cases, rather than on many similar cases. Unknown elements of the present situation are assumed to be the same as known elements of the historical precedent. Investigators may, therefore, reason that the same forces are at work, that the outcome of the present situation is likely to be similar to the outcome of the historical situation, or that a certain policy is required in order to avoid the same outcome as in the past. Reasoning, by comparison, can be chosen when neither data nor theory is available for other analytical strategies, or simply because it is easier and less time-consuming than a more detailed analysis and therefore may be a convenient shortcut. However, a major drawback to this method is the tendency to assume the past is predictive of the future.

In Sum

When evaluating evidence or any information, there is little point in having knowledge of how to minimize bias and objectively analyze it unless the methods are practiced. Herbert Simon noted about management that the principles are relatively simple, even 'trivial', but that it is not enough to know the principles; they must be practiced to the point of habit so that they become the default method and resistant to the normal human urges to do as little as possible.[72]

The same applies to investigating generally and evaluating evidence in particular. At first, it requires conscious effort to avoid comfortable habits and assumptions. Taking prudent steps to generate a number of hypotheses for an event and then testing each one to try to falsify it is the most important habit to develop. Falsification suggests that the most likely hypothesis is usually the one with the least evidence against it, not the one with the most evidence for it. Be careful and methodical in laying out assumptions, especially those that depend upon knowledge of a different national culture. Biases are unconscious processing and affect everyone. People may believe that these biases only affect others and that they themselves are immune to them, even when self-serving attributions are being made.[73] Over time, as good habits develop, an investigator should strive to be skeptical of all information, be careful to assign sole blame, and be willing to look deeper and challenge the system further than others may think necessary. Moreover, the investigator should remain conscious that a lot of information will remain hidden, and a complete understanding may not be possible. In particular, encourage yourself and others to make assumptions explicit and try to specify the degree of uncertainty involved in conclusions. Be willing to ask someone else to examine the problem with a fresh pair of eyes to minimize the effect of incremental approaches to knowledge formation and the ownership that often comes from being too close to an investigation. Likewise, encourage alternative points of view and engage other outside experts for the same reason. Finally, be realistic about expectations, both your own and what others, including your client, expect from you. Understand the limitations of information analysis.[74]

To emphasize, the single most effective way to attain objectivity is by striving to make assumptions explicit so that they may be examined and challenged, not by vain efforts to eliminate them from analysis. Visual aids are good for this, and a simple timeline is a powerful visualization tool to identify known information and gaps in knowledge as well as helping overall understanding of events. John Boyd, the developer of the *observe, orientate, decide, and act loop* (OODA) concept, referred to this process as *deductive destruction*. Boyd described his approach as a method of pulling things apart (analysis) and putting them back together (synthesis) in new combinations which permits apparently unrelated ideas and actions to be discovered and the relationships between them become visible.[75] This method is similar to 'reasoning from first principles' where complicated problems are broken down to the most basic elements to eliminate assumptions. The problem is examined from the foundation level, so deep expertise is essential. Asking questions of yourself, looking for corroborating evidence, being aware of biases, considering alternative perspectives, considering relationships between perspectives, and generally using the five 'whys' all help. Putting time into reflection afterward pays dividends. It is the reflection time spent where alternative options are mentally examined that leads to better decisions and processes over time. Ultimately, an investigator must approach an investigation like a scientist, because as Carl Sagan stated 'Science is a way of thinking much more than it is a body of knowledge'.[76]

Conclusion

While gathering information and evidence is important, it must also be evaluated and interpreted. Evaluation is a vital step to obtain the maximum from what has been gathered. Too often this critical step is overlooked, often because investigators have already prejudged the outcome. Evidence should be examined as objectively as possible. Rushing to judgment can invariably lead to biases creeping into the evaluation of evidence, meaning decisions are made from habit not intentionally and deliberately. It appears that the most effective way to attain objectivity is by making assumptions explicit so that they may be examined and challenged. Practice evaluation as a conscious and deliberate process.

In many investigations, the evidence is straightforward, but maintaining the discipline of objectivity will always pay dividends. Making it a habit to question all evidence, to examine it critically, to avoid jumping to conclusions, and to be comfortable making judgments in the absence of all information are all positive strengths to have as an investigator. In my experience, understanding the skills outlined permits the identification of biases including groupthink that often signal negative corporate culture dynamics. It is this process that can add extra value to the commissioning client from an investigator's perspective as these insights allow mitigation interventions to be developed. Once evaluated, evidence will be used in the report to support conclusions reached. However, it serves another critical function. Evidence is a core part of interviewing. As will be discussed in Chapter 8, it helps to detect deception, and more importantly, the careful use of evidence can move a person from denials to telling the truth. Therefore, the more effort put into the examination and analysis of information, the more effective the interviewer will ultimately be.

Notes

1   Panksepp, J. and Biven, L., *The Archaeology of the Mind: Neuroevolutionary Origins of Human Emotions*, (W.W. Norton, New York, 2012): 160.

2   Damasio, A., *Descartes Error: Emotion, Reason and the Human Brain*, (Vintage, London, 1994); Stanovich, K. E., *Rationality and the Reflective Mind*, (Oxford University Press, Oxford, 2011).

3   Rational choice theory has had a phenomenal impact on political, social science, and economic fields partly because of the work of people such as John von Neumann, Oskar Morgenstern, Kenneth Arrow, and Thomas Schelling, see Amadae, S. M., *Rationalizing Capitalist Democracy: The Cold War Origins of Rational Choice Liberalism*, (University of Chicago, Chicago, 2003). The rational expectations model of Robert Lucas that was developed in the 1970s was particularly influential in American economic policies. RCT was particularly favored by economists as it permitted simplified modeling, even if inaccurate. Taleb, N., *The Black Swan: The Impact of the Highly Improbable*, (Penguin, London, 2008). Another influential model, Efficient Markets Theory, held that investors are rational, and all relevant information is factored into share price. This theory underpinned financial deregulation and the decision not to regulate the derivative market which ultimately led to the 2008 crash, see Madrick, J., *Seven Bad Ideas: How Mainstream Economists Have Damaged America and the World*, (Alfred A. Knopf, New York, 2014).

4   Stanovich, K. E., *The Robot's Rebellion: Finding Meaning in the Age of Darwin*, (University of Chicago, Chicago 2004).

5   Haidt, J., "The Emotional Dog and Its Rational Tail: A Social Intuitionist Approach to Moral Judgment", *Psychological Review*, (2001), 108(4), pp 814; Haidt, J., "Morality", *Perspectives on Psychological Science (Wiley-Blackwell)*, (2008), 3(1), pp 65–72; Haidt, J., *The Righteous Mind*, (Allen Lane, London, 2012).

6   Atran, S., *Talking to the Enemy*, (Allen Lane, London, 2010): 210; Atran, S., *In Gods We Trust: The Evolutionary Landscape of Religion*, (Oxford University Press, Oxford, 2002); Sageman, M., *Misunderstanding Terrorism*, (Pennsylvania University Press, Philadelphia, PA, 2017).

7   Benkler, Y., Farris, R. and Roberts, H., *Network Propaganda: Manipulation, Disinformation, and Radicalization in American Politics*, (Oxford University Press, 2018): 77.

8   Kahneman, D., *Maps of Bounded Rationality: A Perspective on Intuitive Judgement and Choice*, (Princeton University, Department of Psychology, Princeton, 2002); Simon, H. A., 'Theories of Bounded Rationality', (eds) McGuire and Roy, in *Decision and Organization*, (North-Holland, 1972) pp 161–176.

9   Stanovich, K. E., *Rationality and the Reflective Mind*, (2011), Tversky, A. and Kahneman, D., "Judgment under Uncertainty—Heuristics and Biases", *Science*, (1974), 185(4157), pp 1124–1131.

10 Tversky, A. and Kahneman, D., 'Causal Schemas in Judgements under Uncertainty', (eds) Slovic, Tversksy and Kahneman, in *Judgement under Uncertainty: Heuristics and Biases*, (Cambridge University Press, Cambridge, 1982) pp 117–128; Kahneman, D. and Tversky, A., "Prospect Theory: An Analysis of Decision under Risk", *Econometrica*, (1979), 47(2), pp 263–291.

11 Panksepp, J. and Biven, L., *The Archaeology of the Mind: Neuroevolutionary Origins of Human Emotions*, (2012): 20.

12 Stanovich, K. E., *Rationality and the Reflective Mind*, (2011): 19.

13 Langer, E., "The Mindlessness of Ostensibly Thoughtful Action. The Role of 'Placebic' Information in Interpersonal Interaction", *Journal of Personality and Social Psychology*, (1978), 36(6), pp 632–642: 635.

14 Stanovich, K. E., *Rationality and the Reflective Mind*, (2011): 30.

15 Slovic, P., Finucane, M. L., Peters, E. and MacGregor, D. G., "Risk as Analysis and Risk as Feelings: Some Thoughts about Affect, Reason, Risk, and Rationality", *Risk Analysis: An International Journal*, (2004), 24(2), pp 311–322: 319.

16 Stanovich, K. E., *Rationality and the Reflective Mind*, (2011): 104.

17 Haidt, J., "The Emotional Dog and Its Rational Tail: A Social Intuitionist Approach to Moral Judgment", *Psychological Review*, (2001).

18 Stanovich, K. E., *Rationality and the Reflective Mind*, (2011): 102.

19 Kirsch, I., "Response Expectancy as a Determinant of Experience and Behavior", *American Psychologist*, (1985), 40(11), pp 1189–1202.

20 Lord, C. G., Ross, L. and Lepper, M. R., "Biased Assimilation and Attitude Polarization: The Effects of Prior Theories on Subsequently Considered Evidence", *Journal of Personality and Social Psychology*, (1979), 37(11), pp 2098–2109.

21 Bazerman, M. H., Loewenstein, G. and Moore, D. A., "Why Good Accountants Do Bad Audits", *Harvard Business Review*, (2002), 80(11), pp 96–103.

22 See also Arkes, H. R. and Ayton, P., "The Sunk Cost and Concorde Effects: Are Humans Less Rational Than Lower Animals?", *Psychological Bulletin*, (1999), 125(5), pp 591–600.

23 Matthew Syed in Chapter 4 of *Black Box Thinking* (2015) covers a number of failures in the criminal justice system, including DNA exonerations of persons found guilty by the Innocence Project. A common response to this new contradictory evidence is denial by prosecutors and an effort to dismiss the new evidence. In some cases, this has resulted in years between the findings and eventual release from prison. In some cases with prosecutors still insisting in guilt.

24 Kahneman, D., "Maps of Bounded Rationality: Psychology for Behavioral Economics", *The American Economic Review*, (2003), 93(5), pp 1449–1475: 1468.

25 Taleb, N., *The Black Swan: The Impact of the Highly Improbable*, (2008).

26 I am referring here to conspiracy theories around the origin of the disease, conspiracy theories around vaccinations, and alleged cures being promoted contrary to good public health advice.

27 Fenton-O'Creevy, M., Soane, E., Nicholson, N. and Willman, P., "Thinking, Feeling and Deciding: The Influence of Emotions on the Decision Making and Performance of Traders", *Journal of Organizational Behavior*, (2011), 32(8), pp 1044–1061.

28 Kruger, J. and Dunning, D., "Unskilled and Unaware of It: How Difficulties in Recognizing One's Own Incompetence Lead to Inflated Self-Assessments", *Journal of Personality and Social Psychology*, (1999), 77(6), pp 1121–1134. An often-misused term. It has nothing to do with foolish or dumb people failing to recognize that fact. More recent research suggests that the effect may not have been real, rather it was an artifact of data.

29 Cabrera, D. and Cabrera, L., *Systems Thinking Made Simple: New Hope for Solving Wicked Problems*, 2 ed., (Plectica Publishing, 2018): 72.

30 Johnson-Laird, P. N., "Deductive Reasoning", *Annual Review of Psychology*, (1999), 50(1), pp 109–135.

31 Simon, M. A., "Beyond Inductive and Deductive Reasoning: The Search for a Sense of Knowing", *Educational Studies in Mathematics*, (1996), 30(2), pp 197–209.

32 Nisbett, R. E. and Borgida, E., "Attribution and the Psychology of Prediction", *Journal of Personality and Social Psychology*, (1975), 32(5), pp 932–943: 939.

33 This philosophical point is known as Hume's turkey problem, see Taleb, N., *The Black Swan: The Impact of the Highly Improbable*, (2008) for greater discussion.

34 Blalock, G., Kadiyali, V. and Simon, D., "Driving Fatalities After 9/11: A Hidden Cost of Terrorism", *Applied Economics*, (2009), 41, pp 1717–1729.

35 Kahneman, D., *Thinking, Fast and Slow*, (Penguin, London, 2012).

36 Popper, K., *The Logic of Scientific Discovery*, (Routledge, London, 1935[2004]). Carl Sagan's baloney detection method (in *The Demon-Haunted World*) is similarly applicable here. Essentially, it's the basis of scientific thinking in order to eliminate distortion and biases.

37 Heuer, R. J., *Psychology of Intelligence Analysis*, (Central Intelligence Agency, Center for the Study of Intelligence, 1999): 43.

38 Heuer, R. J., *Psychology of Intelligence Analysis*, (1999).

39 Sutmuller, A. D., den Hengst, M., Barros, A. I. and van Gelder, P. H. A. J. M., "Comparison of Methodologies Used in Homicide Investigations to Collect, Prioritize, and Eliminate Persons of Interest: A Case Study of Three Dutch Real-World Homicide Cases", *Policing: A Journal of Policy and Practice*, (2018), 14(4), pp 1166–1181.

40 Investigative methodologies such as ACH and also Trace and Eliminate (TIE), the Persons of Interest Priority Assessment Tool (POIPAT), dragnet investigation (called Rasterfahndung in Germany), help to progress important investigations in the real world where anyone could be a suspect.

41 Heuer, R. J., *Psychology of Intelligence Analysis*, (1999).

42 Heuer, R. J., *Psychology of Intelligence Analysis*, (1999): 89.

43 Systems thinking DSRP has specific rules about the use of lines and arrows when mapping out relationships. See Cabrera, D. and Cabrera, L., *Systems Thinking Made Simple: New Hope for Solving Wicked Problems*, 2nd ed., (2018).

44 Cabrera, D. and Cabrera, L., *Systems Thinking Made Simple: New Hope for Solving Wicked Problems*, 2nd ed., (2018).

45 Cabrera, D. and Cabrera, L., *Systems Thinking Made Simple: New Hope for Solving Wicked Problems*, 2nd ed., (2018): 12.

46 Heuer, R. J., *Psychology of Intelligence Analysis*, (1999).

47 As noted, this concept of falsification was first developed by Karl Popper; see Popper, K., *The Logic of Scientific Discovery*, (1935[2004]).

48 Ross, L. and Anderson, C. A., 'Shortcomings in the Attribution Process: On the Origins and Maintenance of Erroneous Social Assessments', (eds) Kahneman, Slovic and Tversksy, in *Judgement under Uncertainty: Heuristics and Biases*, 2008 ed., (Cambridge University Press, Cambridge, 1982) pp 129–152.

49 Heuer, R. J., *Psychology of Intelligence Analysis*, (1999): 70.

50 Wikström, P.-O. H., 'Why Crime Happens: A Situational Action Theory', (ed) Manzo, in *Analytical Sociology*, (Wiley, Chichester, 2014) pp 71–94; Lenconi, P., *The Five Dysfunctions of a Team*, (John Wiley & Sons, Chichester, 2002).

51 For instance, Social Identity Theory. See Tajfel, H., "Social Psychology of Intergroup Relations", *Annual Review of Psychology*, (1982), 33(1), p 1; Tajfel, H. and Turner, J. C., 'An Integrative Theory of Intergroup Conflict.', (eds) Austin and Worchel, in *The Social Psychology of Intergroup Relations*, (Brooks/Cole, Monterey, CA, 1979) pp 33–47. This theory has been adapted and used to explain terrorism by Sageman, M., *Misunderstanding Terrorism*, (2017) and Atran, S., *Talking to the Enemy*, (2010). The work of Schein, E. H., *Organisational Culture and Leadership*, 5th ed., (Wiley, Hoboken, NJ, 2017) around underlying beliefs and group dynamics is also relevant.

52 Levy, P. F., "The Nut Island Effect: When Good Teams Go Wrong. Teams Pitted Against Distracted Senior Management; Operation of Wastewater Treatment Plant in Quincy, Mass.", *Harvard Business Review*, (2001), 79(3), pp 51–59.

53 Schein, E. H., *Organisational Culture and Leadership*, 5th ed., (2017): 83.

54 Janis, I., *Victims of Groupthink*, (Houghton Miffin, Boston, 1972); Atran, S., *Talking to the Enemy*, (2010); Tajfel, H., "Social Psychology of Intergroup Relations", *Annual Review of Psychology*, (1982); Zimbardo, P., *The Lucifer Effect*, (The Random House Group, London, 2007).

55 This replicates the lack of trust dynamic in Lenconi's (2002) five dysfunctions model.

56 Vaughan, D., *The Challenger Launch Decision: Risky Technology, Culture, and Deviance at NASA* (Chicago University Press, Chicago, 2016).

57 Sutherland, E. H., "Is 'White Collar Crime' Crime?", *American Sociological Review*, (1944), 10(2), pp 132–139.

58 Shiller, R., *Irrational Exuberance*, (Princeton University Press, Princeton, 2005): 77.

59 van Rooij, B. and Fine, A., "Toxic Corporate Culture: Assessing Organizational Processes of Deviancy", *Administrative Sciences*, (2018), 8(23), pp 1–38.

60 Sparrow, M. K., *The Character of Harms: Operational Challenges in Control*, (Cambridge University Press, Cambridge, 2008).

61 Sparrow, M. K., *The Character of Harms: Operational Challenges in Control*, (2008): 243.

62 For example, see Reader, T. W. and O'Connor, P., "The Deepwater Horizon Explosion: Non-Technical Skills, Safety Culture, and System Complexity", *Journal of Risk Research*, (2014), 17(3), pp 405–424.

63 McBarnet, D., "After Enron Will 'Whiter Than White Collar Crime' Still Wash?", *British Journal of Criminology*, (2006), 46(6), pp 1091–1109.

64 Palazzo, G., Krings, F. and Hoffrage, U., "Ethical Blindness", *Journal of Business Ethics*, (2012), 109(3), pp 323–338.

65 Umphress, E. E. and Bingham, J. B., "When Employees Do Bad Things for Good Reasons: Examining Unethical Pro-Organizational Behaviors", *Organization Science*, (2011), 22(3), pp 621–640.

66 Sparrow, M. K., *The Character of Harms: Operational Challenges in Control*, (2008): 244.

67 van Rooij, B. and Fine, A., "Toxic Corporate Culture: Assessing Organizational Processes of Deviancy", *Administrative Sciences*, (2018).

68 Sparrow, M. K., *The Character of Harms: Operational Challenges in Control*, (2008): 247. Copyright, reproduced with permission of the Licensor through PLSclear.

69 See also Vaughan, D., *The Challenger Launch Decision: Risky Technology, Culture, and Deviance at NASA* (2016). Such a phenomenon is also reflected in Robert Merton's "Social Structure and Anomie", *American Sociological Review*, (1938), 3(5), pp 672–682, *Strain Theory*: when the achievement of the desired goals receive strong cultural emphasis and where it is easier to achieve legitimate ends through illegitimate means, people will take the easier route, see also Agnew, R., "Foundations for a General Strain Theory of Crime and Delinquency", *Criminology*, (1992), 30(1), pp 47–88. This finding has been replicated many times, and even juvenile delinquents chase the 'American Dream' through any means necessary. VanderPyl, T., "'I Want to Have the American Dream': Messages of Materialism as a Driving Force in Juvenile Recidivism", *Criminal Justice and Behavior*, (2019), 46(5), pp 718–731.

70 van Rooij, B. and Fine, A., "Toxic Corporate Culture: Assessing Organizational Processes of Deviancy", *Administrative Sciences*, (2018). The Ford Pinto safety issue is almost a paradigmatic illustration of this type of rigid framing in cost–benefit analysis, in that the costs of upgrading an unsafe car in 1971 was $11, as against the projected costs of an estimated death of 180 people which would include items such as funeral expenses. For more detail, see the memo 'Fatalities Associated with Crash-Induced Fuel Leakage and Fires' is available at www.autosafety.org/wp-content/uploads/import/phpq3mJ7F_FordMemo.pdf. [Accessed February 23, 2021].

71 Independent Directors of the Board of Wells Fargo & Company Sales Practices Investigation Report, April 2017. Available at www08.wellsfargomedia.com/assets/pdf/about/investor-relations/presentations/2017/board-report.pdf. [Accessed February 8, 2021].

72 Simon, H. A., *Models of My Life*, (Massachusetts Institute of Technology, Cambridge, MA, 1996): 150.

73 Pronin, E., Lin, D. Y. and Ross, L., "The Bias Blind Spot: Perceptions of Bias in Self versus Others", *Personality and Social Psychology Bulletin*, (2002), 28(3), pp 369–381.

74 Heuer, R. J., *Psychology of Intelligence Analysis*, (1999).

75 The observe, orientate, decide, and act loop (OODA) is another methodology like the *intelligence cycle* or TPED (tasking, processing, exploitation, and dissemination) that concerns the gathering of information and acting on it. OODA was originally developed for US fighter pilots to assist with rapid decision-making. The observation part is about taking in information, the situational awareness element, that determines what is happening. Of particular importance at this point is the ability to filter out noise and focus only on relevant information. The information must be placed in context. Orientation means connecting with reality and seeing the world as it really is, as free as possible from the influence of cognitive biases and shortcuts. The impact of culture and skills at analyzing information are important constraints here, as is a constantly changing situation. Once the information is evaluated in this way, a decision is taken which leads to action. The outcome is then evaluated, and the cycle begins again. See Boyd, J. R., *A Discourse on Winning and Losing*, (Air University Press, Maxwell AFB, Montgomery, AL, 2018): 265.

76 Sagan, C., *Broca's Brain: Reflections on the Romance of Science*, (Random House, New York, NY, 1974).

Bibliography

Agnew, R., "Foundations for a General Strain Theory of Crime and Delinquency", *Criminology*, (1992), 30(1), pp 47–88.

Amadae, S. M., *Rationalizing Capitalist Democracy: The Cold War Origins of Rational Choice Liberalism*, (University of Chicago, Chicago, 2003).

Arkes, H. R. and Ayton, P., "The Sunk Cost and Concorde Effects: Are Humans Less Rational Than Lower Animals?", *Psychological Bulletin*, (1999), 125(5), pp 591–600.

Atran, S., *In Gods We Trust: The Evolutionary Landscape of Religion*, (Oxford University Press, Oxford, 2002).

Atran, S., *Talking to the Enemy*, (Allen Lane, London, 2010).

Bazerman, M. H., Loewenstein, G. and Moore, D. A., "Why Good Accountants Do Bad Audits", *Harvard Business Review*, (2002), 80(11), pp 96–103.

Benkler, Y., Farris, R. and Roberts, H., *Network Propaganda: Manipulation, Disinformation, and Radicalization in American Politics*, (Oxford University Press, 2018).

Blalock, G., Kadiyali, V. and Simon, D., "Driving Fatalities After 9/11: A Hidden Cost of Terrorism", *Applied Economics*, (2009), 41, pp 1717–1729.

Boyd, J. R., *A Discourse on Winning and Losing*, (Air University Press, Maxwell AFB, Montgomery, AL, 2018).

Cabrera, D. and Cabrera, L., *Systems Thinking Made Simple: New Hope for Solving Wicked Problems*, 2 ed., (Plectica Publishing, New York, 2018).

Damasio, A., *Descartes Error: Emotion, Reason and the Human Brain* (Vintage, London, 1994).

Fenton-O'Creevy, M., Soane, E., Nicholson, N. and Willman, P., "Thinking, Feeling and Deciding: The Influence of Emotions on the Decision Making and Performance of Traders", *Journal of Organizational Behavior*, (2011), 32(8), pp 1044–1061.

Haidt, J., "The Emotional Dog and Its Rational Tail: A Social Intuitionist Approach to Moral Judgment", *Psychological Review*, (2001), 108(4), p 814.

Haidt, J., "Morality", *Perspectives on Psychological Science (Wiley-Blackwell)*, (2008), 3(1), pp 65–72.

Haidt, J., *The Righteous Mind*, (Allen Lane, London, 2012).

Hedström, P. and Ylikoski, P., 'Analytical Sociology and Rational-Choice Theory', (ed) Manzo, in *Analytical Sociology*, (Wiley, Chichester, 2014) pp 53–70.

Heuer, R. J., *Psychology of Intelligence Analysis*, (Central Intelligence Agency, Center for the Study of Intelligence, 1999).

Janis, I., *Victims of Groupthink*, (Houghton Miffin, Boston, 1972).

Johnson-Laird, P. N., "Deductive Reasoning", *Annual Review of Psychology*, (1999), 50(1), pp 109–135.

Kahneman, D., *Maps of Bounded Rationality: A Perspective on Intuitive Judgement and Choice*, (Princeton University, Department of Psychology, Princeton, 2002).

Kahneman, D., "Maps of Bounded Rationality: Psychology for Behavioral Economics", *The American Economic Review*, (2003), 93(5), pp 1449–1475.

Kahneman, D., *Thinking, Fast and Slow*, (Penguin, London, 2012).

Kahneman, D. and Tversky, A., "Prospect Theory: An Analysis of Decision under Risk", *Econometrica*, (1979), 47(2), pp 263–291.

Kirsch, I., "Response Expectancy as a Determinant of Experience and Behavior", *American Psychologist*, (1985), 40(11), pp 1189–1202.

Kruger, J. and Dunning, D., "Unskilled and Unaware of It: How Difficulties in Recognizing One's Own Incompetence Lead to Inflated Self-Assessments", *Journal of Personality and Social Psychology*, (1999), 77(6), pp 1121–1134.

Langer, E., "The Mindlessness of Ostensibly Thoughtful Action. The Role of 'Placebic' Information in Interpersonal Interaction", *Journal of Personality and Social Psychology*, (1978), 36(6), pp 632–642.

Lenconi, P., *The Five Dysfunctions of a Team*, (John Wiley & Sons, Chichester, 2002).

Levy, P. F., "The Nut Island Effect: When Good Teams Go Wrong. Teams Pitted Against Distracted Senior Management; Operation of Wastewater Treatment Plant in Quincy, Mass", *Harvard Business Review*, (2001), 79 (3), pp 51–59.

Lord, C. G., Ross, L. and Lepper, M. R., "Biased Assimilation and Attitude Polarization: The Effects of Prior Theories on Subsequently Considered Evidence", *Journal of Personality and Social Psychology*, (1979), 37(11), pp 2098–2109.

Madrick, J., *Seven Bad Ideas: How Mainstream Economists have damaged America and the World*, (Alfred A. Knopf, New York, NY, 2014).

McBarnet, D., "After Enron Will 'Whiter Than White Collar Crime' Still Wash?", *British Journal of Criminology*, (2006), 46(6), pp 1091–1109.

Merton, R., "Social Structure and Anomie", *American Sociological Review*, (1938), 3(5), pp 672–682.

Nisbett, R. E. and Borgida, E., "Attribution and the Psychology of Prediction", *Journal of Personality and Social Psychology*, (1975), 32(5), pp 932–943.

Palazzo, G., Krings, F. and Hoffrage, U., "Ethical Blindness", *Journal of Business Ethics*, (2012), 109(3), pp 323–338.

Panksepp, J. and Biven, L., *The Archaeology of the Mind: Neuroevolutionary Origins of Human Emotions*, (W. W. Norton, New York, NY, 2012).

Popper, K., *The Logic of Scientific Discovery*, (Routledge, London, 1935[2004]).

Pronin, E., Lin, D. Y. and Ross, L., "The Bias Blind Spot: Perceptions of Bias in Self Versus Others", *Personality and Social Psychology Bulletin*, (2002), 28(3), pp 369–381.

Reader, T. W. and O'Connor, P., "The Deepwater Horizon Explosion: Non-Technical Skills, Safety Culture, and System Complexity", *Journal of Risk Research*, (2014), 17(3), pp 405–424.

Ross, L. and Anderson, C. A., 'Shortcomings in the Attribution Process: On the Origins and Maintenance of Erroneous Social Assessments', (eds) Kahneman, Slovic and Tversksy, in *Judgement under Uncertainty: Heuristics and Biases*, 2008 ed., (Cambridge University Press, Cambridge, 1982) pp 129–152.

Sagan, C., *Broca's Brain: Reflections on the Romance of Science*, (Random House, New York, NY, 1974).

Sageman, M., *Misunderstanding Terrorism*, (Pennsylvania University Press, Philadelphia, PA, 2017).

Schein, E. H., *Organisational Culture and Leadership*, 5th ed., (Wiley, Hoboken, NJ, 2017).

Shiller, R., *Irrational Exuberance*, (Princeton University Press, Princeton, 2005).

Simon, H. A., 'Theories of Bounded Rationality', (eds) McGuire and Radner, in *Decision and Organization*, (Elsevier, Amsterdam, 1972) pp 161–176.

Simon, H. A., *Models of My Life*, (Massachusetts Institute of Technology, Cambridge, MA, 1996).

Simon, M. A., "Beyond Inductive and Deductive Reasoning: The Search for a Sense of Knowing", *Educational Studies in Mathematics*, (1996), 30(2), pp 197–209.

Slovic, P., Finucane, M. L., Peters, E. and MacGregor, D. G., "Risk as Analysis and Risk as Feelings: Some Thoughts about Affect, Reason, Risk, and Rationality", *Risk Analysis: An International Journal*, (2004), 24(2), pp 311–322.

Sparrow, M. K., *The Character of Harms: Operational Challenges in Control*, (Cambridge University Press, Cambridge, 2008).

Stanovich, K. E., *The Robot's Rebellion: Finding Meaning in the Age of Darwin*, (University of Chicago, Chicago, 2004).

Stanovich, K. E., *Rationality and the Reflective Mind*, (Oxford University Press, Oxford, 2011).

Sutherland, E. H., "Is 'White Collar Crime' Crime?", *American Sociological Review*, (1944), 10(2), pp 132–139.

Sutmuller, A. D., den Hengst, M., Barros, A. I. and van Gelder, P. H. A. J. M., "Comparison of Methodologies Used in Homicide Investigations to Collect, Prioritize, and Eliminate Persons of Interest: A Case Study of Three Dutch Real-World Homicide Cases", *Policing: A Journal of Policy and Practice*, (2018), 14(4), pp 1166–1181.

Tajfel, H., "Social Psychology of Intergroup Relations", *Annual Review of Psychology*, (1982), 33(1), p 1.

Tajfel, H. and Turner, J. C., 'An Integrative Theory of Intergroup Conflict', (eds) Austin and Worchel, in *The Social Psychology of Intergroup Relations*, (Brooks/Cole, Monterey, CA, 1979) pp 33–47.

Taleb, N., *The Black Swan: The Impact of the Highly Improbable*, (Penguin, London, 2008).

Tversky, A. and Kahneman, D., "Judgment under Uncertainty—Heuristics and Biases", *Science*, (1974), 185(4157), pp 1124–1131.

Tversky, A. and Kahneman, D., 'Causal Schemas in Judgements under Uncertainty', (eds) Slovic, Tversksy and Kahneman, in *Judgement under Uncertainty: Heuristics and Biases*, (Cambridge University Press, Cambridge, 1982) pp 117–128.

Umphress, E. E. and Bingham, J. B., "When Employees Do Bad Things for Good Reasons: Examining Unethical Pro-Organizational Behaviors", *Organization Science*, (2011), 22(3), pp 621–640.

VanderPyl, T., "'I Want to Have the American Dream': Messages of Materialism as a Driving Force in Juvenile Recidivism", *Criminal Justice and Behavior*, (2019), 46(5), pp 718–731.

van Rooij, B. and Fine, A., "Toxic Corporate Culture: Assessing Organizational Processes of Deviancy", *Administrative Sciences*, (2018), 8(23), pp 1–38.

Vaughan, D., *The Challenger Launch Decision: Risky Technology, Culture, and Deviance at NASA* (Chicago University Press, Chicago, 2016).

Wikström, P.-O. H., 'Why Crime Happens: A Situational Action Theory', (ed) Manzo, in *Analytical Sociology*, (Wiley, Chichester, 2014) pp 71–94.

Zimbardo, P., *The Lucifer Effect*, (The Random House Group, London, 2007).

Chapter 8

Detecting and Countering Deceit

Introduction

On the one hand, using rapport to build trust and open communication with the interviewee is the most effective way to interview. On the other hand, it may have the potential to lull the interviewer into believing that the interviewee is also being open and honest in their communication. Interviewees will sometimes try to deceive the interviewer. That is the nature of investigative interviewing, and this chapter examines how to identify deception and how to respond to it.

Deception is a routine aspect of social life. Such deception is not always negative and frequently social harmony needs some white lies to smooth over fractures in relationships; indeed, a world where everyone is brutally honest might not be as benevolent as one might assume. From our perspective, the world is complex, people often have competing agendas, and telling lies to an investigator is a common phenomenon. Moreover, as human nature tends to put a personal public relations spin on most things, it may not be possible to get a fully objective, truthful narrative ever! The main issue that concerns us are that lies are told, or information is withheld, with an intention to deceive or to protect someone from the consequences of deviant behavior. As a result, the ability to detect deceit is important as it prevents an interviewee providing a falsified account of the matter under investigation. Lies can be time consuming as they lead down false paths, taking time to remedy. Undiscovered lies may corrupt the facts, thereby biasing the investigation outcome. This chapter looks at the detection of deceit through two primary routes: verbal and nonverbal indicators. Verbal indicators examine the language used in deception, including phrases and tone. Nonverbal indicators include body language and posture and changes in these.

Unfortunately, knowing someone is lying does not necessarily mean that the truth will be forthcoming. There is usually an amount of work to be done from recognizing any deceit to getting a truthful account, and most certainly, knowing someone is lying is not the same as proving it. When someone gives a false account, there will be situations, that without objective evidence to prove

DOI: 10.4324/9781003269489-8

the contrary, that knowing that information is relatively useless to you. Therefore, the most powerful tool for separating out fact from fiction and getting an interviewee to move from their deceitful account to acknowledge the truth is the skillful use of available evidence. While some people are driven to admit the truth by a strong conscience, for many, it is only after strong, incontrovertible evidence has been shown to them that the futility of lying becomes obvious to them and they change strategy. The utilization of evidence as effectively as possible to obtain maximum results in the interview is an essential part of both lie detection and getting the person to recount a truthful account.

Unintended Deception

Socially, it is considered impolite behavior to be an overt skeptic, and our default social mode is to be trusting of presented information, especially in pleasant surroundings.[1] Instinctively, we are morally inclined to assume lies are negative social phenomena even though we know lies are part of social life, and everyone lies in some form or another. One needs to distinguish between the 'big secrets' and the 'little lies' that are often so ubiquitous in social situations that the telling of them involves little guilt; on the contrary, they may as likely induce positive emotions. Indeed, in certain circumstances, lies and deceit often serve useful social purposes by making our friends feel better about themselves, calming a dangerous or threatening situation, or provide comfort after a tragedy. More formal mythologies are powerful in generating unity in groups.[2]

As in all human interactions, different personalities can be an important factor in how each individual approaches the exchange. In a social context, the use of lies as a social lubricant indicates a more socially sophisticated and confident person. As a general rule, extroverts are more socially competent and thus are inclined to lie more often than introverts.[3] This type of lying is more flattery and lavish praise that make extroverts such good company, if often shallow. These skills of social intelligence can be considered charming and indeed the ability to spin a yarn well often serves as a proxy for the person's intelligence.[4] In social situations, such lies leave little trace of deception. Additionally, most socially competent people develop counter skills to identify and enable them to take a lot of such deception with a grain of salt, while also being able to even enjoy it.

Outside of such social interactions, trying to obtain an accurate account of some event can encounter other obstacles. For instance, even when a person is actively trying to provide a truthful account, there is still a strong possibility of some falsehoods or more accurately, confabulation. Confabulation is not necessarily deliberate; a person may subconsciously fill in the gaps in the narrative that arise from the failings of memory. People simply use their imagination to cobble together a coherent account from fragments of memory based on their own experiences, mental models, and most probable explanations.[5] People do not like gaps in knowledge and make assumptions to fill these gaps, unfortunately these additions are then subsumed into the memory. Memory is not overly reliable and is both fallible and malleable. The memory process is fallible as it involves a number of distinct steps: first, noticing the event is necessary to begin the input process; maintaining it in working memory, then considering it noteworthy enough to encode the event into long-term memory; and then being able to accurately recall the memory; all these stages are vulnerable to biases and exogenous interferences.[6] Even the first step of perceiving something is subject to the limits of human attention, which acts as a filter, allowing in some information while ignoring other stimuli.[7] This can result in a phenomenon known as *inattentional blindness* where preoccupation with one task removes the ability to notice anything else.[8] Once noticed, perceptions must be filtered through an individual's mental model which often determine what to expect. As a result, the inability to identify the incident correctly and the calibration of our perceptions mean that we are even unreliable about what we have witnessed in our own lives. Witnesses therefore can be inherently unreliable or unhelpful because of these failings. Research reveals that even detailed personal memories held by people are often imagined, non-experienced events and that even adults can be confused between witnessed and imagined events held in memory.[9] Moreover, people often forget the reasons for their own behavior or distort the memory of what they did and why.[10]

The malleability of memory means that memories are not like CCTV footage, rather they are originally constructed from perceptions, mental models, experience, and already existing knowledge, so they are created through various subjective lens, not objectively assimilated. Memory processes tend to work with generalized categories to store information. If a person does not have an appropriate category for something, he or she is unlikely to perceive it, store it in memory, or be able to retrieve it correctly from memory later. This partly relates to *epistemic rationality*, a term to describe the factual reality of beliefs.[11] Many people maintain false beliefs that can influence how they categorize information. If something is remembered through an unsuitable category, then recall will also be inaccurate. Therefore, people who think they saw or heard something that did not happen will remember it inaccurately through no deliberate—or conscious—fault. Even when events are highly emotionally charged, it does not mean that they can be accurately recalled and various exogenous sources for information may result in *source confusion* that means the original source for the memory is lost.[12] Source confusion explains how witnesses can contaminate each other's memories if allowed to communicate prior to interviewing. One witness may provide some details that another witness did not have, or possibly could not have. The receiving witness nevertheless incorporates the information into their own memory without realizing it is not from the original memory and the memory is unknowingly contaminated. Witnesses discussing the matter also results in confabulation as efforts to construct a plausible narrative occurs. Even in instances of high emotion, memory may be affected. Emotional arousal can reduce completeness of memory while also increasing accuracy across a much narrower range.[13] As a result, people may genuinely misremember an event or falsely believe something happened that did not. It is noteworthy to comment that a difference in two accounts of the same event may not involve deception but mistaken belief in what happened or was witnessed. In fact, statements taken from supposedly independent witnesses that match in every detail should be regarded with some suspicion, as independent witnesses should never remember the same event in exactly the same way. In sum, memories are unreliable and even well-intentioned interviewees may inadvertently mislead because of memory issues or confusion over what they actually saw or heard. Nonetheless, a combination of wanting to help and the natural process of filling in gaps by using past experiences can generate a plausible memory but that is inaccurate. In this category, one could also put interviewees who tell you information that they think you want to hear, as they believe this is helpful. Similarly, somebody who answers a question with what they think is the correct way to answer the question may be doing so from loyalty to the organization, in such a situation, you may get a quote from a company policy when you ask how something is done instead of the reality. This is not deliberate deception, usually. But such instances highlight why corroborating information received from witnesses through other evidence is vital and why maintaining skepticism is essential to obtaining the truth.

Deliberate Deception

Such unintended deception can be difficult to overcome as the person may genuinely believe that they are telling the truth. Careful questioning through probing the account and the careful use of evidence can help to identify where the account has strayed when you are dealing with a cooperative interviewee. Of course, on other occasions, the deception is intentional with a desire to supply false information to protect the interviewee or someone else. Sometimes, the deception is about falsely accusing someone. For our purposes, lying is a deliberate effort to deceive in investigative matters and this includes the giving of literal truths, or the omission of important information.

Fabricating stories and keeping them straight under questioning is cognitively demanding and takes considerable mental effort to achieve effectively, a phenomenon known as *cognitive load*, as the person must factor in both truth and lies into their reasoning. An alternative to complete fabrication is to blend in as much truth as possible as this makes the deception harder to detect and the less fabrication needed, the easier it is to keep a story straight. Accordingly, a good liar will use as much truth as possible, possibly the truthful events of another time or place, for example, as a template on which to build the lie. The less that has to be added to alter the account necessary to deceive, the better from the deceiver's perspective. Consequently, the interviewer should be alert for subtle efforts to misrepresent the truth; literal truths, evading the question asked, using ambiguous language, and omitting relevant details, which are all examples of more subtle mendacity that can be easier to disguise as less guilt is involved than a barefaced full lie. Nevertheless, the more serious the matter under investigation, and the more at stake for the deceiver in terms of reputation and other potential adverse outcomes, the greater the psychological pressure on the deceiver, which is important from a detection standpoint. In general, the higher the motivation to complete the deception, the more emotion that is involved and the more likely it is that this high emotional arousal will reveal the deception. This is known as the *motivational impairment effect,* as the harder someone tries, the poorer their performance may potentially be.[14]

Detecting deceit is as old as deceit itself. Over the years, detecting deceit has attracted folk wisdom and many fallacies. Freud believed that people found keeping secrets difficult and that even when the lips were silent the fingers would chatter to relieve anxiety, he further believed people found confessing a tremendous psychological relief.[15] Recent research does seem to suggest that carrying a deep secret involves extra cognitive work and which may mean that concomitant physical tasks also require additional effort, almost as if a person was carrying additional physical weight.[16] Some of the misconceptions around the manifested signals of lying can cause people to overestimate their own skill at detecting lies, believing themselves more astute at spotting the behavioral signs than they really are.[17] One common folk wisdom deceit 'tell' is gaze aversion or the inability to look someone in the eye. This is a particularly poor indicator of deception, but it is not that some people do not avert their gaze when they lie, rather that other liars do the exact opposite when lying and instead intentionally stare. People engaged in deception must adopt countermeasures to prevent detection and may deliberately use the strategy of looking their conversation partner in the eye when trying to convince them of something false. Gaze aversion might also be related to unconnected factors such as embarrassment, and like or dislike of the interviewer. Another factor to bear in mind is that in some cultures holding a person's gaze is considered rude. There are other misleading beliefs about what happens when someone is lying. Some literature, for instance, neuro-linguistic programming (NLP) literature suggests that eye movement is up and to the left when someone is trying to construct an account (which has been interpreted to mean lies) but there is no academic evidence of such movement linked to deceit.[18] Another fallacious belief is that liars are less helpful than truthtellers, but liars may in fact try to be even more helpful than usual and there have been many incidences of killers joining in the search for the victim. Such misconceptions have unfortunately entered mainstream consciousness with poor scientific grounding.[19] To compound matters, many academic studies utilize college students in low stake situations to examine detection indicators and are therefore poorly constructed in relation to real-world situations. Compared to students, research has established that criminals, who often are immersed in deceit, have heightened skills in their ability to lie, to maintain a lie, and to detect deceit as a result.[20] On the flip side, this is achieved because of a bias toward disbelieving. In other words, one can be very good at detecting deceit if you never believe anyone. This can be effective, but such cynicism can be damaging to rapport. To maintain an objective position is to accept that some people can be very good liars and appear very credible, that it can be difficult to pinpoint the often subtle signs of deception, and that there is unlikely to be consistent reliable feedback to improve one's abilities. Unfortunately, this simple reality does not stop even professionals from overestimating their lie detection skills.[21]

As even truthful people can exhibit deception signals if they are anxious to be believed, it is important to treat any signals or signs of lying as worthy of suspicion but never as conclusive proof. In addition, one should always be aware of idiosyncratic differences such as social anxiety levels as not everyone is comfortable in social exchanges. There is even a phenomenon known as the 'Othello error' that refers to socially anxious people exhibiting signs of nervousness that create an impression of deception.[22] As a result, any such indicators are 'hot spots' that are not conclusive in themselves but are worthy of further probing.

The most important indicator of deception is a change in behavior during the interview. The rapport stage will be a generally neutral or positive encounter, possibly with some signs of nervousness, which the interviewer will try to alleviate, and this helps to create a good baseline of individual behavior. This also establishes individual idiosyncrasies which may be of relevance, such as anxiety, as well as the interviewee's gestures and posture. That said, it is important to be aware that using the rapport or small talk phase of an interview to provide a baseline for behavior to compare to when the interviewee is under psychological pressure is problematic as they are two very different contexts. Ideally, an important contributor to establishing a baseline is to note changes under comparable contentious segments to note variations. Noticing changes in behavior is the first step in detecting deceit. Next is interpreting the meaning behind those changes. The deceiver must respond to challenges or requests for clarification. All of it while under the stress of discovery and any possible consequences. In other words, some behavioral indicators are likely the consequence of the cognitive load of maintaining deception while being challenged.

This behavioral change falls into two broad categories, verbal and nonverbal behavior. There is a tremendous advantage in having two interviewers with both listening to the account for contradictions, vague replies, long pauses, or other indications of thinking hard, while also watching for nonverbal indicators. Watching for deception therefore requires a holistic approach with attention to multiple channels of an interviewee's behavior.[23] The timing of behavioral changes is also important. Houston et al argue that as we think ten times the speed that we speak then the congruence of deception indicators and stimulus must happen within 5 seconds of the question. As importantly, to be of significance, the indicators should appear as a cluster, so a cluster of verbal and nonverbal changes occurring within 5 seconds is a good indicator of deception.[24] However, pay particular attention as you ask the question. When it is a particularly contentious question and the interviewee understands what you are about to ask, you may see behavioral changes before you have even finished talking, as he or she struggles to formulate a response. This behavioral change may be as subtle as a widening of the eyes. The more of the following indicators present, the more likely deceit is deliberate, but an investigator must probe further with more questioning to confirm this suspicion.

Verbal Indicators

The best verbal indicators of attempted deceit are answers to questions that are contradictory. Another good indicator is an interviewee continually changing their account, possibly with contradictions as well. Unfortunately, not every liar is careless, and some deceptive accounts are carefully planned. Nonetheless, keeping all elements of the deception together can be cognitively demanding and this may result in various verbal indicators. These may include long pauses, word repetitions, or errors, sometimes in conjunction with nonverbal behaviors such as a decrease in hand and finger movements. The behavioral pattern impression given overall by the deceiver may be that of someone who is having to think very hard in answering.[25] This phenomenon may be a more useful observation to reflect on than trying to answer: 'is this person lying to me?' Importantly, the way someone is interviewed is going to be important in helping to reveal deception; the non-accusatory fact-finding interview is preferable to the accusatory interview model as with the accusatory model or with closed questions generally fewer nonverbal signals are available as a guide and both innocent and guilty will be affected by negative emotions.[26] Therefore, the more freedom the speaker has to construct long answers, the more the language will indicate deception. Using open questioning is to allow more developed answers from the interviewee; consequently, a reluctance to expand on answers by the interviewee but instead, staying with short and factual answers may serve as another useful hot spot indicator.

Pauses may be the result as the interviewee tries to formulate an answer or loses cognitive coherence in the middle of sentences. Repeating the question is a common tactic as it disguises this cognitive struggle somewhat. Similarly, non-answer statements such as: 'that's a good question' or 'I'm glad you asked me that' are all methods of fudging to allow more time to think.[27] Guilt and fear are both negative emotions and may also leak into language used by the liar. This may include negative comments—words such as *hate, useless, dislike*—and a tendency to dissociate themselves from statements that they make. This means the replies may seem more impersonal; 'someone did it' rather than 'I did it'. Liars use linguistic constructions to distance themselves from their listeners or the contents of their accounts. This may result in the account, in general, sounding more evasive, unclear, and impersonal. It is difficult to suppress emotions while focusing on a higher executive brain function such as keeping your story straight. In one study of real-life high stakes interviews, the telling differences noted were that liars blinked less and paused more often in answering, with greater use of verbal fillers such as 'ah' or 'um' type language.[28] Liars, as a result, sound more reluctant with an overall increase in disfluency.

As well as little information, an interviewee may provide too much irrelevant information. This is padding and is an attempt to fill time as well as to keep talking but avoid the question. An interviewee may also try to pivot away from the difficult subject by bolstering something that he or she is proud of, such as charity work or rewards received. It's almost a subconscious attempt to say: 'you couldn't possibly think a nice and good person as me would be deviant, could you?'[29] It is therefore critical to pay particular attention to any misalignment between the answer given and the question asked, a person may give an answer, it may even be comprehensive and informative, but it may not actually answer the question that you asked. Another tactic often used is lying by omission by excluding important details and many people find it much easier to lie by omission than commission. If the question is too general or not precise enough, then the deceiver may give an honest answer to a very specific question. In other words, if the question allows some wiggle room or is not quite on the mark, people will provide the answer to the question that suits them to answer. It may involve answering with qualified language, that is, an answer that is overly specific and provides for wiggle room in its exactness. For example, if when answering the question: 'where you ever in London?' the answer given is: 'I was never there in August', suggests there is a qualified answer and careful listening is important to hear that qualification. The answer is not to the question exactly but an answer to another more defined question, one that the person can be truthful about. The qualified answer may be preceded by a pause as the person struggles to frame an evasive answer. Consequently, listening carefully is one of the most important skills in interviewing somebody. Framing questions is also important but being so fixated on the next question you want to ask is going to give unsatisfactory results. Ensure you have been given a full answer to your question. It helps to allow long pauses before asking the next question, especially during critical phases of the interview. Asking the same question in a different format is also a useful tactic, sometimes dispersing them throughout the interview. The deceiver must keep all the details of the lie straight and making it harder for him or her by jumping in and out of the narrative at various points is a good strategy. Likewise, asking the person to provide the narrative in reverse chronological order is another useful counter-deception tactic.[30]

Habitual liars often avoid cognitive load by being generally evasive thereby never committing to any position. This often works superficially, but careful and methodical probing usually exposes the shallowness. On the other hand, good deception involves blending in as much truth as possible into the narrative as this too lessens cognitive load. The person only needs to recall a remembered event and change one or two details. This also has an advantage to the liar in that they are not expressing any signs of deception for most of the account. In other words, lies may be based on personal experiences with some critical details altered. Both the verbal and nonverbal indicators of deception risk giving the game away so minimizing those are important to the deceiver. If an account can be genuinely comprised of mainly truthful memories, the deceiver has an advantage. From an investigator's perspective, therefore it is imperative to ignore truthful behaviors when accessing truthfulness.[31] However, most deception scripts are not deep, so probing and consistent questioning over time may reveal discrepancies in accounts given. Truthtellers often appear less concerned with minor mistakes resulting from a fallible memory than liars who can be anxious to maintain consistency and may become defensive about uncertainties, an inability to remember or being asked to clarify.[32] Truthtellers will usually admit a lack of memory, willingly correct imperfections in the narrative, or express self-doubts.

While there may be a change in vocal tone and pitch with a slowing down of pace in many instances of deception, where someone has had time to prepare their script, the effect may appear to be opposite; talking speed may increase with fewer natural pauses, as if the person is anxious to get the story out quickly before it is forgotten. Naturally, the more time a person has to prepare his or her deception, the more consistent the account. Therefore, if serious matters are under investigation, it makes strategic sense to avoid revealing information about the investigation that gives perpetrators an opportunity to work, individually or collectively, on a constructed account. Careful listening is the essential skill in interviewing and in detecting deception.[33]

Nonverbal Indicators

The detecting of deception involves two separate components, listening to the language spoken and watching for the nonverbal indicators, so it requires strenuous effort on the interviewer's part to both listen and watch at the same time. As previously mentioned, most human communication is nonverbal so watching is very important; body posture, hand and facial gestures, sounds, and gaze are all useful indicators of the emotional state of the person exhibiting those behaviors. This will appear as behavior that may unconsciously trigger warnings in the observer, although it may be difficult to articulate what is the trigger other than using a word like 'hinky' or suspicious. Nonverbal indicators can therefore be of particular use in trying to establish if someone is being dishonest when they communicate. Unfortunately, this aspect of behavior is notoriously difficult to accurately describe and there are no studies showing any definitive results. This is not helped by idiosyncratic responses to stress. When someone is trying to be deceptive in their communication, they will consciously be trying to hide important emotions. The most common emotion likely to be involved is fear as hiding a secret involves deception that if uncovered may have serious consequences for the deceiver. Many people also experience guilt or shame when they do something wrong or believe other people think that they have. These emotions can result from conflict with the self-esteem of the person and this conflict may result in physiological changes throughout the body.[34] Shame seems to have a characteristic demeanor that includes gaze aversion, a closed posture, and a tendency to withdraw.[35] Negative personality traits such as narcissists react particularly badly to being challenged.[36] Moreover, in many cases, such negative personalities may have come to believe their own lies. Generally though, the act of lying may activate such emotions that threaten to reveal incongruous emotions to the account being given and reveal the lie. These emotional indicators may be the result of 'leakage' which is the unintended expression of emotion. It should not be expected that any account be emotion free, but it is normally the presence of emotional indicators incongruent to the words being spoken that is the useful indicator of deceit.

Emotional leakage may occur through the limbs, such as nervous tapping of fingers or legs. The person may begin shifting in their chair or fidgeting excessively when an uncomfortable question is being asked, even before the question is finished. A person may exhibit nonverbal agitation with the questioning by shaking their head or grimacing before the question is even finished, or by a widening of the eyes. The dilation (opening) of the pupil in the eyes itself is a strong indicator of cognitive processing effort and may provide a rapid visible response, although the difference between dilation and contraction may be very small and probably undetectable realistically.[37]

The most useful source of information about emotions is the face. Research and lived experience suggest that the physiological manifestations of most emotional activation include a corresponding facial expression.[38] The muscles involved in many of these expressions are beyond our conscious control, thus it is difficult to activate them unless there is the underlying emotion. For many, these display as macro emotions which last some time and are relatively easy to interpret. Liars may try to prevent these expressions by exerting self-control to prevent leaking these physical signals of emotions. This can result in a wooden appearance as a person tries to control the expression of body language. However, it can be difficult to achieve complete control especially in a cognitive load condition. As a result, sometimes, the facial expression may appear only fleetingly, perhaps for as little as 1/25th of a second. This is very little time to even consciously process the expression, but it suggests closely monitoring an interviewee may reveal incongruous emotional leakage, especially in facial expressions.[39] This is not without controversy and these micro-expressions are difficult to definitively rely on as they can be relatively rare; moreover, frequently, they can lead to false positives.[40]

When speaking, it is common that the hands are also moving and making gestures, known as illustrators, such as for emphasis. Individuals vary in the use of these, so comparison with the same individual is important.[41] In an effort to appear calm, liars may deliberately try to reduce or eliminate entirely these illustrators. However, the use of the hands to touch the face, to rub the neck, sweep back the hair, or to fix up clothing are known as self-grooming gestures, and it is likely that there will be an increase in these at times of high cognitive load.[42] Efforts to maintain a tight control over nonverbal behavior may again make the interviewee appear wooden or otherwise unusually restrained. It is difficult to control everything though and even when the upper body and face is under tight control, the lower limbs may still be communicating.[43] Watching the feet and legs is therefore a good idea as the feet may literally be dancing even as the upper body is immobile. An unusual nonverbal indicator that DePaulo et al discovered was that more often than truth tellers, liars raised their chins up while staring into the other person's eye with medially raised brows. This corresponds to studies of facial expressions in conflict situations, where a similar facial constellation, called a *plus face*, has been identified.[44] This suggests that sometimes the deceiver is almost aggressive in their efforts at deception.

It will not be unusual for liars to be anxious to manage their image and will therefore try to impress the interviewers with their honesty and sincerity. A frequently used proxy for both is friendliness. Smiling and being agreeable is one tactic to disarm investigators. Liars may also display more fake smiles than truthtellers, to encourage a positive perception in the eyes of the receiver.[45] It is therefore important to compare the same person across the interview for any noticeable changes in body language and behaviors. This does not mean that everyone who is being friendly is being deceitful, rather a deceitful person will try to appear friendly. Of course, it is difficult to feel genuine enjoyment when stressed as liars usually are in such situations, so liars will fake the smile. A genuine smile involves the orbicularis oculi muscle that produces laughter lines around the eyes when a person is reacting joyfully to a stimulus. It is not possible to consciously control the orbicularis oculi muscle, but it is easy to produce an artificial smile using just the lips without the wrinkles around the eyes and this may indicate that the smile is not genuine.[46] However, in some circumstances, the liar may also produce a genuine smile because they are enjoying themselves; '*duping delight*' is a term used to describe a smile given in an inappropriate situation by the deceiver, possibly as a result of the pleasure he or she is getting from succeeding in his or her deceit or believing it to be successful.[47]

A word of caution about nonverbal behaviors as indicators of deception is necessary—especially visual cues. There is less accuracy and a tendency to be biased toward believing deception is present when using such indicators exclusively.[48] Furthermore, it is also possible that a good liar displays none of these indicators and it is foolish to be overly reliant on their presence or absence. Individuals differ significantly in behavior when under stress of being questioned and it is probably impossible to identify any consistent cue in all (or most) liars.[49] Heuristics and the various judgment biases are as relevant here as everywhere else. It is therefore important to be alert to the clustering of both verbal and nonverbal behaviors and to note them as 'hot spots' of possible indicators of deception through demeanor. These indicators are then probed further in much greater depth with any available evidence used. In other words, rather than simply relying on passive observation, an interactive approach where critical thinking, careful questioning, and using available evidence is much more likely to reveal deception in an interviewee.[50]

Evidence in the Interview

As important as detecting deceit is, it is usually not enough to know that someone is lying. On occasions, it is sufficient and may lead to an important breakthrough but too often it does not really move the investigation on. There are a lot of difficulties in relying on detecting deceit with too many professional investigators being (erroneously) highly overconfident in their ability to detect deceit.[51] Moving the investigation from suspecting the interviewee is lying to getting a truthful account requires much more work from the interviewer as without some incentive, many will continue to stick to the lie. One of the advantages of the funnel questioning method, by starting broad and slowly beginning to focus the probing questions on smaller and smaller details, is that most people do not prepare their lies comprehensively enough and inconsistencies begin to emerge. I recommend not jumping on the first one or two inconsistencies. It is better to tackle them as a cluster. This probing should be done cautiously, without any accusations of deceit. It is important to realize that memory failings, nervousness, or simple verbal ability to explain may be responsible for the inconsistencies. Therefore, the usual: 'I don't quite understand what you meant by…' or 'I am confused by…' allows rapport to be maintained. Given sufficient time and dedication, few deceitful accounts will stand up to such detailed probing.

Ideally, however, the interviewer has additional information that can be leveraged in the interview. Thus, the careful gathering of evidence is very important. Having evidence is the most effective way both to uncover deceit and to move a deceitful person to giving a truthful account. In addition, having evidence is a powerful ally when dealing with reluctant interviewees. The Conversation Management method can move the interview toward a traditional police interview with an uncooperative suspect. On most occasions in the organizational sphere, its use is only warranted intermittently, and rarely is its sustained use necessary. Nonetheless, if the interviewee remains combative throughout an interview, there is little choice but to use the formal questioning method of conversation management. When doing so, it becomes even more essential to base the questions around the available evidence gathered. Good prior preparation is always useful, for difficult interviews, it is imperative. There is nothing more disheartening, frustrating (for everyone), and demoralizing than trying to conduct an interview without some evidence to base questions on or challenge accounts with. Such interviews all too often devolve to pantomime assertions made by interviewers of 'you did it' met with denials of 'no I didn't'. Many police interviews were doomed from the beginning because there was little preparation done and no evidence was gathered. Evidence is used to build a hypothesis about the events under investigation, such hypotheses may ultimately be in error, but a hypothesis provides a framework to base questions on. Furthermore, evidence is vital to building a challenge to an account, whether suspected of being deceitful or not.

Nevertheless, there is an important distinction to be made between having evidence and knowing how to use it properly. Evidence must be used strategically to maximize its effectiveness. Generally, it is best to get as full an account as possible before introducing evidence. The account should then be probed, this is partly to verify the account through detailed questioning and to obtain possible alternative explanations for the presence of evidence. It is also about being aware of possible excuses or alibis that might be constructed to explain away the evidence, so challenging and clarifying the account is important before producing any piece of evidence.

As covered, challenging accounts can include asking the subject to reverse the chronology of their account. Starting at the end and working backwards is a very effective technique to test an account as it increases cognitive load significantly. Ask event-irrelevant questions. Ask questions in different formats—for example, date of birth and age. Use open questions for longer accounts. Return to a topic after an interval from a different angle and probe deeper. Do not be afraid about repeating certain questions, especially if you are not satisfied with the answers. Such questions as 'what happened then?' or 'why did that happen?' can be used repeatedly to probe. A good memory or short notes are essential in pulling out all the inconsistencies. Hence, good preparation in advance and having a quiet interview room assists in the necessary listening and attention to detail crucial to detecting deceit. In many interviewee-resistant situations or where deception is actively being used, the available evidence is key to getting the truth from the interviewee. Consistently it has been established that the most effective tactic and the single most important determinant in obtaining admissions is the strength of the available evidence.[52] Therefore, the planning about what information to disclose and what to withhold is pivotal to a successful interview.

Strategically Using Evidence

While the purpose of the interview of somebody suspected of deviance is to allow the person suspected an opportunity to offer any explanation that they may have for the evidence available, the evidence should ideally be presented in a coordinated and strategic manner to maximize its potential. It was once a common tactic to reveal all the evidence at the outset of the interview and one study of English police interviewing found almost a third of suspects admitted culpability from the outset, partly as the evidence was also all disclosed at that stage.[53] This strategy is not recommended. It can be very adversarial, even confrontational, and it is unlikely to assist with rapport building. Furthermore, it was used as part of an accusatory approach that assumed guilt while doing nothing to encourage the interviewee to provide an account. Another problem is that it is conceivable that in certain cases such a tactic risks exposing the weakness of the investigation case from the beginning. More importantly, getting an account before introducing evidence has been shown to improve lie detection.[54]

Instead, the strategic disclosure of evidence should be carefully planned at the planning stage to avoid making inappropriate disclosures. For instance, revealing evidence without having asked probing questions to clarify the situation or establish possible alternative explanations may simply require the interviewee to concoct an explanation reasonable in the circumstances or an alibi. Therefore, the investigators should first probe possible innocent explanations for a given piece of evidence, and these should be explored and eliminated with the interviewee before ever revealing the evidence and challenging the interviewee on the discrepancy. For instance, where a statement from an eyewitness makes incriminating claims, the interviewee should be asked about personal relationships or animosities in the workplace generally, then a specific area, before a specific person is mentioned. The objective is to eliminate any possible reason or motive, such as malice, that the interviewee could claim is the real basis of the claims of the eyewitness. Evidence, in this sense, is therefore not just the physical evidence gathered but also witness statements, or indeed, admissions from other interviewees. In a scenario where somebody has done something, such as the creation of a document, in clear violation of written company policies, the questioning should encompass knowledge of company policies, perhaps in an unrelated area, before narrowing down to the area of concern together with training received on the polices. The objective is to avoid a later defense of a fabricated claim of lack of knowledge of procedures and policies or poor training when presenting the documents.

In the Netherlands, the police focus on getting a full written statement of denial before introducing any evidence at the very end of the interview to challenge the account given.[55] However, this method—known as the Strategic Use of Evidence (SUE) method—places a considerable cognitive load on interviewers who need to continue questioning while also developing all discrepancies with the information known to them, so some form of notekeeping is necessary.[56]

In the United Kingdom, enhancements to the PEACE model include an evidence-based questioning method known as GRIMACE.[57] This mnemonic stands for Gathering Reliable Information, Motivating an Account, and then Challenging this Effectively. The GRIMACE technique employs a 'drip feed, gradual' approach to revealing information, in which revelation occurs throughout the questioning phase of an interview rather than at the very end.[58] Ray Bull emphasizes that the successful interviewing of guilty persons involves the minimum use of 'negative feedback' (repeated accusations of lying) as well as the strategic revealing of evidence. While both the SUE method and GRIMACE increase cognitive load in interviewees, Bull claims GRIMACE is more effective as the strategy places the deceptive interviewee in a tactically weak and difficult position, often exposing his deception. Others agree that drip-feeding information to the interviewee is the best method of disclosing evidence and provides useful feedback on the interviewee through its effect on reactions and behaviors.[59]

Either method can be used depending on the situation. And of particular importance is the amount and quality of evidence in the hands of the interviewers. Where a significant piece of evidence is available, it may be more appropriate to disclose it immediately if the person makes a contradictory claim during the account. It depends on the type of investigation and what is needed from the interview. Usually, the concept is to introduce evidence only after a full account has been first given, probed, clarified, and challenged first. The challenge may not be very robust at this point, possibly a question such as: 'are you sure about that?' may be sufficient. Once the free account has been so explored, the interviewer may wish to cover some other areas that were not mentioned by the interviewee first before introducing evidence. Plausibility is an important factor in answers, and it may be appropriate to mention that at certain points with comments such as 'that seems a very unusual occurrence' or 'that just appears somewhat implausible to me' may be useful at this point. Once the interviewer is satisfied that the interviewee will not volunteer any other information, the interviewer returns to some topics and points out what the interviewee said and then incrementally introduces the evidence. This evidence is usually contradictory. Often corroborating evidence need not be mentioned directly to the interviewee, but simply noted by the interviewers. With deceptive interviewees, there is value however in covering all available evidence meticulously. It can be particularly disconcerting for deceptive interviewees to ask questions that you know the answers to and can produce evidence for. Contradictory evidence should be carefully considered. The interviewer should challenge separately for each piece of information disclosed with any contradictions and inconsistencies in the account being raised and carefully pointed out before an explanation is sought for the discrepancy. Again, there is no need for aggression, and a confused 'I'm trying to get to the truth' approach generally works best. Simply point out that 'you have said this happened, yet I have this statement or this item of evidence that says something else happen, why is there this inconsistency?'

As noted, it is important to try to examine other likely explanations for the presence of evidence before disclosing it. For example, it is important to establish if anyone else had access to the interviewee's password or keycard before introducing such evidence. Such questions can be asked to clarify before evidence of relevant access is mentioned. Asking questions related to the evidence before confronting the suspect with the evidence is likely to affect the interviewee's perception of proof, thereby increasing the internal pressure and cognitive load.[60] At this point, where discrepancies are disclosed and no sensible or plausible explanations are offered, it may be useful to point these out somewhat forcefully. Do not be aggressive, but this is a stage of the interview where understatement is not the best course of action! Keep asking for a sensible explanation, if you do not believe the explanation given, point that out by observing that such an answer does not appear credible. Explain slowly and methodically what you believe the evidence is suggesting. Do not accept half answers and be alert to diversionary tactics. The divisionary tactics of whataboutisms or everyone else is doing the same thing or worse claims should be terminated with a 'I'm only interested in your situation right now' statement and point out this interview has a very narrow and specific focus.

In many interview situations, getting an account tying the person to an account or version of events that you can easily disprove with alternative evidence, or an incoherent account with implausible explanations, is good evidence in itself so that when you are unable to get the truth, you are able to get demonstrable lies.[61]

The closure stage of the interview should also then carefully summarize and highlight all these contradictions or inconsistencies revealed along with any narrative changes that occurred when the discrepancies were pointed out. This can become contentious as the interviewee may not like the flip-flopping from account to account that becomes highlighted as he or she tried to fit the evidence into their narrative. It is important to remain calm at this point and explain that the investigators are neutral, simply trying to get the truth, and dependent on the integrity of the interviewee. This method, even if no admissions are forthcoming, presents a powerful piece of evidence where the interview subject is seen as desperately changing his or her story as evidence emerged to challenge their narrative. It may be of use to offer another opportunity to be truthful to the interviewee at this stage, but that is based on the demeanor of the interviewee. Unfortunately, often when people have backed themselves into a corner, it can be difficult for them to reverse course, even when clear and unambiguous evidence shows them to be lying.

Evidence that has been gathered that is presented should be described for the purpose of the electronic recording (if used) and any reference number such as the catalogue/exhibit or statement number cited. If it is a statement from somebody else taken in the investigation, then the necessary passage or phrase should be read over, and an offer made to allow the interviewee to read it for himself or herself. Photos can be used instead of physical evidence. On occasions, it will be necessary to bring in the actual item to be identified by the interviewee and when this is done should be planned but showing a photo first can be effective and more tactically useful.

It is important to bear in mind the need for critical thinking throughout as too often investigators assume that deceit is used only in denying an allegation. Unfortunately, there have been cases where an interviewee admits guilt to something he or she has not done. Generally, this is a result of a deep psychological need to please or gain approval, but other reasons could be trying to protect another. Such interviewees have been very skillful at interpreting and drawing out pertinent information from the interviewers to make the account more credible. Therefore, be very wary of giving out investigative information too easily or allowing a person to gather information from the evidence introduced. This is a particular criticism of using crime scene photographs too early at interviews, as the interviewee now has a lot of useful information with which to build a credible although false confession.

Adverse Inferences

The getting of implausible explanations for solid evidence leads to a situation where there is an inference that the person is lying, otherwise known as an *adverse inference*.[62] In some ways, the increasing use of non-accusatory questioning techniques have also influenced the adoption of legal presumptions. In common-law countries, suspects have a right to silence that is usually interpreted as the right not to answer police questions even if the police have a right to ask them. As police questioning has increasingly focused on fact-finding rather than seeking confessions, the ability of the legal system to penalize a suspect who refuses to answer certain questions by risking an adverse inference being drawn has become a powerful tool in building criminal cases.

The adverse inference might work like this: a suspect is being questioned about a stabbing that occurred the previous night outside a nightclub.[63] The suspect is refusing to answer questions and is simply responding 'no comment' to every question. After making a number of attempts to get an account from the suspect, the investigators will begin to introduce evidence that has been gathered. For illustration purposes, let us assume that a search of the suspect's home has recovered a blood-stained shirt, and CCTV footage shows someone similar to the suspect running from the scene of the stabbing. Obviously, the blood will need to be tested and in an ideal world will match to the victim but that takes time and may not be yet available to investigators. The CCTV, as often happens, is not great quality and too grainy to clearly identify anyone. Throughout the interview, the suspect will be asked questions such as his whereabouts at the time of the stabbing, what he was wearing the previous night, the last time he was in the area, who he was with over last two days, to which the only reply is consistently 'no comment' to every question. The shirt will be produced, but not before questions such as 'do you own a Farah light blue long sleeve cotton shirt?' and 'when was the last time you wore this shirt?' are asked. The shirt is then produced to the suspect, and he is again asked if this is his shirt. The blood stains are referenced, and the suspect will be asked to account for the presence of blood on the shirt. If the suspect continues to refuse or fail to provide an account, then the investigator will explain his or her belief that the blood may be the victim's blood and may thus link the suspect directly to the crime. The investigator will explain that if the suspect fails to provide an alternative explanation, then a court, in deciding any question of guilt, might take an inference from the failure to answer the question that it was because the suspect had no alternative plausible explanation for the presence of the blood other than it being because of the stabbing. A similar method is used to account for the person's presence at the scene.

That is a very basic illustration of the use of adverse inferences for the purposes of a criminal prosecution, but the same approach can be used in the circumstances of a corporate investigation. The evidence is produced only after an opportunity to provide an alternative explanation is examined. Once produced and the person declines to answer, it should be explained what the evidence seems to be telling the investigator. This then is the opportunity for the interviewee to correct the record if there is another plausible explanation. If the person declines to provide an answer, then it should be emphasized that as there seems to be only the investigators interpretation that is available, and the person is not providing any other, then the investigator's interpretation must be correct.

This technique should only be used as a last resort in cases of total uncooperative behavior from the interviewee and where appropriate evidence exists. The investigators try to get an explanation for the available evidence and the interviewee will have been given an opportunity to explain it. The problem-solving approach is probably the best approach to use even in these circumstances. After all, on its own such evidence is at best circumstantial. In criminal cases, there would be no possibility of a conviction based solely on adverse inference references so bear the limitations of them in mind. In my experience, however, I have found the tactic very useful in getting the interviewee to begin talking, which allows a relatively normal interview to be used. So, it is another useful tool in the toolbox and uses the drip feeding of evidence and creates some psychological pressure to provide an alternative answer to the investigator's interpretation, especially if the person has one.

It is also a powerful way to negate the use of non-answers, especially the type such as: 'I don't remember'. In such a case, it is useful to point out that it is not a denial and that it may have been possible that it happened. In such a scenario, the investigator is pointing out the adverse inference that can be taken from the use of memory fault answers. I would caution that it is important to only use this tactic where it is clearly being used as a counter-interview measure, it would not be appropriate to use in genuine cases of lapsed memories. In both cases of claimed memory loss or refusal to provide an explanation or answer, the investigator has an opportunity to provide an interpretation for the available evidence. The interviewee is offered the opportunity to correct the record and provide an alternative explanation again and failure to do so is good evidence.

Conclusion

Detecting deception is difficult. Ideally, a good baseline of behavior can be established and when the interviewee strays into changed behaviors, this is obvious. The liar is under additional cognitive load and sometimes this appears as someone trying to think very hard to answer what should be relatively simple questions. Behavioral indicators may escape from the liar, in the form of verbal cues and nonverbal signs. Listening carefully to the answers you receive and especially to incomplete answers is therefore very effective at detecting deceit. Qualified language in the answer may be an important indicator of deception. A change in the use of illustrators, either less use (more frozen) or increased use is another possible indicator. What is important is the timing of these changes and the appearance of them in clusters. Any signs of deception provide only an indicator as for various reasons, there may exist more innocuous explanations for their presence. Therefore, tread cautiously and probe further.

As important as it is to know someone is lying, getting them to admit the truth is more important. Essentially, the best method is the tactical use of whatever evidence has been uncovered. Using this evidence carefully ensures when it is presented to the interviewee that its effect can be profound. This is often independent proof of their deception. As always, move slowly, maintaining rapport and demonstrating respect as much as possible. Avoid 'gotcha' moments. This is an ongoing process and it's important for the interviewer to maintain his or her professional composure. Unfortunately, there may be times that an interviewee refuses to even acknowledge the evidence you have presented, and it is necessary to change their perceptions that denial is a good strategy to one where they tell the truth. As a result, changing perceptions or using persuasion is the subject of the next chapter.

Notes

1 Bond, C. F. and DePaulo, B. M., "Accuracy in deception judgments", *Personality and Social Psychology Review*, (2006), 10 (3), pp 214–234: 215.

2 Harari, Y. N., *Sapiens: A Brief History of Humankind*, (Harville Secker, London, 2014).

3 Eysenck, H. J., "Biological Basis of Personality", *Nature*, (1963), 199(4898), pp 1031–1034.

4 Turpin, M. H., Kara-Yakoubian, M., Walker, A. C., Walker, H. E. K., Fugelsang, J. A. and Stolz, J. A., "Bullshit Ability as an Honest Signal of Intelligence", *Evolutionary Psychology*, (2021), 19(2), pp 1–10.

5 Stanovich, K. E., *The Robot's Rebellion: Finding Meaning in the Age of Darwin*, (University of Chicago, Chicago 2004); Mlodinow, L., *The Drunkards walk: How randomness rules our lives*, (Allen Lane, London, 2008).

6 Shaw, J., *The Memory Illusion*, (Penguin, London, 2016).

7 Dennett, D. C., Cohen, M. and Kanwisher, N., "What Is the Bandwidth of Perceptual Experience?", *Trends in Cognitive Sciences*, (2016), 20(5), pp 324–335.

8 Chabris, C. and Simons, D., *The Invisible Gorilla*, (HarperCollins, London, 2011).

9 Vrij, A., *Detecting Lies and Deceit*, (Wiley, Chichester, 2008): 248; Sacchi, D. L. M., Agnoli, F. and Loftus, E. F., "Changing History: Doctored Photographs Affect Memory for Past Public Events", *Applied Cognitive Psychology*, (2007), 21(8), pp 1005–1022.

10 Kaasa, S. O., Morris, E. K. and Loftus, E. F., "Remembering Why: Can People Consistently Recall Reasons for Their Behaviour?", *Applied Cognitive Psychology*, (2011), 25(1), pp 35–42.

11 Stanovich, K. E., *The Robot's Rebellion: Finding Meaning in the Age of Darwin,* (2004).

12 Kaasa, S. O., Morris, E. K. and Loftus, E. F., "Remembering Why: Can People Consistently Recall Reasons for Their Behaviour?", *Applied Cognitive Psychology,* (2011).

13 Nashiro, K. & Mather, M. 2011. How Arousal Affects Younger and Older Adults' Memory Binding. *Experimental aging research,* 37, pp 108–128.

14 Vrij, A., *Detecting Lies and Deceit,* (2008): 76.

15 Webster, R., *Why Freud was Wrong: Sin, Sex and Psychoanalysis,* (Orwell Press, Oxford, 2005).

16 Slepian, M. L., Masicampo, E. J., Toosi, N. R. and Ambady, N., "The Physical Burdens of Secrecy", *J Exp Psychol Gen,* (2012), 141(4), pp 619–24: 619.

17 Leach, A.-M., Lindsay, R. C. L., Koehler, R., Beaudry, J. L., Bala, N. C., Lee, K. and Talwar, V., "The Reliability of Lie Detection Performance", *Law & Human Behavior,* (2009), 33(1), pp 96–109: 96.

18 Wiseman, R., Watt, C., ten Brinke, L., Porter, S., Couper, S.-L. and Rankin, C., "The Eyes Don't Have It: Lie Detection and Neuro-Linguistic Programming", *PloS one,* (2012), 7(7), pp e40259–e40259.

19 Vrij, A., *Detecting Lies and Deceit,* (2008).

20 Hartwig, M., Granhag, P. A., Stromwall, L. A. and Kronkvist, O., "Strategic Use of Evidence During Police Interviews: When Training to Detect Deception Works", *Law & Human Behavior,* (2006), 30(5), pp 603–619: 604.

21 Vrij, A., Granhag, P. A. and Porter, S., "Pitfalls and Opportunities in Nonverbal and Verbal Lie Detection", *Psychological Science in the Public Interest,* (2010), 11(3), pp 89–121.

22 Vrij, A., Granhag, P. A. and Porter, S., "Pitfalls and Opportunities in Nonverbal and Verbal Lie Detection", *Psychological Science in the Public Interest,* (2010).

23 Porter, S. and ten Brinke, L., "The Truth About Lies: What Works in Detecting High-Stakes Deception?", *Legal and Criminological Psychology,* (2010), 15(1), pp 57–75: 57.

24 Houston, P., Floyd, M. and Carnicero, S., *Spy the Lie,* (St. Martins Press, New York, 2012).

25 Vrij, A., *Detecting Lies and Deceit,* (2008): 85.

26 Leach, A.-M., Lindsay, R. C. L., Koehler, R., Beaudry, J. L., Bala, N. C., Lee, K. and Talwar, V., "The Reliability of Lie Detection Performance", *Law & Human Behavior,* (2009).

27 Houston, P., Floyd, M. and Carnicero, S., *Spy the Lie,* (2012): 61.

28 Vrij, A., Mann, S. and Bull, R., "Suspects, Lies, and Videotape: An Analysis of Authentic High-Stake Liars", *Law & Human Behavior,* (2002), 26(3), pp 365–376: 371.

29 Houston, P., Floyd, M. and Carnicero, S., *Spy the Lie,* (2012).

30 Vrij, A., Granhag, P. A. and Porter, S., "Pitfalls and Opportunities in Nonverbal and Verbal Lie Detection", *Psychological Science in the Public Interest,* (2010).

31 Houston, P., Floyd, M. and Carnicero, S., *Spy the Lie,* (2012): 48.

32 Hartwig, M., Granhag, P. A., Stromwall, L. A. and Kronkvist, O., "Strategic Use of Evidence During Police Interviews: When Training to Detect Deception Works", *Law & Human Behavior,* (2006).

33 Porter, S. and ten Brinke, L., "The Truth About Lies: What Works in Detecting High-Stakes Deception?", *Legal and Criminological Psychology,* (2010).

34 A polygraph machine is designed to detect the subsequent physiological changes such as in perspiration, skin conductivity, heart rate, and breathing.

35 DePaulo, B. M., Lindsay, J. J., Malone, B. E., Muhlenbruck, L., Charlton, K. and Cooper, H., "Cues to Deception", *Psychological Bulletin*, (2003), 129(1), pp 74: 81.

36 Initially, narcissism is one of the Dark Triad of negative personality traits that also includes psychopathy and Machiavellianism. Sadism has been added to make it a Dark Tetrad. See Paulhus, D. L. and Williams, K. M., "The Dark Triad of Personality: Narcissism, Machiavellianism, and Psychopathy", *Journal of Research in Personality*, (2002), 36(6), pp 556–563, Buckels, E. E., Trapnell, P. D. and Paulhus, D. L., "Trolls Just Want To Have Fun", *Personality and Individual Differences*, (2014), 67, pp 97–102.

37 Hess, E. H., "Attitude and Pupil Size", *Scientific American*, (1965), 212, pp 46–54.

38 Ekman, P., "An Argument for Basic Emotions", *Cognition and Emotion*, (1992), 6(3/4), pp 169–200; Ekman, P., *Emotions Revealed: Understanding Faces and Feelings*, (Weidenfeld and Nicolson, London, 2003); Ekman, P., Friesen, W. V. and Ellsworth, P., *Emotion in the Human Face: Guidelines for Research and an Integration of Findings*, (Pergamon Press, New York, 1972).

39 Frank, M. G., Yarbrough, J. D. and Ekman, P., 'Investigative Interviewing and the Detection of Deception', (eds) Williamson, in *Investigative Interviewing: Rights, Research and Regulation*, (Willan, Cullompton, 2006) pp 229–255. Ekman suggests that with the proper training, success in spotting deception through monitoring facial micro-expressions can be brought as high as 80%, although this is considerably contested by other researchers.

40 Porter, S. and ten Brinke, L., "The Truth About Lies: What Works in Detecting High-Stakes Deception?", *Legal and Criminological Psychology*, (2010): 60. There is also controversy about the inherent reliability of the face as an emotional indicator, e.g., see Barrett, L. F., *How Emotions are made*, (Macmillan, London, 2017).

41 Porter, S. and ten Brinke, L., "The Truth About Lies: What Works in Detecting High-Stakes Deception?", *Legal and Criminological Psychology*, (2010): 64.

42 Navarro, J., *What Every Body Is Saying*, (William Morrow, New York, 2008).

43 Navarro, J., *What Every Body Is Saying*, (2008).

44 DePaulo, B. M., Lindsay, J. J., Malone, B. E., Muhlenbruck, L., Charlton, K. and Cooper, H., "Cues to Deception", *Psychological Bulletin*, (2003): 94.

45 Houston, P., Floyd, M. and Carnicero, S., *Spy the Lie*, (2012).

46 Vrij, A., *Detecting Lies and Deceit*, (2008): 76.

47 Ekman, P., "An Argument for Basic Emotions", *Cognition and Emotion*, (1992).

48 Vrij, A., "Nonverbal Dominance versus Verbal Accuracy in Lie Detection: A Plea to Change Police Practice", *Criminal Justice and Behavior*, (2008), 35(10), pp 1323–1336.

49 DePaulo, B. M., Lindsay, J. J., Malone, B. E., Muhlenbruck, L., Charlton, K. and Cooper, H., "Cues to Deception", *Psychological Bulletin*, (2003).

50 Levine, T. R., "Active Deception Detection", *Policy Insights from the Behavioral and Brain Sciences*, (2014), 1(1), pp 122–128, Levine, T. R., "Five Reasons Why I Am Skeptical That Indirect or Unconscious Lie Detection Is Superior to Direct Deception Detection", *Frontiers in Psychology*, (2019), 10(1354), pp 1–5.

51 Bond, C. F. and DePaulo, B. M., "Accuracy in Deception Judgments", *Personality and Social Psychology Review*, (2006), Vrij, A., Granhag, P. A. and Porter, S., "Pitfalls and Opportunities in Nonverbal and Verbal Lie Detection", *Psychological Science in the Public Interest*, (2010).

52 Moston, S., Stephenson, G. M. and Williamson, T. M., "The Effects of Case Characteristics on Suspect Behaviour During Police Questioning", *The British Journal of Criminology*, (1992), 32(1), pp 23–40, Pearse, J., 'Challenge, Compromise and Collaboration: Part of the Skill Set Necessary for Interviewing a Failed Suicide Bomber', (eds) Pearse, in *Investigating Terrorism: Current Political, Legal and Psychological Issues*, (John Wiley, Chichester, 2015) pp 45–66, Leo, R. A., "Inside the Interrogation Room", *Journal of Criminal Law & Criminology*, (1996), 86(2), pp 266–303, Williamson, T. M., 'Towards Greater Professionalism: Minimizing Miscarriages of Justice', (eds) Williamson, in *Investigative Interviewing: Rights, Research, Regulation*, (Willan, Cullompton, 2006) pp 147–166.

53 Baldwin, J., "Police Interview Techniques—Establishing Truth or Proof", *British Journal of Criminology*, (1993), 33(3), pp 325–352.

54 Vrij, A., Mann, S. A., Fisher, R. P., Leal, S., Milne, R. and Bull, R., "Increasing Cognitive Load to Facilitate Lie Detection: The Benefit of Recalling an Event in Reverse Order", *Law & Human Behavior*, (2008), 32(3), pp 253–265; Levine, T. R., "Active Deception Detection", *Policy Insights from the Behavioral and Brain Sciences*, (2014); Hartwig, M., Granhag, P. A., Stromwall, L. A. and Kronkvist, O., "Strategic Use of Evidence During Police Interviews: When Training to Detect Deception Works", *Law & Human Behavior*, (2006).

55 Sleen, J. V., 'A Structured Model for Investigative Interviewing of Suspects', (eds) Bull, Valentine and Williamson, in *Handbook of Psychology of Investigative Interviewing*, (Wiey-Blackwell, Chichester, 2009) pp 25–52: 38; Hartwig, M., Granhag, P. A., Stromwall, L. A. and Kronkvist, O., "Strategic Use of Evidence During Police Interviews: When Training to Detect Deception Works", *Law & Human Behavior*, (2006).

56 Dando, C. J. and Bull, R., "Maximising Opportunities to Detect Verbal Deception: Training Police Officers to Interview Tactically", *Journal of Investigative Psychology & Offender Profiling*, (2011), 8, pp 189–202: 192.

57 Bull, R., 'When in Interviews to Disclose Information to Suspects and to Challenge Them?', (eds) Bull, in *Investigative Interviewing*, (Springer, New York, 2014) pp 167–181.

58 Dando, C. J. and Bull, R., "Maximising Opportunities to Detect Verbal Deception: Training Police Officers to Interview Tactically", *Journal of Investigative Psychology & Offender Profiling*, (2011): 191.

59 Carter, P., 'Defence Counsel in Terrorism Trials', (eds) Pearse, in *Investigating Terrorism: Current Political, Legal and Psychological Issues*, (John Wiley, Chichester, 2015) pp 80–99.

60 Sleen, J. V., *A Structured Model for Investigative Interviewing of Suspects*, Bull, Valentine and Williamson, *Handbook of Psychology of Investigative Interviewing*, (2009): 46.

61 Hawkins, N., "Prosecution Perspectives", *The Investigator.*, (2012), (2), pp 31–33: 32.

62 Adverse inference is a legal term that has been used routinely over the last few decades in the United Kingdom. This has been partly as a result of the influence of European law that has impacted all criminal justice systems in the European Union through the decisions of the European Court of Human Rights. In most European countries, the criminal law uses presumptions, and the adverse inferences are a version of such presumptions. The civil regulatory and legal system, such as company regulatory inspectors or tax inspectors, have far wider scope in both the use of presumptions and powers to compel answers to questions. Generally, however, any

answers obtained cannot then be used in the criminal justice system. For example, judgment in *Saunders v UK* (1997) 23 EHRR 313.

63 In the United States, an accused or suspect in a criminal trial or during the investigation process may invoke the Fifth Amendment of the Constitution that protect against self-incrimination. No comment can be made on using this strategy and no adverse inference can be drawn. However, during civil litigation process in Federal court, pleading the fifth may result in an adverse inference being drawn, e.g., see Doe ex rel. Rudy-Glanzer v. Glanzer, 232 F.3d 1258, 1264 (9th Cir. 2000). Some states likewise have similar provisions.

Bibliography

Baldwin, J., "Police Interview Techniques—Establishing Truth Or Proof", *British Journal of Criminology*, (1993), 33(3), pp 325–352.

Barrett, L. F., *How Emotions Are Made*, (Macmillan, London, 2017).

Bond, C. F. and DePaulo, B. M., "Accuracy in Deception Judgments", *Personality and Social Psychology Review*, (2006), 10 (3), pp 214–234.

Buckels, E. E., Trapnell, P. D. and Paulhus, D. L., "Trolls Just Want to Have Fun", *Personality and Individual Differences*, (2014), 67, pp 97–102.

Bull, R., 'When in Interviews to Disclose Information to Suspects and to Challenge Them?', (ed) Bull, in *Investigative Interviewing*, (Springer, New York, NY, 2014) pp 167–181.

Carter, P., 'Defence Counsel in Terrorism Trials', (ed) Pearse, in *Investigating Terrorism: Current Political, Legal and Psychological Issues*, (John Wiley, Chichester, 2015) pp 80–99.

Chabris, C. and Simons, D., *The Invisible Gorilla*, (HarperCollins, London, 2011).

Dando, C. J. and Bull, R., "Maximising Opportunities to Detect Verbal Deception: Training Police Officers to Interview Tactically", *Journal of Investigative Psychology & Offender Profiling*, (2011), 8, pp 189–202.

Dennett, D. C., Cohen, M. and Kanwisher, N., "What Is the Bandwidth of Perceptual Experience?", *Trends in Cognitive Sciences*, (2016), 20(5), pp 324–335.

DePaulo, B. M., Lindsay, J. J., Malone, B. E., Muhlenbruck, L., Charlton, K. and Cooper, H., "Cues to Deception", *Psychological Bulletin*, (2003), 129(1), pp 74.

Ekman, P., "An Argument for Basic Emotions", *Cognition and Emotion*, (1992), 6(3/4), pp 169–200.

Ekman, P., *Emotions Revealed: Understanding Faces and Feelings*, (Weidenfeld and Nicolson, London, 2003).

Ekman, P., Friesen, W. V. and Ellsworth, P., *Emotion in the Human Face: Guidelines for Research and an Integration of Findings*, (Pergamon Press, New York, NY, 1972).

Eysenck, H. J., "Biological Basis of Personality", *Nature*, (1963), 199(4898), pp 1031–1034.

Frank, M. G., Yarbrough, J. D. and Ekman, P., 'Investigative Interviewing and the Detection of Deception', (ed) Williamson, in *Investigative Interviewing: Rights, Research and Regulation*, (Willan, Cullompton, 2006) pp 229–255.

Harari, Y. N., *Sapiens: A Brief History of Humankind*, (Harville Secker, London, 2014).

Hartwig, M., Granhag, P. A., Stromwall, L. A. and Kronkvist, O., "Strategic Use of Evidence During Police Interviews: When Training to Detect Deception Works", *Law & Human Behavior*, (2006), 30(5), pp 603–619.

Hawkins, N., "Prosecution Perspectives", *The Investigator*, (2012), 2, pp 31–33.

Hess, E. H., "Attitude and Pupil Size", *Scientific American*, (1965), 212, pp 46–54.

Houston, P., Floyd, M. and Carnicero, S., *Spy the Lie*, (St. Martins Press, New York, NY, 2012).

Kaasa, S. O., Morris, E. K. and Loftus, E. F., "Remembering Why: Can People Consistently Recall Reasons for Their Behaviour?", *Applied Cognitive Psychology*, (2011), 25(1), pp 35–42.

Leach, A.-M., Lindsay, R. C. L., Koehler, R., Beaudry, J. L., Bala, N. C., Lee, K. and Talwar, V., "The Reliability of Lie Detection Performance", *Law & Human Behavior*, (2009), 33(1), pp 96–109.

Leo, R. A., "Inside the Interrogation Room", *Journal of Criminal Law & Criminology*, (1996), 86(2), pp 266–303.

Levine, T. R., "Active Deception Detection", *Policy Insights from the Behavioral and Brain Sciences*, (2014), 1(1), pp 122–128.

Levine, T. R., "Five Reasons Why I Am Skeptical That Indirect or Unconscious Lie Detection Is Superior to Direct Deception Detection", *Frontiers in Psychology*, (2019), 10(1354), pp 1–5.

Milne, R. and Griffiths, A., 'Will it All End in Tiers? Police Interviews with Suspects in Britain', (ed) Williamson, in *Investigative Interviewing: Rights, Research, Regulation* (Willan, Cullompton, 2006) pp 167–188.

Mlodinow, L., *The Drunkards Walk: How Randomness Rules Our Lives*, (Allen Lane, London, 2008).

Moston, S., Stephenson, G. M. and Williamson, T. M., "The Effects of Case Characteristics on Suspect Behaviour During Police Questioning", *The British Journal of Criminology*, (1992), 32(1), pp 23–40.

Nashiro, K. & Mather, M. 2011. How Arousal Affects Younger and Older Adults' Memory Binding. *Experimental Aging Research*, 37, pp 108–128.

Navarro, J., *What Every Body is Saying*, (William Morrow, New York, 2008).

Paulhus, D. L. and Williams, K. M., "The Dark Triad of Personality: Narcissism, Machiavellianism, and Psychopathy", *Journal of Research in Personality*, (2002), 36(6), pp 556–563.

Pearse, J., 'Challenge, Compromise and Collaboration: Part of the Skill Set Necessary for Interviewing a Failed Suicide Bomber', (ed) Pearse, in *Investigating Terrorism: Current Political, Legal and Psychological Issues*, (John Wiley, Chichester, 2015) pp 45–66.

Porter, S. and ten Brinke, L., "The Truth About Lies: What Works in Detecting High-Stakes Deception?", *Legal and Criminological Psychology*, (2010), 15(1), pp 57–75.

Sacchi, D. L. M., Agnoli, F. and Loftus, E. F., "Changing History: Doctored Photographs Affect Memory for Past Public Events", *Applied Cognitive Psychology*, (2007), 21(8), pp 1005–1022.

Shaw, J., *The Memory Illusion*, (Penguin, London, 2016).

Sleen, J. V., 'A Structured Model for Investigative Interviewing of Suspects', (ed) Bull, Valentine and Williamson, in *Handbook of Psychology of Investigative Interviewing*, (Wiley-Blackwell, Chichester, 2009) pp 25–52.

Slepian, M. L., Masicampo, E. J., Toosi, N. R. and Ambady, N., "The Physical Burdens of Secrecy", *Journal of Experimental Psychology: General*, (2012), 141(4), pp 619–624.

Stanovich, K. E., *The Robot's Rebellion: Finding Meaning in the Age of Darwin*, (University of Chicago, Chicago, 2004).

Turpin, M. H., Kara-Yakoubian, M., Walker, A. C., Walker, H. E. K., Fugelsang, J. A. and Stolz, J. A., "Bullshit Ability as an Honest Signal of Intelligence", *Evolutionary Psychology*, (2021), 19(2), pp 1–10.

Vrij, A., *Detecting Lies and Deceit*, (Wiley, Chichester, 2008).

Vrij, A., "Nonverbal Dominance versus Verbal Accuracy in Lie Detection: A Plea to Change Police Practice", *Criminal Justice and Behavior*, (2008), 35(10), pp 1323–1336.

Vrij, A., Granhag, P. A. and Porter, S., "Pitfalls and Opportunities in Nonverbal and Verbal Lie Detection", *Psychological Science in the Public Interest*, (2010), 11(3), pp 89–121.

Vrij, A., Mann, S. and Bull, R., "Suspects, Lies, and Videotape: An Analysis of Authentic High-Stake Liars", *Law & Human Behavior*, (2002), 26(3), pp 365–376.

Vrij, A., Mann, S. A., Fisher, R. P., Leal, S., Milne, R. and Bull, R., "Increasing Cognitive Load to Facilitate Lie Detection: The Benefit of Recalling an Event in Reverse Order", *Law & Human Behavior*, (2008), 32(3), pp 253–265.

Webster, R., *Why Freud was Wrong: Sin, Sex and Psychoanalysis*, (Orwell Press, Oxford, 2005).

Williamson, T. M., 'Towards Greater Professionalism: Minimizing Miscarriages of Justice', (ed) Williamson, in *Investigative Interviewing: Rights, Research, Regulation*, (Willan, Cullompton, 2006) pp 147–166.

Wiseman, R., Watt, C., ten Brinke, L., Porter, S., Couper, S.-L. and Rankin, C., "The Eyes Don't Have it: Lie Detection and Neuro-Linguistic Programming", *PloS one*, (2012), 7(7), pp e40259–e40259.

Chapter 9

Mental Models, Persuasion, and Influence

Introduction

As discussed in Chapter 7, careful analysis is important, but many human decisions are based on heuristics or rules of thumb that are automated responses. Intuition or 'gut feelings' is a term often synonymous with this type of response. Emotions are also a fundamental driver of our decision-making process. In this chapter, we look deeper into motivated reasoning, which is making decisions based on how it makes us feel and how the mental models of the world impact our decision-making. Two centuries ago, David Hume argued that our reason is simply the slave to our passions and emotions continue to play a dominant role in our decision making. Mental models comprise our deepest assumptions and beliefs and are the lens that we view reality through. Important information may be ignored in favor of feeling good about the decision, if it ties into our deepest beliefs. This inevitably is dangerous as emotions are easily manipulated. It also works in the interviewers favor as it is the primary reason why techniques such as rapport are so effective in establishing communication because rapport creates an emotional connection. For humans probably the most important environment is our social world. Certain emotions evolved to help us navigate our social environment and understanding these can help an interviewer to get a truthful account. As a result, how we feel about someone is important to the influence they have over our decisions. When we like someone, we are more inclined to trust them. Trustworthiness and friendliness are going to increase the likelihood of a person confiding in the interviewer. An emotional feeling of trust between the interviewee and interviewer is important in getting a truthful account and in preventing someone becoming defensive and closing down because they feel threatened.

Additionally, this chapter looks at why people can refuse to acknowledge the reality of evidence presented to them. Sometimes, a person is struggling with the emotion of acknowledging the truth, and in such situations, it is important to use emotion and the subtle influence of persuasion to get openness from the interviewee. This technique is used to counter the trait some people exhibit of deceiving themselves by refusing to incorporate new information to change

DOI: 10.4324/9781003269489-9

their beliefs. Persuasion in the interview context is the reframing of evidence to make it more salient or emotionally relevant in a person's decision-making. Persuasion is usually unnecessary in corporate investigations as, in many circumstances, failing to provide credible answers to questions asked can be sufficient from an investigative standpoint. Nonetheless, there may be occasions when that is simply insufficient, for instance, an investigator may need some cooperation and compliance in answering questions to understand how much damage has been done, where stolen funds may be recovered, or how controls were circumvented. In such cases, it may be necessary to deploy some type of persuasion to get answers. Persuasion may also be useful in encouraging a witness to make a full and honest disclosure, as often personal loyalties because of group membership can cloud coworker's judgments and prevent openness.

Emotion

Emotion is an inbuilt evolutionary mechanism to assist with survival. Threat avoidance is a major concern of all living organisms. As a consequence, we are constantly monitoring our environment for any signs of threat.[1] The basic emotional 'systems' include fear, as well as rage, joy, panic/grief, seeking, and play.[2] The areas responsible for emotional responses are located in the sub-cortical regions of the brain such as the brain stem region and the limbic system. The thalamus, the amygdala, and the hippocampus are part of the limbic system. The limbic system controls the autonomic nervous system (ANS) with its key task to attend to the welfare of the organism.[3] The amygdala is one of the major emotional processing centers, especially of fear. Together, the amygdala and hippocampus are an important component in the acquisition, storage, and expression of fear memories and in establishing conditioned responses, including phobias.[4]

Panksepp and Biven refer to three emotional levels: first, the primary-process level responsible for survival. At this level, in response to external stimuli, emotions arise in the subcortical region, outside conscious awareness, but that signal up to more conscious levels and down to bodily organs.[5] Our external environment is monitored by our senses in a form of perception known as *neuroception* that can trigger or inhibit defensive strategies.[6] All sense perception (except smell) arrives first at the thalamus before traveling onto various processing parts of the brain.[7] The cognitive processing areas of the brain react far slower than the ANS, which may already have the body reacting and readying for fight or flight by the time the mind becomes aware. The secondary-process level of emotion is involved in classic conditioning and implicit learning as well as learned behavioral regulation, so there is a mix of habit forming, automated processing, and conscious awareness. Here, early childhood influences generate beliefs and behavior that can remain throughout life.[8] Learning is an important part of adaptation and emotional development, that is built on innate emotional systems, and which is an iterative process so that the systems become intertwined over time into complicated emotional responses.[9] Some learning is easier as we come with a *learned preparedness*, such as for a fear of snakes or spiders, for instance.[10] Learning itself will involve morphological brain changes. Each new experience, if it provides a lesson worth remembering—or learned because of necessity—creates new neurological links, a term known as *plasticity*.[11] Consequently, when behaviors are learned earlier in life, the physiological changes become a fundamental structure on which further learning is built. Finally, the tertiary-process is where emotions are processed by the higher executive cognitive brain, responsible for rational thought and where emotions can be mediated.[12] This level is also known as feelings and is where the subjective interpretation of emotions occur.[13] This processing occurs in the neocortex, an evolutionary more recent part of the brain. In particular, the prefrontal cortex (PFC) is important for analytical and conscious thought; the dorsolateral PFC guides thoughts, attention, and actions, while the orbital and ventromedial PFC regulates emotion.[14] However, it is important to understand that input from the emotions is essential for the analytical brain for all decisions, as without it, the rational mind would be overwhelmed by possible options.[15] The PFC potentially can override an emotional response, if it is consciously and actively engaged. The ability to understand your own feelings enables you to empathize with another person and to take the perspective of that person, a mechanism known as Theory of Mind.[16] This ability is particularly important for an interviewer to nurture as it is used in reflecting back emotions to the interviewee.

While opportunities are readily sought by an organism, threats are always privileged in the real world. You can survive missing a meal, you cannot survive becoming one. When the body perceives a threat, it responds with a stress response, involving the limbic system. Stress forces our body's regulating systems outside normal dynamic activity to maintain *homeostasis* to enable survival.[17] The emotions rapidly activate predetermined physiological changes, including the ANS that controls visceral functions of the body.[18] The physiological results include the gut-wrenching sensations, pounding heart, and fast and shallow breathing in preparation of fight or flight.[19] Fighting, fleeing, or freezing (in very high-stress situations) are common responses to perceived stressful events, but when physical action is not possible, people use avoidant and psychological fleeing mechanisms that are dissociative.[20] Stress therefore causes behavioral and physiological responses and may generate strong defensive negative feelings.[21] Such behavior might include withdrawal or aggression in an interview by an interviewee.

Stress can inhibit the functioning of the PFC and significantly reduce the ability to inhibit emotions or make calculated decisions. Stress may therefore induce an almost regressive thinking style as the more threatened an individual feels, the more 'regressed' the style of thinking and behaving may become.[22] Accordingly, it is important to minimize stress levels in an interviewee to prevent such regressive thinking or habitual responding. Moreover, as we saw with heuristics in Chapter 7 the involvement of the conscious thinking brain in the PFC does not necessarily preclude reflexive thinking. For a calculated evaluation of options available, the analytical/reflexive thinking mode has to be actively engaged which is itself effortful.[23] Frequently, this analytical part is often used instead after the decision has been made to simply provide justification and a post-hoc rationalization for an emotional decision.[24]

Social Emotions and Group Dynamics

In addition to the basic emotional 'systems', other emotions known as social emotions help to regulate interpersonal relationships.[25] Indeed, it is possible that human intelligence evolved to predict and respond to complex behavior of other human beings of our own social groups.[26] In our evolutionary past, group membership was vital to survival. Being a group member requires cooperative, altruistic behavior that lets other members know you can be trusted to behave for the benefit of the group and not selfishly. Trust is based on important forms of social preferences such as betrayal aversion and feeling safe when vulnerable.[27] It remains a critical part of employee satisfaction and effectiveness.[28] Therefore, emotions, including friendship, dislike, moralistic aggression, gratitude, trust, shame, suspicion, and some types of guilt can be explained as important evolutionary adaptions to regulate the altruistic system that facilitates cooperation.[29] We feel pleasure with people who show signs that they can be trusted to reciprocate with pleasant social company releasing endogenous opioids.[30] Earning a reputation as a trustworthy group member enhances self-esteem.[31] As a consequence, other peer group member's likes or dislikes create a constant influence on our own behavior with social pressure or the need to conform, a powerful, if often subconscious, motivation.[32] In sum, we have a brain that scans our internal environment and external environment, but which also monitors our social status through the gauge of self-esteem. Emotions in this way direct behavior by nonconsciously guiding one to personally attractive options and away from repulsive ones.[33] It does not matter how the group is perceived by outsiders, it is how the group members perceive and value their group that determines the strength of their attachment to the group, as well as its norms and values. This is why group culture has such a profound effect in generating criminogenic environments and why conspiracy groups and cults can be so difficult to leave.

Worldview

Although we become acculturated when we join any organization or group, many beliefs and values have already been acquired from our childhood. Because information is cognitively expensive to store, even infants begin to categorize information into concepts that are then used as predictive models of the world.[34] Some of these concepts are the basis of lifelong patterns of behavior.[35] The family, the peer group, institutions—such as religion and education—all provide information to build these concepts. Although effective in storage and transmission of information, the categorization of information into concepts is dangerous in that there is a risk of creating stereotypes and categorical thinking, a form of reductionism. The world can seem much less complex as a result.[36] These concepts nevertheless become habits, ways of behaving, ways of viewing the world, and intuitive responses that are often inaccessible to conscious thought. Our memories and past experiences thus build a subconscious filter through which all new information is processed. This is one's worldview, a collection of mental models of how the world operates, that may sometimes conflict with each other. It is relatively easy to feel that we control what we learn; that it is an active and participatory event, one that we consciously control, but this ignores the inductive learning experience that often happens nonconsciously. People tend to hold tightly to beliefs once formed and be reluctant to reevaluate these beliefs, a phenomenon known as *belief perseverance*.[37] Many of our beliefs are layered on earlier ones and combined with strong emotional attachments in our mind such that we do not want to discard them. A mental model thus creates a 'version of reality' that decides what information to pay attention to, how it is perceived, how it is organized, and the meaning attributed to it.[38] Logical consistency between mental models is not relevant for belief perseverance.[39] The result is that new information can have little or no impact on belief perseverance.[40] Moreover, the influence of group membership has a profound effect on what we can believe.[41]

Individual life stories then create personal *narratives* that are constructed to provide meaning and identity in the world.[42] Narrative understandings of the self are strongly influenced by culture—that is, by the images, metaphors, symbols, and stories that gain currency and affirmation in a given social and historical milieu.[43] These cultural stories and values bias the interpretation of an individual's experience and narrative and generate adaptations that reflect an individual's goals, virtues, and self-image.[44] No person presents the same facet of their personality all the time. We all have different identities or 'faces' that we can present to the world.[45] Through these identities, an individual attempts to make sense of their world and their place within it. Not all of these identities are consistent with each other, but each has behavioral scripts attached consistent with whichever identity is most salient. Accordingly, the same person can make different decisions depending on the mindset he or she is in. This is partly the result of the ability to rationalize as well as our innate ability to compartmentalize different parts of our personality and beliefs.

But mental models in long-term memory that are so essential and adaptive to rapid stimuli responses are also the principal source of inertia in recognizing and adapting to a changing environment. People prefer to remain consistent even if the habits they have are maladaptive. This is because people tend to restrict their reasoning to what is contained in their mental models, refraining from overtaxing their working memory by ignoring alternative states of the world, and tending to accept presented information as truth rather than try to determine falsity.[46] New ideas are thus rejected simply because they conflict with old ideas, not because of their merit. Likewise, the tendency to use a *rigid frame* perspective, a form of categorical thinking, can reduce alternative, unfavorable, or competing perspectives.[47] A rigid frame is an unyielding perspective that someone uses to evaluate choices. For example, a lawyer may view all decisions from the context of whether the act is legal, if you can do it legally, you should. An accountant might consider only whether accountancy rules are applicable. A banker may say that decisions are based on a 'only business' philosophy which negates having to examine the origins of cash, no matter how pernicious the source, thereby avoiding any moral conflict. Where decisions are viewed from a transactional perspective, there is no right or wrong, but a cost–benefit analysis of what you get against what does it cost. Such logic can easily accommodate any scenario to ensure that there is a coherent argument to bolster the desired outcome. In all scenarios, there is never a view considered from an ethical perspective.[48] Rigid frames mean we can avoid triggering conflicting values and maintain consistency with the person we believe ourselves to be by using such rationalizations.

Rationalization

It does happen that when objective reality conflicts with our worldview, we change our worldview to accommodate the new information. Unfortunately, more often, we have a tremendous ability to denigrate objective reality to avoid having to change our beliefs, especially core beliefs. We all have an ability to rationalize that is a critical part of self-deception.[49] The ability to deny the obvious helps to protect self-esteem as self-esteem is critical for personal well-being as it promotes happiness and good mental health.[50] Such denial is not actually lying, rather it is a perceptual incapacity—the most primitive of the psychological defences to protect oneself.[51] Both the ability to compartmentalize information and the denial of facts are fundamental to the ability to rationalize. Moreover, an individual constructs their personal narrative through their unique mental models using a memory that is itself fallible and unreliable. Perpetrators can thus redefine their reality through blatant denial to sophisticated rationalization that is not necessarily deliberate deception, sometimes their mental model is simply so skewed that the resulting narrative is effortlessly self-serving and self-justifying, while ignoring contradictory evidence.

This phenomenon has a profound impact in the interview room. Few criminals accept the reality that they are in fact criminals, there is always someone else to blame or some situation that was responsible. Rationalization is assisted by *techniques of neutralization* such as the denial of responsibility, an appeal to higher loyalties, and the condemnation of condemners, that help the individual free themselves from a large measure of social control and personal responsibility.[52] In some interpersonal conflicts, the primary tools perpetrators use are silence and secrecy, if that fails, attacks on the credibility of accusers are the next line of defense, trying to ensure that few listen to or take the allegations seriously.[53]

More generally, people will often attribute personal successes to dispositional factors (personal skills or knowledge) while blaming exogenous sources (bad luck, randomness, others malicious motives) for failures but use the inverse premise for others; referred to as the *fundamental attribution error*.[54] People easily revise their subjective reality to abrogate all blame and culpability for themselves, while being dogmatic about other's failings. Rationalization is so powerful that when information contrary to strongly held beliefs is presented, not only are the beliefs left unchallenged, but they may actually be strengthened.[55] It's why the terms *cognitive dissonance* and *confirmation bias* were coined.[56] These cognitive distortions help to maintain beliefs despite contradictory evidence, as previously noted. Such biases may also be related to the need for cognitive closure, which is a dislike of uncertainty with a need for a clear-cut opinion on a topic.[57] People dislike doubt so any decision is better than none, and once reached, it can be easily rationalized and then maintained. Normally, there is a negative correlation between biases and intelligence; more intelligent people are less susceptible to biases with higher intelligence generally correlated with better higher executive functioning of the analytical system. However, one bias, *myside bias*, which is a subclass of confirmation bias, is unlike many other biases.[58] Myside bias is heavily influenced by ingroup membership, and the beliefs attached to such membership thus cause a person to evaluate evidence, generate evidence, and test hypotheses in a manner biased toward their own prior opinions and attitudes. Myside bias is not negatively correlated to intelligence, meaning that highly sophisticated thinkers, such as group leaders, are as likely to display it as anyone else. In fact, because sophisticated thinkers are inclined to believe that they actively construct their beliefs and as they can provide more coherent and logical arguments to support them, they may actually be more susceptible. As a result, the more developed the analytical system the better the reasoning and post-hoc rationalizations.

However, it demonstrates that for persuasion, an appeal to personal interests and emotions rather than logical reasoning is always more likely to be successful in changing a person's perception of facts. Moreover, the investigator must tailor his or her own behavior to make the interviewee's cooperative identities salient such as caring father, husband, friend, conscientious employee, or dutiful son or daughter, at the expense of other, more challenging identities, by which the investigator maximizes compliance and minimizes confrontation.[59]

Intuition

Understanding emotion allows us to understand intuition, sometimes referred to a sixth sense, which it can be, and often referred to as a *gut instinct* as it involves the visceral organs as in a stress response. The innate survival mechanism humans have is important to understand for various reasons, firstly, it is of use to the investigator to understand his or her own responses to situations. Secondly, it is essential to understand that the interviewee is likewise appraising the situation. Thirdly, intuition is also about the integration of previous learning and knowledge into our adaptive responses to situations.

If the interviewer is sensing a strong gut reaction, then understanding why is important, as the emotional visceral responses to a perceived threat may be the cause. Understanding may provide valuable information about the person or situation you are in. The gut instinct reaction could mean you are being lied to, or that the interviewee is hostile toward you but trying to disguise it. Something is happening that you are perceiving at an unconscious level as a threat. Identifying what it is may provide valuable insight. The ability to incorporate emotion in this way is a useful skill, as is the ability to recognize its limits.[60] The interviewee likewise is likely to be stressed and stress tends to close down executive cognitive functioning and lead to perceptual narrowing. It may even make listening difficult.[61] The fact that listening when stressed is difficult means it may be impossible to integrate new information as it cannot even begin to be processed. Combined with the perceptual incapacity of denial and other cognitive biases, this makes logical reasoning virtually impossible with someone who is stressed. This is one major reason why the rapport phase of the interview is so important as it is designed to minimize any negative emotional stimuli, thus avoiding triggering defensive emotional reactions in the interviewee. The ability to recognize emotions in others and the ability to respond appropriately is an important tool in social intelligence and vital in the interview situation.

However, intuition has other dimensions other than the innate emotional reaction to danger, including the subconscious retrieval of long forgotten information that has nonetheless become integrated into personal skills or actions. Herbert Simon suggested that intuition is *nothing more and nothing less than the recognition* of cues from other experiences that the person has previously encountered and learned something from.[62] This view of intuition could be considered a form of tacit or implicit knowledge. Intuition could naturally fit into a discussion of heuristics and biases, as many decisions are made based on cues from long held experience reflexively because of an implicit assumption that this is a similar situation. This is not unique to humans; all animals integrate learning and experience into their emotional responses. Evolution gives us the emotional tools, but experience provides the triggers for many emotions and over time, an animal can adapt to new threats or positive experiences. With this information sorted into concepts, the brain uses these and new inputs to predict what is about to happen and the appropriate necessary behavior in response.[63] The acquired knowledge adapts our emotional responses and increases the efficiency of our reasoning processes.[64]

Intuition as this skill could potentially be developed and strengthened. For instance, many experts develop a sharp sense of intuition in their area of specialization, but this does not occur in all fields of expertise. To develop intuition, there is a need for a high degree of regularity, prompt accurate feedback, and plenty of opportunity for practice in a skill.[65] Many practical skills are learned inductively without conscious awareness. Examples are provided in Malcolm Gladwell's book *Blink,* which focused on this intuitive mastery among various experts who had developed reflexive actions over years of experience.[66] Among these types of experts, intuition functions as a form of recognition because some cue from the situation triggers associative memory, which has information about similar previously encountered situations stored in memory which then provides useful information to assist a decision. Gerd Gigerenzer suggests that complex decision-making processes can be deconstructed into simple cues resulting in swift and accurate responses as a heuristic. This is achieved by reducing the complexity of information processing resulting in better decisions overall.[67] Therefore, in occupations or professions that provide an opportunity to experience learning opportunities with such cues, intuition may provide a valuable sixth sense enabling a rapid cognitive response.

Unfortunately, investigation is rarely such an environment because the ground truth is normally uncertain to begin with; feedback is often poor or even deceptive, and complete information may never be known. This fact may not affect confidence in one's judgment however, and often the high degree of confidence associated with a belief has little to do with the reliability of the belief used to make the judgment.[68] Confidence in a belief is related to two related impressions: *cognitive ease* and *coherence.*[69] We can be confident in our story or theory when it comes easily to mind and is not contradicted by any competing scenario. The ease or availability with which a scenario comes to mind serves as an answer to the question of probability of an event and tends to replace the more difficult question in objective terms. The associative mind then suppresses doubt and provides information and ideas that are compatible with the story; it also tends to ignore information that it does not know.[70] Even compelling causal statistics or base rate probabilities will not change long held beliefs or beliefs rooted in personal experience. In other words, judgments based on 'gut instincts' can be notoriously unreliable. I am not saying that intuition does not develop in investigators, it certainly does. One gets better at reading people and situations, it is just that too often investigators run with their gut decisions to the exclusion of all other possibilities, which they ignore completely. Intuition is a valuable tool, once judiciously used. By acknowledging the inherent risks, intuition can be used carefully as subtle cues can provide guidance that helps the investigator to hone his or her instincts. It is vitally important not to confuse intuition for facts, but intuition can be very useful as long as the limitations are understood. The major limitation is that too often people confuse the stress response of the gut instincts for a cognitive cue and react accordingly. One all too common consequence of this is investigators being convinced someone is lying to them, and then using misinformed nonverbal behavioral cues to confirm this biased response.[71]

In other words, relying on your feelings is unlikely to be wise in every situation. Moreover, the recognition of some cue from a situation may simply and automatically activate a behavior script from habit. As a result, the response is one that is the same one used many times in the past, even though the new situation may bear little semblance to previous situations and the responsive may be counterproductive. Additionally, reinforcing this script makes it even more powerful. As a result, patterns of behavior, especially negative ones, have a habit of reappearing throughout a person's life. Frustratingly, even when those negative patterns are recognized, changing them is a tough task.

Persuasion

People are therefore reluctant to change their mind especially if it means changing a deeply held belief. They may listen to a logical argument as to why it makes sense to do so, but usually only as they simultaneously prepare their counterargument. They may not go far enough to even listen if the person speaking is not considered trustworthy. Thus, the rapport phase is so important in establishing that trust connection. It does not overcome the problem that a person is not going to change their thinking based on logic. It is necessary to appeal to emotional interests to get a person to change and motivational interviewing uses that strategy by listening carefully and utilizing the person's own words to frame questions, that the person answers and thereby begins to change their own minds by having to construct answers and question their own beliefs. It is a powerful method of getting fundamental change. Nevertheless, entrenched individuals may require additional incentives. What we are trying to achieve in the interview room is to encourage the interviewee to give a truthful account, and unlike therapy, within a very finite timeframe. As noted in Chapter 2, incentives such as promises of leniency may allow a deal in return for cooperation to be made. In many scenarios, there may be little to offer as leniency in return for the truth or it may not be appropriate to make such an offer. Therefore, getting someone to be truthful by persuasion may be the only strategy available to the interviewer.

Persuasion is a form of communication where one person seeks to influence another to voluntarily adopt a different viewpoint or behavior by changing their perceptions.[72] Persuasion is an essential part of social life, and it may be the reason why human language evolved: to convince others of the rightness of our arguments.[73] To achieve perception or behavior change, the persuader tries to meet the needs or desires of the person to be persuaded by understanding what their beliefs are and what they want—or at least, believe they want. Because of this, it is a reciprocal process where both parties are dependent on each other. In many ways, it is similar to motivational interviewing in this respect. Likewise, to be most effective, the person should feel the change has come from within as distinct from being imposed from outside.[74]

In the case of the interview, persuasion can be used to get the full facts. Consequently, it is critical that persuasion is only used to make existing evidence salient or available to the reflective mind. Persuasion remains an important feature of many social interactions being used in negotiation, the advertising business, even education, and on the darker side, it is present in propaganda, radicalization, and in computer hacking through social engineering techniques. Persuasion is using framing and communication skills to make certain information more prominent to the interviewee. It is not about manipulation, which is the use of misinformation, lies, deceit, or otherwise false information designed to create a false impression in the mind of the interviewee. Manipulation includes the fabrication or misuse of objectively false information, or coercive techniques to generate emotional feelings. Some police interrogation techniques are based principally on using forms of persuasion and manipulation to convince a person to confess. The fact that so many innocent people have confessed to crimes that they did not do is testament to the effectiveness of the techniques. Persuasion is an effective technique but often the problem of false confessions is one of biased investigators who are convinced of the accuracy of their beliefs who then push suspects (and witnesses) into giving them the narrative they want.

In accusatory interrogation models, the interviewer generally does most of the talking, trying to persuade the suspect to confess by gradually introducing various themes that can be taken as justifiable reasons for committing the crime by the suspect.[75] The objective is to have the subject placed in a cooperative frame of mind and use careful verbal framing to maintain that mindset. The subject will continue to rely on their feelings as cues for how to respond.[76] However, most such models also use manipulation by inventing evidence, if necessary, that claims to contradict the person's account. In addition, the refusal to listen to any denials can be extremely coercive, particularly when dealing with vulnerable interviewees. Such tactics cannot be considered ethical in any organizational interviewing context.

Accusatory interrogation methods suggest that one way to overcome rationalizations is to apply psychological pressure on the suspect by maximizing the negative outcomes or the worst possible narrative when denials continue, while minimizing the outcome if an admission is made. For instance, a lighter sentence. One human factor that assists is a feature of perception, what is referred to as *the contrast principle*, where one item is compared to another; so if a trader offers his most expensive item first, any subsequent items appear cheap.[77] Therefore, an interrogation using such a maximization technique, followed by the minimization of the offense through alternative motives, would incline the suspect to view the alternative motives in a much more positive light than if the motives had been presented in a standalone version. There is wisdom in rapidly overcoming rationalizations as if they are left unchallenged, the person making them will come to accept them as truth. When making a decision, people often only use the most salient information that comes easiest to mind, known as the *availability bias*.[78] Having the rationalizations available as uppermost in the interviewee's mind may make obtaining the truth difficult. By using persuasion, the interviewer will attempt to make the choice of information available to the person the most relevant and pertinent to the decision to tell the truth. Persuasion will also use emotion to make the person feel positive about disclosing the truth.

Robert Cialdini has identified six key principles of persuasion used to get compliance: reciprocation or give and take; commitment and consistency; social proof; liking, authority; and the scarcity principle.[79] The key to persuasion is to generate agreement through raising the saliency of any principle that already exists; with liking, reciprocation, and commitment particularly important in interviewing. The primary influencer are the personal feelings toward the interviewer; positive feelings make influencing easier; people are more likely to comply with a request by someone they like, and someone they sense some commonalities with. The use of small gestures to give something to the interviewee is a subtle tool often used to establish a sense of reciprocity. Reciprocity is a fundamental hard-wired human response, when someone gives us something, then we feel socially obligated to return the favor. The favor does not necessarily have to be tangible; even a compliment or small gestures such as holding a door open all activate the obligation. The repayment does not have to be in kind, but the person has a sense of debt to repay the gesture. The presenting of refreshments without solicitation is a favored technique by many police interviewers.

Rapport is the major factor in generating this positive affect and in building trust. It also helps in understanding an interviewee's core beliefs, which is essential as people are more interested in communication that aligns with these beliefs and rapport builds the necessary sense of common identity between both the interviewer and interviewee.[80] It therefore permits the interviewer to establish what is important to the interviewee and hence useful later when likely motivations are being examined.

Using reasoned argument or logic are far less powerful in persuasion than the communicator's communication style and often irrational elements.[81] As noted, logic often causes a person to engage their reflective PFC to develop counterarguments which is a poor strategy in persuasion. In general, it is easier for the interviewee to process positive information than negative.[82] Just as importantly, positive emotions, such as a smile, can be perceived as rewards or incentives toward the behavior desired by the persuader and work much better than a threat.[83]

Context is an important part of the communication landscape and the decision-making process. Of course, the context can be changed by the interviewer to make salient the perspective required. The careful use of imagery and indirect associations can link concepts without directly communicating such links.[84] *Framing* is utilizing careful scripting or semantics to paint the scene that allows people to see what they expect to see or believe what they already believe.[85] In some ways, it is similar to creating what Thaler and Sunstein describe as the choice architecture of decision-making.[86] This is where certain configurations of our environment influence our decisions nonconsciously by leveraging our emotions, memories, expectations, and the opinions of others. Language is therefore important. People give different meanings to words or concepts based on their own beliefs, attitudes, and experience.[87] The meaning of words is usually determined by what is or is not loaded into them through context, by any other words used to modify it, and by the intent or ignorance of the speaker and receiver.[88] Understanding a person's beliefs and framing the concepts around them makes it is easier for a person to accept and assimilate new ideas as they correspond to already held beliefs.[89] Therefore, not just the words used but how they are conveyed sends a subliminal message to the receiver. For instance, the same choice can be interpreted differently, resulting in a different decision being made, depending on whether it is framed a loss or a gain.[90] In a study looking at how language impacted on people's assessment of speed of driving involving a collision, the word 'smashed' elicited a higher estimate of speed than words less emotionally charged such as 'collided' or 'bumped'. In an investigation, language such as 'stole' or 'thief' can immediately create defensiveness, even in those not suspected of any wrongdoing. Even using the word 'investigation' may trigger a negative emotional reaction, which the word 'enquiry' may not. Understanding the power of language is second nature to the public relations industry who can develop innocuous sounding euphemisms for tragic outcomes such as using 'self-injurious behavior incidents' to describe suicide by American war captives.[91] Mistakes resulting in death in the healthcare profession are known as 'technical error', 'complication', or 'unanticipated outcome', all of which can be somewhat correct but disguise the full truth.[92] Euphemisms, of course, are the currency of politics.

The timing of when and how to say something therefore becomes as important as what to say. People can say things with a smile that come across as humorous that if said by a dour individual would sound threatening or insulting. The brain is all about associations, so activating the association relative to the message is an effective way to introduce the message in a surreptitious manner and accordingly the request for compliance may be explicit or it may be implicit.[93] For instance, psychology researchers can activate the concept of honesty in participants by priming the subjects first through the introduction of the concept of the Ten Commandments.[94] In this way, the request for assistance causes the receiver to ask herself if she is an honest person. Once the person has put herself into the mindset of an honest person, she is now primed to respond accordingly. The concept of honesty and its synonyms such as morality, ethics, and doing the right thing are powerful tools in interview persuasion, particularly if they can also be related to doing it for some personally important person.

Threats can be effective in some circumstances, such as in preventing someone taking an action in the future.[95] Threats and coercion can be powerful tools and are often used in the recruitment of informants. It may be fair to say that coercion can lead to desired behavior changes, although it rarely leads to a change in perception. People do not like to feel coerced; in fact, it can often be counterproductive.[96] It does work, however, at least in the short-term, even if people tend to chafe under its yolk. Because of its extensive use in police interview rooms, people desperately trying to escape the coercive environment of an interrogation room often make a false confession to do so.[97] In many of these instances, threats were used to force a confession, despite a lack of clear evidence of guilt.

In the police interview room, one popular method of persuasion is the use of the 'good cop, bad cop' technique. It is a very useful technique because it allows the two interviewers to play off each other. Robert Cialdini writes that the good cop/bad cop technique is a powerful example of the potency of combination of the peculiarities of human nature; firstly, through the fear the technique engenders in the threats of the bad cop, which then involves invoking the perpetual contrast principle, as the good cop is especially nice; and finally, the pressure of the reciprocity rule, as the good cop is constantly intervening on behalf of the suspect.[98] The technique is often exaggerated but it has advantages and can be used much more subtly: for instance, when one interviewer tackles the reluctance of an interviewee by calling them out on it, it can be useful for the second interviewer to step in to restore the rapport. Nonetheless, the necessary criticism will have landed, and the interviewee knows this as well as acknowledging that the other interviewer was nicer and stepped in on their behalf. Cialdini emphasizes the rule of reciprocation is that we should repay in some way what another person has given us. When we like the person to whom we owe that favor, we are even more likely to want to comply. Even an unwanted favor once received can produce indebtedness. This reciprocity rule can be further manipulated to force a person to agree to a concession, in what Cialdini refers to as the 'rejection then retreat rule' whereby an extreme first request is turned down, but this is followed immediately by a smaller but real request that is accepted.[99] Although there is a danger in this tactic that if the initial request is too extreme as to appear unreasonable, it may backfire. However, Cialdini notes that a little-appreciated by-product of this type of concession is that it engenders feelings of greater responsibility for and satisfaction with the arrangement. This is as a result of that feature of the human psyche, which is the desire to behave consistently with any choices that we make. If we are not behaving consistently with our beliefs, it can result in cognitive dissonance.[100] This pressure to behave consistently causes us to respond in ways that justify our earlier decisions. This, Cialdini argues, is because most people prefer to avoid the labor of thinking hard and consistency can function as a shield against thought as well as any unpalatable consequences of our actions.[101] Therefore, the offering of motives or themes such as self-defense or provocation to a murder suspect plays to this consistency of the suspect as an honorable man and one he may be willing to maintain, thereby permitting the reframing of choices into personally congruent factors to be acceptable. While framing the murderer as a psychopathic killer is an extreme interpretation and one likely to be rejected. Normally, as noted previously, one should avoid words with very negative connotations, but this is one time when framing something like a motive at one extreme is used to contrast the alternative motive that is offered. Likewise, framing a fraud as someone struggling in a desperate financial situation is more acceptable than when the alternative explanation of a ruthless, cold-hearted conman is posited. The use of hypothetical questions can be a useful way to deliver this dichotomy. For instance: 'what might your wife think about your behavior and your reasons for doing what you did?'

In sum, emotional responses to someone we like will generate an innate desire to be cooperative. Compliance can therefore be subtly induced by friendliness, the careful use of language and imagery, the giving of something to the interviewee, and avoiding confrontation such as argument or logical reasoning. The use of friendliness and subtlety is far more effective than logic in convincing someone to tell the truth. Like all tools of influence, there is potential to misuse it. This is particularly dangerous when the persuader has a hidden agenda. The power of such techniques is too evident in our world where conspiracy theories abound and where intelligent people have adopted bizarre beliefs that often lead them to taking actions that are equally bizarre, misguided, and, too often, damaging to innocent people.

Conclusion

While humans are intelligent animals, we do not use that logical reflective brain as much as we like to believe. Instead, habits, cognitive shortcuts, and laziness are the defining features of human decision-making. Most of the time, this works just fine and usually people know when it is necessary to engage the reflective analytical brain. Indeed, forming good habits is the easier method of developing the discipline to exercise or study than having to face that decision on a regular basis. But many habits that we form young govern how we behave and react for our lives. The difficulties arise when we fail to realize how powerful our emotional desires are, and the control emotions exert over our thinking. Emotions are what we need to make us feel safe, secure, loved, needed, and wanted by our peers. This is the essential element to life. Assuming that emotions have no input into decisions or that they can be switched off is unwise. Persuasion is a skill to leverage those emotions to get compliance from an interviewee. It uses tools like liking, trust, and reciprocation to get the interviewee to engage their own reflective brain by making relevant evidence salient to them. It is a powerful tool but in the hands of a biased investigator, very dangerous. The danger of using manipulation to invent evidence is also present. The investigator must not make assumptions and jump to conclusions. The only way to avoid this is, once again, questioning your assumptions and biases, and evaluating information with a view to trying to falsify it. The next chapter reviews an actual police interview that effectively used many of the techniques discussed in the book.

Notes

1 Porges, S. W., "The Polyvagal Theory: New Insights into Adaptive Reactions of the Autonomic Nervous System", *Cleveland Clinic Journal of Medicine*, (2009), 76 (Suppl 2), pp S86–S90.

2 Panksepp, J. and Biven, L., *The Archaeology of the Mind: Neuroevolutionary Origins of Human Emotions*, (W.W. Norton, New York, 2012). Panksepp and Biven point out that there is a great deal of overlap, and these are not standalone systems, as well as often combining together in activation. For instance, the seeking system is involved in exploring, curiosity, and opportunity seeking, so is essential to many of the other emotions. Ekman, on the other hand, argues that universal facial displays of emotion suggest six universal basic emotions: fear, anger, sadness, disgust, surprise, and joy in Ekman, P., "An Argument for Basic Emotions", *Cognition and Emotion*, (1992), 6(3/4), pp 169–200.

3 van der Kolk, B., *The Body Keeps The Score: Mind, Brain and Body in the Transformation of Trauma*, (Penguin, London, 2015): 57; Porges, S. W., "The Polyvagal Theory: Phylogenetic Contributions to Social Behavior", *Physiology and Behavior*, (2003), 79(3), pp 503–513.

4 LeDoux, J. E., "Emotion Circuits in the Brain", *Annual Review of Neuroscience*, (2000), 23(1), pp 155–184: 161.

5 This account of emotions is disputed. The field is rich with many different accounts of emotions, some more influenced by the academic history of the field, some less. Psychological theories suggest an *Appraisal Theory* of emotions, for review, see Niendenthal, P. M. and Ric, F., *Psychology of Emotion*, (Routledge, London, 2017), and the *Social Construction Theory* suggests that emotions are learned entirely through family interactions, e.g., Barrett, L. F., *How Emotions Are Made*, (Macmillan, London, 2017). The James/Lange theory of emotion, involving feedback from the body, is still spoken of Sapolsky, R., *Behave: The Biology of Humans at Our Best and Worst*, (Vintage, London, 2017). Moreover, some theories discuss emotions as only the conscious awareness of bodily changes in response to a stimulus. Damasio refers to this stage as feelings and Panksepp calls it the tertiary stage of the whole process. The interchangeability of terms such as affect for emotion also militates against consilience. Barret, for instance, uses *Affect* for what Panksepp calls the primary-process emotional reaction. Affect is defined as a simple pleasure/displeasure (valence) response determined by level of arousal. Neuroscientists, however, do agree that emotion/affect is an integral part of all decision making.

6 Porges, S. W., "The Polyvagal Theory: new insights into adaptive reactions of the autonomic nervous system", *Cleveland Clinic Journal of Medicine*, (2009).

7 Sapolsky, R., *Behave: The Biology of Humans at Our Best and Worst,* (2017).

8 See, for instance, Bowlby, J., *Attachment and Loss: Volume 1: Attachment*, (Basic Books, New York, 1969).

9 Panksepp, J. and Biven, L., *The Archaeology of the Mind: Neuroevolutionary Origins of Human Emotions,* (2012).

10 Seligman, M. E. P., "On the Generality of the Laws of Learning", *Psychological Review*, (1970), 77, pp 406–418.

11 Sapolsky, R., *Behave: The Biology of Humans at Our Best and Worst,* (2017).

12 Panksepp, J. and Biven, L., *The Archaeology of the Mind: Neuroevolutionary Origins of Human Emotions,* (2012).

13 Damasio, A., *The Feeling of What Happens: Body, Emotion and the Making of Consciousness*, (Vintage, London, 2000).

14 Arnsten, A. F. T., "Stress Weakens Prefrontal Networks: Molecular Insults to Higher Cognition", *Nature Neuroscience*, (2015), 18(10), pp 1376–1385: 1376.

15 Damasio, A., *Descartes Error: Emotion, Reason and the Human Brain* (Vintage, London, 1994).

16 Baron-Cohen, S., *Mindblindness: An Essay on Autism and Theory of Mind*, (MIT Press, Cambridge, MA, 1995).

17 Perry, B. D., "Fear and Learning: Trauma-Related Factors in the Adult Education Process", *New Directions for Adult and Continuing Education*, (2006), pp 21–27: 22; Girgenti, M. J., Hare, B. D., Ghosal, S. and Duman, R. S., "Molecular and Cellular Effects of Traumatic Stress: Implications for PTSD", *Current Psychiatry Reports*, (2017), 19(11), pp 85–85.

18 Damasio, A., *The Feeling of What Happens: Body, Emotion and the Making of Consciousness*, (2000): 273; Porges, S. W., "The Polyvagal Theory: Phylogenetic Contributions to Social Behavior", *Physiology and Behavior*, (2003); Porges, S. W., "The Polyvagal Theory: New Insights into Adaptive Reactions of the Autonomic Nervous System", *Cleveland Clinic Journal of Medicine*, (2009).

19 van der Kolk, B., *The Body Keeps The Score: Mind, Brain and Body in the Transformation of Trauma*, (2015): 204.

20 Perry, B. D., "Fear and Learning: Trauma-related Factors in the Adult Education Process", *New Directions for Adult and Continuing Education*, (2006): 24.

21 Deater-Deckard, K., Li, M. and Bell, M. A., "Multifaceted Emotion Regulation, Stress and Affect in Mothers of Young Children", *Cognition and Emotion*, (2016), 30(3), pp 444–457: 445; Smith, S. M. and Vale, W. W., "The Role of the Hypothalamic-Pituitary-Adrenal axis in Neuroendocrine Responses to Stress", *Dialogues in Clinical Neuroscience*, (2006), 8(4), pp 383–395.

22 Perry, B. D., Pollard, R. A., Blakely, T. L., Baker, W. L. and Vigilante, D., "Childhood Trauma, the Neurobiology of Adaptation, and 'Use-Dependent' Development of the Brain: How 'States' Become 'Traits'.", *Infant Mental Health Journal*, (1995), 16(4), pp 271–291: 274.

23 Stanovich, K. E., *Rationality and the Reflective Mind*, (Oxford University Press, Oxford, 2011).

24 Haidt, J., *The Righteous Mind*, (Allen Lane, London, 2012); Haidt, J., "The Emotional Dog and Its Rational Tail: A Social Intuitionist Approach to Moral Judgment", *Psychological Review*, (2001), 108(4), p 814.

25 Burnett, S. and Blakemore, S.-J., "Functional Connectivity during a Social Emotion Task in Adolescents and in Adults", *European Journal of Neuroscience*, (2009), 29(6), pp 1294–1301: 1294.

26 Shackelford, T. and Duntley, J., 'Evolutionary Forensic Psychology', (eds) Duntley and Shackelford, in *Evolutionary Forensic Psychology: Darwinian Foundations of Crime and Law*, (Oxford University Press, Oxford, 2008) pp 3–17; Baumeister, R. F. and Leary, M. R., "The Need to Belong: Desire for Interpersonal Attachments as a Fundamental Human Motivation", *Psychological Bulletin*, (1995), 117(3), pp 497–529.

27 Fehr, E., "On the Economics and Biology of Trust", *Journal of European Economic Association*, (2008), 7(2–3), pp 235–266: 2.

28 Project Aristotle. "The Secrets of Effective Teams at Google". The number one finding is that trust is the most important factor in effectiveness, that is in a team

with high psychological safety, colleagues feel safe to take risks around their team members. Available at https://rework.withgoogle.com/print/guides/572131265 5835136/. [Accessed April 10, 2022].

29 Trivers, R. L., "The Evolution of Reciprocal Altruism", *The Quarterly Review of Biology*, (1971), 46(1), pp 35–57.

30 Panksepp, J. and Biven, L., *The Archaeology of the Mind: Neuroevolutionary Origins of Human Emotions*, (2012): 339.

31 As a counterargument, it should be noted that much of the modern western world has displaced being a cooperative member of the group with the seeking of status. This usually translates to accumulating personal wealth. The work of Robert Merton has been particularly influential and remains relevant. Social anomie results from persons pursuing status, if necessary, by crooked means, if legitimate means are unavailable, see Merton, R., "Social Structure and Anomie", *American Sociological Review*, (1938), 3(5), pp 672–682. Status seeking is nonetheless also driven by self-esteem motivations.

32 Tajfel, H., "Social Psychology of Intergroup Relations", *Annual Review of Psychology*, (1982), 33(1), p 1; Tajfel, H. and Turner, J. C., 'An Integrative Theoty of Intergroup conflict.', (eds) Austin and Worchel, in *The Social Psychology of Intergroup Relations*, (Brooks/Cole, Monterey, CA, 1979) pp 33–47.

33 LeDoux, J. E., Wison, D. H. and Gazzaniga, M. S., "A Divided Mind", *Annals of Neurology*, (1977), 2, pp 417–421.

34 Barrett, L. F., *How Emotions are Made,* (2017).

35 An example might be Attachment Theory, where the relationship between primary caregiver and child has an influence in later relationships and coping styles, for more, see Bowlby, J., *Attachment and Loss: Volume 1: Attachment,* (1969); Cicchetti, D. and Doyle, C., "Child Maltreatment, Attachment and Psychopathology: Mediating Relations", *World Psychiatry: Official Journal of the World Psychiatric Association (WPA)*, (2016), 15(2), pp 89–90; Bretherton, I., "The Origins of Attachment Theory: John Bowlby and Mary Ainsworth", *Developmental Psychology*, (1992), 28(5), pp 759–775; Schore, J. R. and Schore, A. N., "Modern Attachment Theory: The Central Role of Affect Regulation in Development and Treatment", *Clinical Social Work Journal*, (2008), 36(1), pp 9–20.

36 Taleb, N., *The Black Swan: The Impact of the Highly Improbable*, (Penguin, London, 2008).

37 Mercier, H. and Sperber, D., "Why do Humans Reason? Arguments for an Argumentative Theory", *Behavioral and Brain Sciences*, (2011), 34(2), pp 57–111: 65.

38 Heuer, R. J., *Psychology of Intelligence Analysis*, (Central Intelligence Agency, Center for the Study of Intelligence, 1999): xxi.

39 Stanovich, K. E., *The Robot's Rebellion: Finding Meaning in the Age of Darwin*, (University of Chicago, Chicago 2004).

40 Ross, L. and Anderson, C. A., 'Shortcomings in the Attribution Process: On the Origins and Maintenance of Erroneous Social Assessments', (eds) Kahneman, Slovic and Tversksy, in *Judgement Under Uncertainty: Heuristics and Biases [2008 ed]*, (Cambridge University press, Cambridge, 1982) pp 129–152: 145.

41 Bourdieu uses the concept of *doxa,* which refers to the unquestioned truths which give rise to the universe of possible discourses (1982: 59). The doxa determine what things are beyond discussion, 'forbidden' or 'taboo' in the group. Scott Atran Atran, S. and Axelrod, R., "Reframing Sacred Values", *Negotiation Journal*, (2008), 24(3), pp 221–246, *In Gods We Trust: The Evolutionary Landscape of Religion*, (Oxford University

Press, Oxford, 2002) describe these sometimes become *sacred values* that are not only beyond debate but of such importance that even a hint of denigration may promote outrage. Many of these unspoken or tacit rules exist beyond the consciousness of group members, who fail to appreciate the hidden power that they exert.

42   Howard, G. S., "Culture Tales: A Narrative Approach to Thinking, Cross-Cultural Psychology, and Psychotherapy", *American Psychologist*, (1991), 46(3), pp 187–197; McAdams, D. P., Albaugh, M., Farber, E., Daniels, J., Logan, R. L. and Olson, B., "Family Metaphors and Moral Intuitions: How Conservatives and Liberals Narrate Their Lives", *Journal of Personality and Social Psychology*, (2008), 95(4), pp 978–990.

43   McAdams, D. P., Albaugh, M., Farber, E., Daniels, J., Logan, R. L. and Olson, B., "Family Metaphors and Moral Intuitions: How Conservatives and Liberals Narrate Their Lives", *Journal of Personality and Social Psychology*, (2008): 979.

44   McAdams, D. P. and Pals, J. L., "A New Big Five: Fundamental Principles for an Integrative Science of Personality", *American Psychologist*, (2006), 61(3), pp 204–217: 207.

45   Goffman, E., *The Presentation of Self in Everyday Life*, (University of Chicago Press, Chicago, 1959).

46   Johnson-Laird, P. N., "Deductive Reasoning", *Annual Review of Psychology*, (1999), 50(1), pp 109–135.

47   Palazzo, G., Krings, F. and Hoffrage, U., "Ethical Blindness", *Journal of Business Ethics*, (2012), 109(3), pp 323–338.

48   Palazzo, G., Krings, F. and Hoffrage, U., "Ethical Blindness", *Journal of Business Ethics*, (2012).

49   Triadis, H. C., *Self-Deception in Politics, Religion, and Terrorism*, (Praeger, London, 2009).

50   Mazar, N., Amir, O. and Ariely, D., "The Dishonesty of Honest People: A Theory of Self-Concept Maintenance", *Journal of Marketing Research (JMR)*, (2008), 45(6), pp 633–644; Cialdini, R. B. and Goldstein, N. J., "Social Influence: Compliance and Conformity", *Annual Review of Psychology*, (2004), 55(1), pp 591–621.

51   Moston, S. and Stephenson, G. M., "A Typology of Denial Strategies by Suspects in Criminal Investigations", (eds) Bull, Valentine and Williamson, in *Handbook of Psychology of Investigative Interviewing*, (Wiley-Blackwell, Chichester, 2009) pp 17–34: 22.

52   Sykes, G. M. and Matza, D., "Techniques of Neutralization: A Theory of Delinquency", *American Sociological Review*, (1957), 22(6), pp 664–670.

53   Herman, J. L., *Trauma and Recovery: The Aftermath of Violence*, (Basic Books, New York, 1992).

54   Nisbett, R. E. and Ross, L., *Human Inference: Strategies and Shortcomings in Social Judgement*, (Prentice-Hall, Englewood Cliffs, NJ, 1980), Ross, L. and Anderson, C. A., *Shortcomings in the Attribution Process: On the Origins and Maintenance of Erroneous Social Assessments*, Kahneman, Slovic and Tversksy, *Judgement Under Uncertainty: Heuristics and Biases* [2008 ed], (1982)

55   Moston, S. and Stephenson, G. M., *A Typology of Denial Strategies by Suspects in Criminal Investigations*, (eds) Bull, Valentine and Williamson, in *Handbook of Psychology of Investigative Interviewing*, (2009); Lord, C. G., Ross, L. and Lepper, M. R., "Biased Assimilation and Attitude Polarization: The Effects of Prior Theories on Subsequently Considered Evidence", *Journal of Personality and Social Psychology*, (1979), 37(11), pp 2098–2109; Miller, W. R. and Rollnick, S., *Motivational Interviewing*, (Guilford Press, New York, 2002).

56 Festinger, L. and Carlsmith, J. M., "Cognitive Consequences of Forced Compliance", *Journal of Abnormal and Social Psychology*, (1959), 58(2), pp 203–210; see Nickerson, R. S., "Confirmation Bias: A Ubiquitous Phenomenon in Many Guises", *Review of General Psychology*, (1998), 2(2), pp 175–220.

57 Vrij, A., *Detecting Lies and Deceit*, (Wiley, Chichester, 2008): 132.

58 Stanovich, K. E., West, R. F. and Toplak, M. E., "Myside Bias, Rational Thinking, and Intelligence", *Current Directions in Psychological Science*, (2013), 22(4), pp 259–264.

59 Roberts, K., "Social Psychology and the Investigation of Terrorism", (ed) Pearse, in *Investigating Terrorism: Current Political, Legal and Psychological Issues*, (John Wiley, Chichester, 2015), pp 202–213: 212.

60 Fenton-O'Creevy, M., Soane, E., Nicholson, N. and Willman, P., "Thinking, Feeling and Deciding: The Influence of Emotions on the Decision Making and Performance of Traders", *Journal of Organizational Behavior*, (2011), 32(8), pp 1044–1061.

61 Stress can narrow all perceptions, including visual fields and auditory senses. The mind tends to prioritize its attention, even more so under stress. In the case of hearing, stress makes the frequency of human speech less salient, being more alert to frequencies of animal noises. For more, see Porges, S. W., "The Polyvagal Theory: Phylogenetic Contributions to Social Behavior", *Physiology and Behavior*, (2003); Porges, S. W., "The Polyvagal Theory: New Insights into Adaptive Reactions of the Autonomic Nervous System", *Cleveland Clinic Journal of Medicine*, (2009), Syed, M., *Black Box Thinking: Marginal Gains and the Secrets of High Performance*, (John Murray, London, 2015).

62 Quoted in Kahneman, D., *Thinking, Fast and Slow*, (Penguin, London, 2012): 237.

63 Barrett, L. F., "Are Emotions Natural Kinds?", *Perspectives on Psychological Science*, (2006), 1(1), pp 28–58.

64 Damasio, A., *Looking for Spinoza*, (Vintage, London, 2004): 148. This is consistent with system one processing, see Kahneman (1982, 2012).

65 Often referred to as 10,000 hours of good practice.

66 Gladwell, M., *Blink: The Power of Thinking Without Thinking*, (Penguin, London, 2006).

67 Gigerenzer, G., "Heuristics", (eds) Gigerenzer and Engel, in *Heuristics and the Law*, (MIT Press, Cambridge, MA, 2006), pp 17–44; Marewski, J. N., Gaissmaier, W. and Gigerenzer, G., "Good Judgments Do Not Require Complex Cognition", *Cognitive Processing*, (2010), 11(2), pp 103–121.

68 Kruger, J. and Dunning, D., "Unskilled and Unaware of It: How Difficulties in Recognizing One's Own Incompetence Lead to Inflated Self-assessments", *Journal of Personality and Social Psychology*, (1999), 77(6), pp 1121–1134.

69 Kahneman, D., *Thinking, Fast and Slow*, (2012).

70 Kahneman, D., *Thinking, Fast and Slow*, (2012): 239.

71 Vrij, A., Granhag, P. A. and Porter, S., "Pitfalls and Opportunities in Nonverbal and Verbal Lie Detection", *Psychological Science in the Public Interest*, (2010), 11(3), pp 89–121.

72 Jowett, G. and O'Donnnell, V., *Propaganda and Persuasion*, (Sage, Thousand Oaks, CA, 2012): 32.

73 Haidt, J., *The Righteous Mind*, (2012). The argument suggests that complex social life requiring tracking of individual relationships, trust, favors owed, and friendships was a major driver in human intelligence. Language then evolved around convincing others.

74 Jowett, G. and O'Donnnell, V., *Propaganda and Persuasion*, (2012): 33.

75 Inbau, F. E., "Police Interrogation—A Practical Necessity", *Journal of Criminal Law & Criminology*, ([1961] 1999), 89(4), pp 1403; Inbau, F. E., Reid, J., Buckley, J. P. and Jayne, B., *Criminal Interrogation and Confessions*, 4th ed., (Aspen, Gaithersburg, MD, 2001).

76 Cialdini, R. B. and Goldstein, N. J., "Social Influence: Compliance and Conformity", *Annual Review of Psychology*, (2004): 593.

77 Cialdini, R. B., *Influence: The Psychology of Persuasion*, (HarperCollins, New York, 2007): 9.

78 Tversky, A. and Kahneman, D., "Availability: A Heuristic for Judging Frequency and Probability", (eds) Kahneman, Slovic and Tversky, in *Judgement Under Uncertainty: Heuristics and Biases*, (Cambridge University Press, Cambridge, 1982) pp 163–178.

79 Cialdini, R. B. and Goldstein, N. J., "Social Influence: Compliance and Conformity", *Annual Review of Psychology*, (2004); Cialdini, R. B., *Influence: The Psychology of Persuasion*, (2007). Similarly, Tali Sharot outlines seven core elements involved in influencing someone and that regulate someone's thoughts and actions. These include the prior beliefs, the emotions involved, the incentives presented, creating a sense of agency, or curiosity, the state of mind, and the knowledge and acts of other people.[79] David Gragg describes how psychological triggers are used in social engineering (cyber hacking) by leveraging strong affect (emotion), overloading, reciprocation, deceptive relationships, the diffusion of responsibility and moral duty, authority, and integrity and consistency. There is obvious congruency between the different research approaches. See also Ferreira, A. and Teles, S., "Persuasion: How Phishing Emails Can Influence Users and Bypass Security Measures", *International Journal of Human-Computer Studies*, (2019), 125, pp 19–31.

80 Jowett, G. and O'Donnell, V., *Propaganda and Persuasion*, (2012): 38; Sharot, T., *The Influential Mind: What the Brain Reveals About Our Power to Change Others*, (Little Brown, London, 2017).

81 Abelson, R. P., "Beliefs Are Like Possessions", *Journal for the Theory of Social Behaviour*, (1986), 16(3), pp 223–250.

82 Gupta, R., Hur, Y. J. and Lavie, N., "Distracted by Pleasure: Effects of Positive versus Negative Valence on Emotional Capture under Load", *Emotion*, (2016), 16(3), pp 328–337.

83 Sharot, T., *The Influential Mind: What the Brain Reveals About Our Power to Change Others*, (2017).

84 Watson, J. M., Balota, D. A. and Roediger III, H. L., "Creating False Memories With Hybrid Lists of Semantic and Phonological Associates: Over-additive False Memories Produced by Converging Associative Networks", *Journal of Memory and Language*, (2003), 49(1), pp 95–118.

85 Loftus, E. F. and Palmer, J. C., "Reconstruction of Automobile Destruction: An Example of the Interaction Between Language and Memory", *Journal of Verbal Learning & Verbal Behavior*, (1974), 13(5), pp 585–589.

86 Thaler, R. H. and Sunstein, C. R., *Nudge: Improving Decisions about Health, Wealth, and Happiness*, (Yale University Press, Yale, 2008). The choice architecture talks about designing in ways to save, have better health, by leveraging our inherent biases. An article by Simon Ruda in February 2022, who was one of the lead scientists in the British government's Behavioral Insights Team established in 2010, cautioned against the risk of using choice architecture at policy level. He warned that nudge

techniques risked being misused by authoritarian regimes and their use can never be considered benign. Article available at https://unherd.com/2022/01/how-the-government-abused-nudge-theory/. [Accessed February 7, 2022].

87 Jowett, G. and O'Donnnell, V., *Propaganda and Persuasion*, (2012): 170. Jowett and O'Donnnell discuss the Semantic Differential which can be used a measure of these differences.

88 Cabrera, D. and Cabrera, L., *Systems Thinking Made Simple: New Hope for Solving Wicked Problems*. 2nd ed, (Plectica Publishing, 2018): 58.

89 Stanovich, K. E., *The Robot's Rebellion: Finding Meaning in the Age of Darwin*, (2004).

90 Kern, M. C. and Chugh, D., "Bounded Ethicality: The Perils of Loss Framing", *Psychological Science (Wiley-Blackwell)*, (2009), 20(3), pp 378–384.

91 Jowett, G. and O'Donnnell, V., *Propaganda and Persuasion*, (2012): 9.

92 Syed, M., *Black Box Thinking: Marginal Gains and the Secrets of High Performance*, (2015): 15.

93 Cialdini, R. B. and Goldstein, N. J., "Social Influence: Compliance and Conformity", *Annual Review of Psychology*, (2004): 592.

94 Mazar, N., Amir, O. and Ariely, D., "The Dishonesty of Honest People: A Theory of Self-Concept Maintenance", *Journal of Marketing Research (JMR)*, (2008).

95 Sharot, T., *The Influential Mind: What the Brain Reveals About Our Power to Change Others*, (2017).

96 Brehm, S. S. and Brehm, J. W., *Psychological Reactance: A Theory of Freedom and Control*, (Academic Press, New York, 1981).

97 Gudjonsson, G. H., *The Psychology of Interrogations and Confessions: A Handbook*, (Wiley, Chichester, 2003); Kassin, S. M., Drizin, S. A., Grisso, T., Gudjonsson, G. H., Leo, R. A. and Redlich, A. D., "Police-Induced Confessions: Risk Factors and Recommendations", *Law and Human Behavior*, (2010), 34(1), pp 3–38; Kassin, S. M., Meissner, C. A. and Norwick, R. J., ""I'd Know a False Confession if I Saw One": A Comparative Study of College Students and Police Investigators", *Law & Human Behavior*, (2005), 29(2), pp 211–227.

98 Cialdini, R. B., *Influence: The Psychology of Persuasion*, (2007): 140.

99 Cialdini, R. B., *Influence: The Psychology of Persuasion*, (2007): 28.

100 Jowett, G. and O'Donnnell, V., *Propaganda and Persuasion*, (2012): 178.

101 Cialdini, R. B., *Influence: The Psychology of Persuasion*, (2007): 61. Chinese interrogators used such principles very effectively during the Korean War, see Edgar Schein 1956 "The Chinese Indoctrination Program" Psychiatry 19; also Gudjonsson 2010, Interviewing Suspects: Practice, Science, and Future Directions, discusses theories of why suspects falsely confess, including coerced-compliant treatment where the suspect eventually internalizes the behavior ascribed to him by interrogators.

Bibliography

Abelson, R. P., "Beliefs Are Like Possessions", *Journal for the Theory of Social Behaviour*, (1986), 16(3), pp 223–250.

Arnsten, A. F. T., "Stress Weakens Prefrontal Networks: Molecular Insults to Higher Cognition", *Nature Neuroscience*, (2015), 18(10), pp 1376–1385.

Atran, S., *In Gods We Trust: The Evolutionary Landscape of Religion*, (Oxford University Press, Oxford, 2002).

Atran, S. and Axelrod, R., "Reframing Sacred Values", *Negotiation Journal*, (2008), 24(3), pp 221–246.

Baron-Cohen, S., *Mindblindness: An Essay on Autism and Theory of Mind*, (MIT Press, Cambridge, MA, 1995).

Barrett, L. F., "Are Emotions Natural Kinds?", *Perspectives on Psychological Science*, (2006), 1(1), pp 28–58.

Barrett, L. F., *How Emotions Are Made*, (Macmillan, London, 2017).

Baumeister, R. F. and Leary, M. R., "The Need to Belong: Desire for Interpersonal Attachments as a Fundamental Human Motivation", *Psychological Bulletin*, (1995), 117(3), pp 497–529.

Bowlby, J., *Attachment and Loss: Volume 1: Attachment*, (Basic Books, New York, NY, 1969).

Brehm, S. S. and Brehm, J. W., *Psychological Reactance: A Theory of Freedom and Control*, (Academic Press, New York, NY, 1981).

Bretherton, I., "The Origins of Attachment Theory: John Bowlby and Mary Ainsworth", *Developmental Psychology*, (1992), 28(5), pp 759–775.

Burnett, S. and Blakemore, S.-J., "Functional Connectivity during a Social Emotion Task in Adolescents and in Adults", *European Journal of Neuroscience*, (2009), 29(6), pp 1294–1301.

Cabrera, D. and Cabrera, L., *Systems Thinking Made Simple: New Hope for Solving Wicked Problems.* 2nd ed, (Plectica Publishing, 2018).

Cialdini, R. B., *Influence: The Psychology of Persuasion*, (HarperCollins, New York, NY, 2007).

Cialdini, R. B. and Goldstein, N. J., "Social Influence: Compliance and Conformity", *Annual Review of Psychology*, (2004), 55(1), pp 591–621.

Cicchetti, D. and Doyle, C., "Child Maltreatment, Attachment and Psychopathology: Mediating Relations", *World Psychiatry: Official Journal of the World Psychiatric Association (WPA)*, (2016), 15(2), pp 89–90.

Damasio, A., *Descartes Error: Emotion, Reason and the Human Brain* (Vintage, London, 1994).

Damasio, A., *The Feeling of What Happens: Body, Emotion and the Making of Consciousness*, (Vintage, London, 2000).

Damasio, A., *Looking for Spinoza*, (Vintage, London, 2004).

Deater-Deckard, K., Li, M. and Bell, M. A., "Multifaceted Emotion Regulation, Stress and Affect in Mothers of Young Children", *Cognition and Emotion*, (2016), 30(3), pp 444–457.

Ekman, P., "An Argument for Basic Emotions", *Cognition and Emotion*, (1992), 6(3/4), pp 169–200.

Fehr, E., "On the Economics and Biology of Trust", *Journal of European Economic Association*, (2008), 7(2–3), pp 235–266.

Fenton-O'Creevy, M., Soane, E., Nicholson, N. and Willman, P., "Thinking, Feeling and Deciding: The Influence of Emotions on the Decision Making and Performance of Traders", *Journal of Organizational Behavior*, (2011), 32(8), pp 1044–1061.

Ferreira, A. and Teles, S., "Persuasion: How Phishing Emails Can Influence Users and Bypass Security Measures", *International Journal of Human-Computer Studies*, (2019), 125, pp 19–31.

Festinger, L. and Carlsmith, J. M., "Cognitive Consequences of Forced Compliance", *Journal of Abnormal and Social Psychology*, (1959), 58(2), pp 203–210.

Gigerenzer, G., 'Heuristics', (eds) Gigerenzer and Engel, in *Heuristics and the Law*, (MIT Press, Cambridge, MA, 2006) pp 17–44.

Girgenti, M. J., Hare, B. D., Ghosal, S. and Duman, R. S., "Molecular and Cellular Effects of Traumatic Stress: Implications for PTSD", *Current Psychiatry Reports*, (2017), 19(11), pp 85–85.

Gladwell, M., *Blink: The Power of Thinking Without Thinking*, (Penguin, London, 2006).

Goffman, E., *The Presentation of Self in Everyday Life*, (University of Chicago Press, Chicago, 1959).

Gudjonsson, G. H., *The Psychology of Interrogations and Confessions: A Handbook*, (Wiley, Chichester, 2003).

Gupta, R., Hur, Y. J. and Lavie, N., "Distracted by Pleasure: Effects of Positive Versus Negative Valence on Emotional Capture under Load", *Emotion*, (2016), 16(3), pp 328–337.

Haidt, J., "The Emotional Dog and Its Rational Tail: A Social Intuitionist Approach to Moral Judgment", *Psychological Review*, (2001), 108(4), p 814.

Haidt, J., *The Righteous Mind*, (Allen Lane, London, 2012).

Herman, J. L., *Trauma and Recovery: The Aftermath of Violence*, (Basic Books, New York, NY, 1992).

Heuer, R. J., *Psychology of Intelligence Analysis*, (Central Intelligence Agency, Center for the Study of Intelligence, Langley, VA, 1999).

Howard, G. S., "Culture Tales: A Narrative Approach to Thinking, Cross-Cultural Psychology, and Psychotherapy", *American Psychologist*, (1991), 46(3), pp 187–197.

Inbau, F. E., "Police Interrogation—A Practical Necessity", *Journal of Criminal Law & Criminology*, ([1961] 1999), 89(4), p 1403.

Inbau, F. E., Reid, J., Buckley, J. P. and Jayne, B., *Criminal Interrogation and Confessions*, 4th ed., (Aspen, Gaithersburg, MD, 2001).

Johnson-Laird, P. N., "Deductive Reasoning", *Annual Review of Psychology*, (1999), 50(1), pp 109–135.

Jowett, G. and O'Donnnell, V., *Propaganda and Persuasion*, (Sage, Thousand Oaks, CA, 2012).

Kahneman, D., *Thinking, Fast and Slow*, (Penguin, London, 2012).

Kassin, S. M., Drizin, S. A., Grisso, T., Gudjonsson, G. H., Leo, R. A. and Redlich, A. D., "Police-Induced Confessions: Risk Factors and Recommendations", *Law and Human Behavior*, (2010), 34(1), pp 3–38.

Kassin, S. M., Meissner, C. A. and Norwick, R. J., ""I'd Know a False Confession if I Saw One": A Comparative Study of College Students and Police Investigators", *Law & Human Behavior*, (2005), 29(2), pp 211–227.

Kern, M. C. and Chugh, D., "Bounded Ethicality: The Perils of Loss Framing", *Psychological Science (Wiley-Blackwell)*, (2009), 20(3), pp 378–384.

Kruger, J. and Dunning, D., "Unskilled and Unaware of It: How Difficulties in Recognizing One's Own Incompetence Lead to Inflated Self-assessments", *Journal of Personality and Social Psychology*, (1999), 77(6), pp 1121–1134.

LeDoux, J. E., "Emotion Circuits in the Brain", *Annual Review of Neuroscience*, (2000), 23(1), pp 155–184.

LeDoux, J. E., Wilson, D. H. and Gazzaniga, M. S., "A Divided Mind", *Annals of Neurology*, (1977), 2, pp 417–421

Loftus, E. F. and Palmer, J. C., "Reconstruction of Automobile Destruction: An Example of the Interaction Between Language and Memory", *Journal of Verbal Learning & Verbal Behavior*, (1974), 13(5), pp 585–589.

Lord, C. G., Ross, L. and Lepper, M. R., "Biased Assimilation and Attitude Polarization: The Effects of Prior Theories on Subsequently Considered Evidence", *Journal of Personality and Social Psychology*, (1979), 37(11), pp 2098–2109.

Marewski, J. N., Gaissmaier, W. and Gigerenzer, G., "Good Judgments Do Not Require Complex Cognition", *Cognitive Processing*, (2010), 11(2), pp 103–121.

Mazar, N., Amir, O. and Ariely, D., "The Dishonesty of Honest People: A Theory of Self-Concept Maintenance", *Journal of Marketing Research (JMR)*, (2008), 45(6), pp 633–644.

McAdams, D. P., Albaugh, M., Farber, E., Daniels, J., Logan, R. L. and Olson, B., "Family Metaphors and Moral Intuitions: How Conservatives and Liberals Narrate Their Lives", *Journal of Personality and Social Psychology*, (2008), 95(4), pp 978–990.

McAdams, D. P. and Pals, J. L., "A New Big Five: Fundamental Principles for an Integrative Science of Personality", *American Psychologist*, (2006), 61(3), pp 204–217.

Mercier, H. and Sperber, D., "Why Do Humans Reason? Arguments for an Argumentative Theory", *Behavioral and Brain Sciences*, (2011), 34(2), pp 57–111.

Merton, R., "Social Structure and Anomie", *American Sociological Review*, (1938), 3(5), pp 672–682.

Miller, W. R. and Rollnick, S., *Motivational Interviewing*, (Guilford Press, New York, NY, 2002).

Moston, S. and Stephenson, G. M., 'A Typology of Denial Strategies by Suspects in Criminal Investigations', (eds) Bull, Valentine and Williamson, in *Handbook of Psychology of Investigative Interviewing*, (Wiley-Blackwell, Chichester, 2009) pp 17–34.

Nickerson, R. S., "Confirmation Bias: A Ubiquitous Phenomenon in Many Guises", *Review of General Psychology*, (1998), 2(2), pp 175–220.

Niendenthal, P. M. and Ric, F., *Psychology of Emotion*, (Routledge, London, 2017).

Nisbett, R. E. and Ross, L., *Human Inference: Strategies and Shortcomings in Social Judgement*, (Prentice-Hall, Englewood Cliffs, NJ, 1980).

Palazzo, G., Krings, F. and Hoffrage, U., "Ethical Blindness", *Journal of Business Ethics*, (2012), 109(3), pp 323–338.

Panksepp, J. and Biven, L., *The Archaeology of the Mind: Neuroevolutionary Origins of Human Emotions*, (W. W. Norton, New York, NY, 2012).

Perry, B. D., "Fear and Learning: Trauma-related Factors in the Adult Education Process", *New Directions for Adult and Continuing Education*, (2006), 110, pp 21–27.

Perry, B. D., Pollard, R. A., Blakely, T. L., Baker, W. L. and Vigilante, D., "Childhood Trauma, the Neurobiology of Adaptation, and 'Use-Dependent' Development of the Brain: How 'States' Become 'Traits'.", *Infant Mental Health Journal*, (1995), 16(4), pp 271–291.

Porges, S. W., "The Polyvagal Theory: Phylogenetic Contributions to Social Behavior", *Physiology and Behavior*, (2003), 79(3), pp 503–513.

Porges, S. W., "The Polyvagal Theory: New Insights into Adaptive Reactions of the Autonomic Nervous System", *Cleveland Clinic Journal of Medicine*, (2009), 76 (Suppl 2), pp S86–S90.

Pronin, E., Lin, D. Y. and Ross, L., "The Bias Blind Spot: Perceptions of Bias in Self Versus Others", *Personality and Social Psychology Bulletin*, (2002), 28(3), pp 369–381.

Roberts, K., 'Social Psychology and the Investigation of Terrorism', (ed) Pearse, in *Investigating Terrorism: Current Political, Legal and Psychological Issues*, (John Wiley, Chichester, 2015) pp 202–213.

Ross, L. and Anderson, C. A., 'Shortcomings in the Attribution Process: On the Origins and Maintenance of Erroneous Social Assessments', (eds) Kahneman, Slovic and Tverksy, in *Judgement under Uncertainty: Heuristics and Biases [2008 ed]*, (Cambridge University press, Cambridge, 1982) pp 129–152

Sapolsky, R., *Behave: The Biology of Humans at Our Best and Worst*, (Vintage, London, 2017)

Schore, J. R. and Schore, A. N., "Modern Attachment Theory: The Central Role of Affect Regulation in Development and Treatment", *Clinical Social Work Journal*, (2008), 36(1), pp 9–20.

Seligman, M. E. P., "On the Generality of the Laws of Learning", *Psychological Review*, (1970), 77, pp 406–418.

Shackelford, T. and Duntley, J., 'Evolutionary Forensic Psychology', (eds) Duntley and Shackelford, in *Evolutionary Forensic Psychology: Darwinian Foundations of Crime and Law*, (Oxford University Press, Oxford, 2008) pp 3–17.

Sharot, T., *The Influential Mind: What the Brain Reveals About Our Power to Change Others*, (Little Brown, London, 2017).

Smith, S. M. and Vale, W. W., "The Role of the Hypothalamic-Pituitary-Adrenal Axis in Neuroendocrine Responses to Stress", *Dialogues in Clinical Neuroscience*, (2006), 8(4), pp 383–395.

Stanovich, K. E., *Rationality and the Reflective Mind*, (Oxford University Press, Oxford, 2011).

Stanovich, K. E., *The Robot's Rebellion: Finding Meaning in the Age of Darwin*, (University of Chicago, Chicago 2004).

Stanovich, K. E., West, R. F. and Toplak, M. E., "Myside Bias, Rational Thinking, and Intelligence", *Current Directions in Psychological Science*, (2013), 22(4), pp 259–264.

Syed, M., *Black Box Thinking: Marginal Gains and the Secrets of High Performance*, (John Murray, London, 2015).

Sykes, G. M. and Matza, D., "Techniques of Neutralization: A Theory of Delinquency", *American Sociological Review*, (1957), 22(6), pp 664–670.

Tajfel, H., "Social Psychology of Intergroup Relations", *Annual Review of Psychology*, (1982), 33(1), p 1.

Tajfel, H. and Turner, J. C., "An Integrative Theory of Intergroup Conflict.", (eds) Austin and Worchel, in *The Social Psychology of Intergroup Relations*, (Brooks/Cole, Monterey, CA, 1979) pp 33–47.

Taleb, N., *The Black Swan: The Impact of the Highly Improbable*, (Penguin, London, 2008).

Thaler, R. H. and Sunstein, C. R., *Nudge: Improving Decisions about Health, Wealth, and Happiness*, (Yale University Press, Yale, 2008).

Triadis, H. C., *Self-Deception in Politics, Religion, and Terrorism*, (Praeger, London, 2009).

Trivers, R. L., "The Evolution of Reciprocal Altruism", *The Quarterly Review of Biology*, (1971), 46(1), pp 35–57.

Tversky, A. and Kahneman, D., 'Availability: A Heuristic for Judging Frequency and Probability', (eds) Kahneman, Slovic and Tversky, in *Judgement under Uncertainty: Heuristics and Biases*, (Cambridge University press, Cambridge, 1982), pp 163–178.

van der Kolk, B., *The Body Keeps The Score: Mind, Brain and Body in the Transformation of Trauma*, (Penguin, London, 2015).

Vrij, A., *Detecting Lies and Deceit*, (Wiley, Chichester, 2008).

Vrij, A., Granhag, P. A. and Porter, S., "Pitfalls and Opportunities in Nonverbal and Verbal Lie Detection", *Psychological Science in the Public Interest*, (2010), 11(3), pp 89–121.

Watson, J. M., Balota, D. A. and Roediger III, H. L., "Creating False Memories With Hybrid Lists of Semantic and Phonological Associates: Over-additive False Memories Produced by Converging Associative Networks", *Journal of Memory and Language*, (2003), 49(1), pp 95–118.

Chapter 10

Review of the Colonel Interview

Introduction

It is difficult to adequately describe an interview method by talking abstractly about it. It is much better to watch the technique in actual use. Fortunately, the Internet offers many examples of interviewing, some good, some less so. One of the better examples of multiple techniques discussed in this book is the Canadian police interview of air force Colonel Russell Williams, who committed two murders of women after sexually assaulting them.[1] Obviously, this is a murder investigation and does differ somewhat from an organizational interview. Although the actual video shown is edited by the trial court, there is sufficient detail to identify how many of the techniques outlined in this book are used, although obtaining the initial account phase is limited. The most important observations to make is the friendly tone of the interview throughout, and the use of rapport to maintain communication throughout the interview, even after admissions are obtained. I describe some of these techniques below as it was an excellent police interview that shows the effectiveness of these types of technique. Not every technique used is elaborated, as it would mean rewriting the book to do so.[2]

Interview Tone

The most important aspect to be taken from the video is the lack of confrontation or aggression. Even though it is a multiple homicide investigation, the suspect is always treated with respect and courtesy. Sergeant Smyth is almost friendly and conversational. The sergeant is constantly working with the suspect throughout the interview to try to problem solve and begins by extending his gratitude for the voluntary assistance that the colonel has given by attending at the police station. This is continued from the first meeting outside the interview room and into the room itself. Note the sitting arrangements in the room, the desk is not between them and permits full body scanning and leaning into the interviewee when necessary. Before he even starts the interview, he has brought coffee for them both. Sergeant Smyth lays out the ground rules for the

DOI: 10.4324/9781003269489-10

interview that he treats everyone with respect and expects to be treated like-wise. In particular, watch the elegant way the sergeant starts the interview by a constant focus on rapport and is able to advise the suspect of his rights while keeping him at ease. He does this by explaining the purpose of the interview and how important talking to police is because of the gravity of the investi-gation. Sergeant Smyth never points out the fact that the Colonel is the sus-pect. Rather the police are following all leads and Colonel Williams is but one person, nonetheless, sergeant Smyth carefully and patiently explains the voluntariness nature of the interview and his rights, including to legal advice, but it is all in a narrative style that is nonconfrontational and never seems to threaten Williams. Indeed, the explanation actually builds rapport because it emphasizes fairness, and the respect sergeant Smyth has for treating everyone fairly. Williams remains relatively relaxed even though he has actually been told that he is a suspect, does not need to talk to the police, has rights, including the right to free legal advice, and this is a taped recording which might be used in evidence. Note also that although Williams appears calm and his body posture is relaxed, he is chewing gum ferociously.

Sergeant Smyth reflects back William's own words to point out why he is an important person for the investigators to talk to, but it is framed in a way that almost seems perfunctory and simply part of methodical police work. Sergeant Smyth then moves to getting an account, starting with rela-tively lowball account-for-your-movement's type questions. Sergeant Smyth clarifies some points around time and dates issues as the suspect progresses through the account but again in an almost casual 'just trying to be precise' manner.

The body language is striking. Sergeant Smyth sits closely and leans in some-times toward Williams for emphasis. As Williams is asked to account for knowing the victims, his body language changes, and he begins using his left hand to rub his right elbow and bicep. He uses his right hand for emphasis at certain points but mainly about ancillary points such as activities at the base when the report of murder came in. At times later on, he begins to rub his neck and shirt collar. As sergeant Smyth probes Williams account of his movements more deeply just after 15 minutes, Williams folds his arms into a tighter defensive posture. Sergeant Smyth carefully frames the narrative to get the cooperation of Williams to provide DNA and other forensic samples. He asks first if he has watched CSI programs and knows about forensic evidence. He then asks what Williams would do to help the investigation; he clarifies this when asked: 'what do you mean?' by responding if you would be willing to give samples. Williams is anxious to appear cooperative and says he would be. Sergeant Smyth then cleverly and immediately says that yes, we will do that. He has used a hypothet-ical question to get agreement and then sealed that with a definite course of action. Humor and social intelligence are used throughout to get cooperation and it is the way the suspect is persuaded to voluntarily supply DNA and other forensics.

The available evidence is carefully presented in tactical ways. Sergeant Smyth first asks questions to examine alternative explanations for evidence that he already has before introducing it. The suspect is asked is there any reason that his DNA might appear at any crime scene, but it is again couched in language of cooperation and helping the investigation. The suspect is encouraged to be open and honest and to be frank about any reason for DNA at the crime scene, such as an affair. The sergeant is covering off any possible alternative explanations comprehensively for recovered evidence early before any such evidence is presented. Once Williams has denied it completely, the sergeant checks his interview plan and then casually but quickly changes subject to ask the suspect for the make of vehicle tires and when fitted. The sergeant then changes subject again to the use of Williams swipe card and a deeper probe of his movements at the relevant times. Sergeant Smyth then carefully introduces his evidence of Williams tire tracks close to the house of the victims, suggesting but never accusing Williams that it was his vehicle. Sergeant Smyth then changes subject again to introduce diary evidence from one of the victims and asks for an explanation.

The importance of mutual respect is constantly emphasized and is used to frame to Williams the subject of being dishonest, rather than ever accusing him of lying. This is an example of a subtle use of the DEAL technique. At 35 minutes in the video, as he returns to the room, sergeant Smyth talks about the need for mutual respect and how the police have tried to meet Williams's desire for discretion, but issues keep coming up that are pointing to Williams. The implication is that the police are doing their best for Williams, but he is not fulfilling his part of the agreement. So, when footprint impressions of Williams at the rear of Jessica Llyod's house are produced, it is this approach of respect that primes Williams that he has been lying. Watch William's body language as this evidence is put to him and honesty is asked for. He sits forward and makes a show of carefully examining the photocopied impression. Sergeant Smyth uses silence and then points out what this and other evidence seems to be saying. He states that it appears that Williams was at the house despite denying it and he wants to know why. A small admission to be obtained first. There is nothing in this about murder or anything else, just confusion about disparity between the account given and contradictory evidence. Sergeant Smyth appears to be waiting for a plausible explanation that he would happily accept and move on.

When Williams claims lack of knowledge, more pressure is applied, search warrants are being executed and likely to find more evidence linking Williams to these 'situations'; the word crime scene or murder locations is not used. Likewise, the phrase 'evidence that supports an investigative position' is used rather than 'links you to these crimes' that would have much more negative connotations. The evidence is beginning to pile up, even though it is only potential. Subtle persuasion suggests that an understanding of Williams's need for control is known and planned for. Williams is advised that denial will only lose him control. He needs to provide a plausible explanation now to retain control before the evidence provides it. Williams is now still sitting forward, nodding his head and grunting as if he understands the issue he is facing. The sergeant raises the issue of credibility and believability. He uses persuasion and hypothetical questions to show Williams the best option from the alternatives available.

Sergeant Smyth asks Williams 'what are we going to do?' at 44 minutes in the tape and then stays silent for over 30 seconds until Williams who is clearly thinking hard looks away and down. Sergeant Smyth then repeats the question, to which Williams asks to be called 'Russ' instead of 'Russell'. The question is repeated again, more silence. Sergeant Smyth then makes a bold change of tack, asking Williams if the body of Jessica (one of the victims) can be found easily. The emphasis is on doing the right thing, an appeal to self-esteem and ideology, to help bring closure by recovering the victim's body for the family. More lengthy silence follows. Williams body language goes from defensive to struggling, and sergeant Smyth asks what issue he is struggling with. The tactic hasn't worked, and Williams withdraws somewhat but sergeant Smyth adapts, rolls with it, and keeps up the pressure by continuing to use persuasion, even using the word 'bud' to maintain solidarity and then agrees to a request to help minimize the impact on Williams's wife. This is an appeal to Williams's ego to minimize the effect on his wife. Smyth keeps suggesting that he is trying to help Williams. Minimizing the impact on Williams's wife remains the anchor that gives Williams the illusion he is exercising some control over his current situation.

At 54 minutes, Williams asks how to minimize the impact on his wife, Smyth suggests starting by telling the truth. Williams says OK, to which the first question asked immediately is 'where is she?' After a short silence, Williams asks for a map. At this point, Smyth wants to get a concrete admission first and asks for general location to get the right map. Smyth is fully aware that the suspect may retract and retreat if given time to think and therefore pushes to get a committed admission. Commitment to the new position is important to firmly establish, once that is done, the interviewee is more likely to behave consistently with the new mindset. Smyth asks for general location and then 'is the body inside or outside'. Williams responds outside and gives a location of body. Now that he has made some admissions about where the body is, sergeant Smyth follows up with other investigative important questions, even though he rises ostensibly to get a map. Once admissions are made to the first victim, follow-up questions get admissions to the other murder and sexual assault victims. Williams now insists he only wants to talk to sergeant Smyth and reveals all the details of his breaking and entering, kidnapping, and murder. Sergeant Smyth's tone hardly changes, and he remains calm and professional even as he listens to the graphic details. Sergeant Smyth takes it slowly and it is only after getting sufficient details on one crime that a second one is discussed. Although he does return for more extensive information, the previous patterns of behavior prior to these murders are only raised toward the end after the initial admissions.

Once some admissions are gained, follow-up questions can clarify the matters further and get further admissions. A person will generally behave consistently once he or she has begun making admissions. Although that may be limited to one's own involvement, depending on the relationship, interviewees can be reluctant to implicate accomplices.

Throughout the sergeant is constantly trying to be fair to the suspect and his memory. He is friendly and uses rapport to build and maintain trust. Colonel Williams' body language does become defensive, but for some time at the beginning, he seems assured and confident that he has the upper hand. Sergeant Smyth uses enough formality with 'Russell' but never referred to the suspect as colonel, thus depriving Williams of that authority. The fact that Williams was casually dressed compared to sergeant Smyth's suit also helped. The main thrust of the approach initially was the cooperative nature of the interaction, Williams graciously assisting the police to advance their enquiries. Sergeant Smyth was fully prepared for the interview, although at times in the earlier part, he appeared casual and just needed to check details, this was probably a tactical decision to take the interview slowly. It was probably also a deliberate tactical decision to have only one interviewer rather than have two. Confident, powerful personalities such as colonel Williams, used to being dominant, might have found two interviewers more of a threat and been much more defensive. One interviewer, who is clearly not seeking dominance, on the contrary, almost appears submissive, is not a threat. Sergeant Smyth is formally dressed and stays that way and looks almost like a bookkeeper. The Colonel feels in control. Many powerful individuals in organizations such as CEOs will have a similar attitude and will enter a contest for dominance between himself and the interviewer during the interview which is a waste of time. That applies in particular to strong male personalities.

Conclusion

This is an excellent example of the power of a fact-gathering interview model. Rapport is used to get cooperation, but the interviewer was fully prepared with evidence and a tactical plan about when to use it. There was no aggression used and respect was shown throughout to the interviewee. Gentle persuasion, by combining silence and evidence, was effective at obtaining the admissions, although there was a possibility that the victim was still alive. This type of interview was both effective and ethical, while being an example of excellent interpersonal social skills by the interviewer.

Notes

1 Available on YouTube at www.youtube.com/watch?v=bsLbDzkIy3A. [Accessed September 11, 2021]. A number of different videos are available, this particular one was used in the subsequent court case and edited slightly for it. For instance, 17 and

half minutes on the video is approximately 1 hour 30 minutes into the interview. Williams was subsequently convicted of two counts murder, forcible confinement, sexual assault, and 82 counts of breaking and entering.

2 For instance, Cialdini's 'rejection then retreat' principle.

Chapter 11

Conclusion

Introduction

This book was written to describe an interview technique that can be used in any organization no matter what kind of investigation is required. It is intended to provide an ethical and effective method to obtain information from any individual. The technique emphasizes the importance of evaluating information critically and how to use that information to its best advantage. The importance of thinking critically and being aware of one's own biases is an important part of being an investigator because a major criticism of investigators is that often they have been guided by what they believed to be intuition, which in reality was simple bias. As a result, innocent people have had their lives destroyed. In understanding and investigating organizations, the insight that people operate and learn in the context of organizational culture is a vital component to resolving issues. As a result, even those individuals fully culpable for deviant behavior may merely be the lightning rod for complex causal factors. These factors, if left undisturbed, will resurface again and again. An investigator therefore has an important opportunity to identify and cause positive change in an organization to help it develop in order to fulfill its core mission.

The FIIT

The book was focused on using an investigative interviewing technique, the FIIT. This technique consists of a questioning component and a component that carefully evaluates and utilizes information. The questioning component is grounded in utilizing social intelligence and rapport to create an appropriate environment to talk to the interviewee and encourage the disclosure of information to the investigator. The rapport part of interviewing is worked on throughout the interview and remains fundamental to the honest disclosure from an interviewee of all information. The FIIT uses open questions to get an account from the interviewee in as much detail as possible before using probing questions to go into greater depth. At all times, respect for the interviewee and an awareness of the limitations of memory and cultural context is maintained.

DOI: 10.4324/9781003269489-11

The interview is assisted by careful planning and gathering of evidence. The evaluation and analysis of evidence is critical to objectivity and avoiding pre-judging issues. It accepts that evidence may have multiple explanations and there is a need to examine alternative hypotheses carefully. The book touched on the importance of culture in organizations. Cultures that regard failure as learning opportunities and encourage honest and open reporting of issues are going to be stronger organizations with less problems. Such organizations will promote quality cultures in their companies, which will provide good working environments that employees will value. On the other hand, organizations that regard the ends more important than the means are always going to struggle with honesty. Such organizations create the negative environment or crimino-genic climate that actually encourages dishonest and deviant behavior. Over time, these problems grow in magnitude rather than decrease. The investigator may need to take all this contextual information into the interview as well as any personal information already obtained about the interviewee and build a relationship with the interviewee from that position. No matter how serious the matters under investigation, the interviewer strives to show empathy to the interviewee.

At the beginning of the interview, the interviewer first seeks to explain the reasons for the interview and what the expectations from the interviewee are before asking the interviewee to give a free account of the matter under inves-tigation. The interviewee is guided through nonverbal signaling and encour-agement as well as clarifying questions to give as complete an account as possible. Once this account is obtained, the interviewer goes over the account to clarify fully any ambiguity or potential misunderstandings. More detail is thus obtained. Further open questions may be used together with a combin-ation of other questioning styles such as probing or hypothetical questions. At this point, the account might be corroborated or challenged if evidence exists or if the account is in some way vague or ill-defined despite all other efforts to resolve. This is not done aggressively; rapport is maintained by using a problem-solving approach. Typically, this uses a 'I must have misunderstood what you said earlier' type of style. This may get additional detail, and clari-fication, or it may result in an obvious effort on the part of the interviewee to deceive. It may then be appropriate to introduce additional available evi-dence. Usually, every effort is made to question around this to ensure alternative explanations are covered before the evidence is actually introduced. Again, the same, 'I'm confused' style is effective at introducing it as it maintains rapport and allows the interviewee to maintain self-esteem. Where efforts at deceit are detected, emphasizing mutual respect as a synonym for honesty is an effective method of introducing the DEAL technique from the cognitive interviewing model. Throughout the entire interview, careful and attentive listening and using silence are the best tools in an investigator's toolbox. At times, especially with interview-resistant interviewees, it may be necessary to become more formal with the question and answering styles. The interviewer strives to ensure all interview objectives are achieved and efforts have been made to answer investigatively important questions. Once this is achieved, the interviewer usually recaps the process for the benefit of the interviewee and allows the interviewee an opportunity to ask any questions he or she needs answered. Once the interview is completed, the investigator takes all information gathered back into an evaluation cycle. In large-scale investigations with investigators fulfilling various roles, this may require briefing other team members as well as a written memo. In small investigations, the investigator may be solely responsible and will simply evaluate the memo in light of other evidence available. The investigator tries to ensure objectivity and honesty to eliminate bias from the process as much as possible. Spending time on evaluation and analysis of evidence is time well spent as a thorough understanding of evidence provides the investigator the tools to identify and counter deception as well as developing a better systemic understanding of the organization. As in everything, the investigator understands his or her fallibility and how biases can prejudice the investigation and tries to be honest and fair in the results reported to the client.

Culture

Many investigations will find that the person responsible acted alone. There may have been some personal disgruntlement or disengagement from the organization, there may have been some personal issues such as addiction underlying the behavior, or there may simply have been an opportunist who saw his chance. An investigator must keep an open mind while being willing to ask more questions. People are complex, organizations are complex, the world is complex, and these all interact in various adaptive systems. Complex adaptive systems mean that our mental models of how the world works rarely align with how the world actually works, leading to *wicked problems*.[1] Wicked problems are difficult to solve partly because adaptation means situations evolve and gain complexity over time; our own emotional needs and views complicate the picture even further, as we fail to see objective reality. It can be too easy to look for simple linear causal relationships, particularly when there is an implicit expectation of finding someone to blame but few investigations are that simple, even if they do not go deeper than apportioning blame. The understanding that complex systems are nonlinear with complicated and nuanced causal chains permits a more sophisticated and holistic examination of an organization. Ultimately, this permits bigger problems to be identified as they are developing by recognizing that the initial investigation is merely a symptom, in many organizations, of deeper systemic problems.

The objective analysis of evidence, showing respect for the interviewee, and approaching the investigation from an open mindset are all important skills of any investigator. Investigators in private organizations have the potential to provide additional value by developing the investigation beyond the obvious. Organizations that generate a culture of blame emphasize fear among individuals. In such organizations, there can be a ready willingness to ascribe blame to an individual with the negative consequences often being dismissal. In such organizations, the fear of failure together with the fear of exposure for failing instills an attitude of concealment. It destroys trust in the organization with everybody mindful of their own tenuous positions if failure occurs. Such organizations generally develop only one way and that is toward more deviance rather than less. Many such organizations compound these problems by pushing an efficiency mindset, often using tools such as lean sigma six models. Such models are predicated on eliminating time or resource wastage and can serve a useful function. Nevertheless, it is a fallacy to believe that there will never be negative consequences from their implementation. The underlying assumptions that are rarely examined include the fact that not all workers are willing, still less enthusiastic, about cooperating, and that allowing no margin of error is always a good way to operate. The reality is that individuals can be uncooperative in very imaginative ways and pushing dogmatically for efficiencies may in the long run be a very inefficient endeavor.

Organizations on the other hand that understand that failure is a normal part of the process can develop learning cultures where errors are reframed as learning opportunities. Such cultures are more than simply 'no blame' cultures, responsibility is apportioned, and this includes blame if necessary. But the process is impeccably and transparently fair and individuals are not held accountable for systemic problems. Instead, there is an understanding that, in general, everyone comes to work to do the best job possible. Mistakes will be made but where processes can be improved the organization as a whole can develop and become better. Individuals are seen as an important part of the organization rather than disposable cogs in the machine. Such an organization can develop what Sidney Dekker refers to as a 'just culture' where individuals are treated fairly and with respect.[2] In such a 'just culture', systemic causes are examined together with individual behaviors and there is no rush to judgment. Instead, it is acknowledged that sometimes the person who learns the most from the mistake is the individual who is responsible for the mistake but who may as a result acquire useful knowledge that could benefit the organization. In such a learning organization, others see that making a mistake is not a career killing action, and the organization develops faster and better processes together with more committed employees.

One point I have tried to emphasize throughout is that humans rarely make entirely rational decisions. Instead, emotions motivate reasoning to find a good enough excuse to perform certain actions. Most of us do not understand how deep many of our most profoundly held beliefs are and how they continue to influence much of our day-to-day behavior. Habits continue to repeat, patterns of behavior continue to repeat, even as we change our circumstances and surroundings. Yet, no matter who we are otherwise, being part of a group is fundamental to our wellbeing and health. To be part of a group, we will often conform to the expectations of a group, even if we change our own reasoning to do so. Therefore, the culture that an organization has can profoundly affect how employees engage with their roles. Organizations that provide intrinsic as well as extrinsic motivations provide a better work culture than one focused entirely on extrinsic. Where the culture encourages that the ends justify the means at any cost, then over time, employees will deviate further from the normative values held outside the organization. Even in organizations that have less competitive cultures, aspects of the culture and the inherent expectations in it may represent opportunities to improve through identifying and learning about such influences. Deviance has a complicated pathway. All complex systems have inherent latent failures that are impossible to remove, and the simple solution of the imposition of additional controls, regulations, or guidelines creates additional complexity which in itself only adds to the complexity of the system.[3] An overly complex system can motivate personnel to find ways to work around the complexity, thus negating their effectiveness, encouraging deviance, and introducing more potential random adverse events. This suggests that rather than focus entirely on top-down hierarchical management, the recruitment process, the training and acculturation process, and the monitoring and mentoring process can combine to develop a quality learning organization and deter deviance at each point.

Ironically, all organizations are ultimately learning organizations. Culture is the method through which common mental models spread in an organization, and too often these are suboptimal. The difficulty is to control and direct the learning and culture to be a positive force for an organization. Top-down command and control is not effective at reinforcing positive change, partly because individuals can simply choose to be strategically compliant, to appear as if they are doing what they are directed to do but ultimately if individuals in an organization do not want to they can find some way to obstruct or obfuscate the directions they have received.

None of this is exceptional or new knowledge, the world is full of motivational coaches who encourage team building and personal growth as important contributors to organizational success. The criminological understanding of the potential dark side of inclusive cultures that group members consider important is merely another perspective on the positive aspects of culture. The investigator's role may be to recognize where a potentially positive culture has begun to deviate and to understand why and how to intervene. The difficulty is that people rarely appreciate when they have reached a moral inflection point, the Rubicon that they now stand on the shores of, and potentially are about to cross. The lack of a moral awareness means that it is difficult to reach a moral decision. Without this awareness, it is impossible to evaluate the information or decision to be made from a normative perspective, that makes it impossible to establish a moral intention, thereby rendering an ethical decision also impossible.[4] Where one has the routine activities of the work place,[5] combined with the normalization of deviance[6] then it is often difficult to pause and critically reflect on the underlying ethical decision. The behaviors have often become habitual and are therefore carried out almost automatically.

Conclusion

Law does not tell us how to live. Any law simply sets the threshold beyond which certain behavior will be sanctioned. It is not an invitation to push up to that threshold. Law describes what not to do, the forbidden behaviors. What should guide us to live good lives is a strong ethical drive founded on a moral compass. Too often in organizations, behavior is considered acceptable if it is not illegal, particularly if the organization benefits. The current business model of seeking profit and ever greater efficiencies to achieve it is a paradigm where shortcuts and unethical behavior are not just overlooked but rewarded. This is not true of every organization and individuals are often solely responsible for their behaviors, but an investigator will understand that an organization that lacks a moral compass, that encourages unethical behaviors, and is solely focused on the bottom line will create a toxic culture. This culture will create its own learning environment that will teach employees how to succeed. It is inevitable that sooner or later such an organization is being investigated. What an investigator can potentially do is to recognize the warning signs and suggest culture changes that focus more on ethical success and positive learnings. I hope some of the skills covered in this book provide assistance to investigators in understanding and bringing solutions to these, and other, problems.

Notes

1 A term to describe seeming complex intractable problems. See Cabrera, D. and Cabrera, L., *Systems Thinking Made Simple: New Hope for Solving Wicked Problems.* 2nd ed, (Plectica Publishing, 2018), Sparrow, M. K., *The Character of Harms: Operational Challenges in Control*, (Cambridge University Press, Cambridge, 2008).

2 Dekker, S., *Just Culture: Restoring Trust and Accountability in Your Organization*, (CRC Press, Boca Raton, FL, 2016).

3 Cook, R. I., "How Complex Systems Fail: (Being a Short Treatise on the Nature of Failure; How Failure is Evaluated; How Failure is Attributed to Proximate Cause; and the Resulting New Understanding of Patient Safety)", *Cognitive Technologies Laboratory, University of Chicago*, (2000), https://ckrybus.com/static/papers/how_complex_systems_fail_cook_2000.pdf

4 Palazzo, G., Krings, F. and Hoffrage, U., "Ethical Blindness", *Journal of Business Ethics*, (2012), 109(3), pp 323–338.

5 Routine Activities Theory is a very popular criminological explanation of crime, suggesting the intersection of motivated offender, suitable opportunity, and the lack of a capable guardian. See Cohen, L. E. and Felson, M., "Social Change and Crime Rate Trends: A Routine Activity Approach", *American Sociological Review*,

(1979), 44(4), pp 588–608. The theory suffers, in my opinion, from being some-what vague.

6   Vaughan, D., *The Challenger Launch Decision: Risky Technology, Culture, and Deviance at NASA* (Chicago University Press, Chicago, 2016).

Bibliography

Cabrera, D. and Cabrera, L., *Systems Thinking Made Simple: New Hope for Solving Wicked Problems.* 2nd ed, (Plectica Publishing, New York, 2018).

Cohen, L. E. and Felson, M., "Social Change and Crime Rate Trends: A Routine Activity Approach", *American Sociological Review*, (1979), 44(4), pp 588–608.

Cook, R. I., "How Complex Systems Fail: (Being a Short Treatise on the Nature of Failure; How Failure is Evaluated; How Failure is Attributed to Proximate Cause; and the Resulting New Understanding of Patient Safety)", *Cognitive Technologies Laboratory, University of Chicago*, (2000), https://ckrybus.com/static/papers/how_com plex_systems_fail_cook_2000.pdf

Dekker, S., *Just Culture: Restoring Trust and Accountability in Your Organization*, (CRC Press, Boca Raton, FL, 2016).

Palazzo, G., Krings, F. and Hoffrage, U., "Ethical Blindness", *Journal of Business Ethics*, (2012), 109(3), pp 323–338.

Sparrow, M. K., *The Character of Harms: Operational Challenges in Control*, (Cambridge University Press, Cambridge, 2008).

Vaughan, D., *The Challenger Launch Decision: Risky Technology, Culture, and Deviance at NASA* (Chicago University Press, Chicago, 2016).

Index

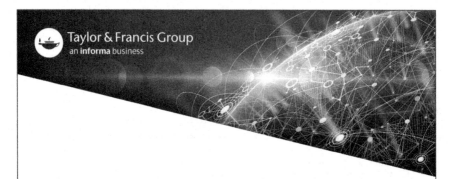

Printed in the United States
by Baker & Taylor Publisher Services